T0179257

A Philosophy of Material Culture

This book focuses on material culture as a subject of philosophical inquiry and promotes the philosophical study of material culture by articulating some of the central and difficult issues raised by this topic and providing innovative solutions to them, most notably an account of improvised action and a non-intentionalist account of function in material culture.

Preston argues that material culture essentially involves activities of production and use; she therefore adopts an action-theoretic foundation for a philosophy of material culture. Part 1 illustrates this foundation through a critique, revision, and extension of existing philosophical theories of action. Part 2 investigates a salient feature of material culture itself—its functionality. A basic account of function in material culture is constructed by revising and extending existing theories of biological function to fit the cultural case. Here the adjustments are for the most part necessitated by special features of function in material culture.

These two parts of the project are held together by a trio of overarching themes: the relationship between individual and society, the problem of centralized control, and creativity.

Beth Preston is Professor of Philosophy at the University of Georgia, USA.

Routledge Studies in Contemporary Philosophy

For a full list of titles in this series, please visit www.routledge.com

First published 2013
by Routledge
711 Third Avenue, New York, NY 10017

Simultaneously published in the UK
by Routledge
2 Park Square, Milton Park, Abingdon, Oxon OX14 4RN

*Routledge is an imprint of the Taylor & Francis Group,
an informa business*

Library of Congress Cataloging-in-Publication Data

Preston, Beth.
A philosophy of material culture : action, function, and mind / by Beth
  Preston. — 1st ed.
    p. cm. — (Routledge studies in contemporary philosophy ; v. 48)
  Includes bibliographical references and index.
  1. Material culture—Philosophy.   I. Title.
  GN406.P74 2012
  306.4′6—dc23
  2012030039

ISBN: 978-0-415-62308-7
ISBN: 978-0-203-06984-4

Typeset in Sabon
by Apex CoVantage, LLC

A Philosophy of Material Culture

Action, Function, and Mind

Beth Preston

Routledge
Taylor & Francis Group

NEW YORK AND LONDON

To the memory of Elizabeth Preston James

Contents

x *Contents*

Acknowledgements

I have been working on this project for a very long time, and a lot of people have helped me along the way. My abject apologies in advance to anyone I forget to mention here. My thanks go, first of all, to those who read all or part of the manuscript in draft and sent me comments—Olle Blomberg, David Chapman, Randolph Clarke, Alan Costall, Robert Cummins, Nathan Crilly, Edward Halper, Risto Hilpinen, Heikki Ikäheimo, Alfred Mele, John Sutton, Raimo Tuomela, and James Wilkinson. Needless to say, any errors that remain are my responsibility. I owe a special debt of gratitude to the songwriters who agreed to be interviewed for the study that forms the basis of Chapter Four, and who patiently put up with what must often have seemed like incomprehensible questions—Mamie Fike Simonds, Russ Hallauer, Kevn Kinney, Kathy Kirbo, Mike Mills, Miria, Kelly Noonan, Debbie Norton, Nathan Sheppard, and Jason Slatton. For generously helping me with this part of the project in other ways, I would like to thank: Anita Blaschak, Bertis Downs, Kenneth Green, Cecilia Herles, Scott Munn, Kevin O'Neil, Judith Preisle, and Meredith Williams. Finally, thanks to Melissa Link, Anne Portman, and Elizabeth Ann Robinson, who helped in the preparation of the manuscript. The writing of this book was supported in part by grants from the Willson Center for Humanities and Arts at the University of Georgia, and by the University of Georgia Research Foundation.

Permission to adapt material from Beth Preston, "The Case of the Recalcitrant Prototype," in *Doing Things with Things,* edited by Alan Costall and Ole Dreier, 15–27 (Farnham: Ashgate, 2006), copyright © 2006, granted by the Publishers.

Permission to adapt material from Beth Preston, "Biological and Cultural Proper Functions in Comparative Perspective," in *Functions in Biological and Artificial Worlds: Comparative Philosophical Perspectives (Vienna Series in Theoretical Biology, Volume 9)*, edited by Ulrich Krohs and Peter Kroes, 37–50 (Cambridge, MA: MIT Press, 2009), granted by MIT Press.

Permission to adapt material from Beth Preston, "Philosophical Theories of Artifact Function," in *Philosophy of Technology and Engineering Sciences (Handbook of the Philosophy of Science, Volume 9)*, volume editor Anthonie Meijers, general editors Dov M. Gabbay, Paul Thagard, and John Woods, 213–233 (Amsterdam: Elsevier, 2009), granted by Elsevier.

Introduction

The subject matter of this book does not fit neatly into the usual labeling scheme of contemporary Anglo-American or Continental philosophy. Its main sections are overtly concerned with action theory and function theory, which are rarely paired to begin with. But its contents range over topics relevant to philosophy of mind and cognitive science, epistemology, social philosophy, and philosophy of technology. The first part of this introduction explains how I came to write this book, and why it has such an odd philosophical profile. The second section explains why I have chosen to use the term 'material culture' instead of the more common 'artifact.' The last section provides a brief overview of the book, with a sketch of what the reader may expect in each chapter.

MEMOIRS OF A MATERIAL GIRL

When I was a graduate student casting about for a dissertation topic, I became interested in the philosophical foundations of artificial intelligence, and in particular in the Martin Heidegger-inspired critiques advanced by Hubert Dreyfus and John Haugeland. In my dissertation I went after this topic in a completely standard philosophy-of-mind sort of way, trying to articulate an account of intentionality consonant with Heidegger's notion of *Dasein*. But in the course of my research, I fell in with Philip Agre and David Chapman, two graduate students at the MIT Artificial Intelligence Laboratory, who were also interested in Heidegger and in the implications of his ideas for their own dissertation research. They were part of a larger group of post-doctoral fellows and graduate students centering around Rodney Brooks and his mobile robotics lab. Through this group—and especially through Agre and Chapman—I learned a lot about artificial intelligence in general, and mobile robotics in particular.[1] And the more I learned, the more it seemed to me that mobile robotics was likely to be where artificial intelligence would experience its most serious reality check, because mobile robots must ultimately act—and even more importantly, interact—in real time and in the same natural and built environments that human beings inhabit.

The robots coming out of Brooks's lab at that time were exemplars of what he later called 'Cambrian AI' (1999). This suggests artificial intelligence at the level of very early, sea-dwelling invertebrates, such as trilobites or sponges. These robots wandered the corridors and offices of the MIT AI Lab without crashing into things, for the most part. One of them even had the useful habit of picking up empty soda cans. But they did not care whether things were animate or inanimate, let alone naturally occurring, as opposed to manufactured. In other words, they were navigating the lab environment without understanding or interacting with it as material culture, specifically.[2] Of course, one important goal of mobile robotics down the road was to build systems that *could* do this—as well as carry on conversations in natural language and engage in the other sorts of activities characteristic of high-level cognition. But the question that began to take form for me then, and that ultimately resulted in the writing of this book, was: What is involved in our *own* production and use of material culture?

When I started looking into this seriously—years later and with tenure making a new project feasible—I discovered that, curiously, neither the history of philosophy nor the recent philosophical literature provided much in the way of an answer.[3] Historically, a fair number of philosophers have had something to say about material culture, but they have done so only in the context of projects focused on something else. Aristotle, for instance, talks about material culture in two contexts. First, in the *Physics* and the *Metaphysics* he uses it as a foil for talking about natural objects and the process of growth, which he takes to be very different from the process of making. Second, in the *Nicomachean Ethics*, he uses production as a foil for talking about what he takes to be the very different phenomenon of practical action. In neither case does he have any interest in material culture in its own right. Karl Marx and Friedrich Engels, on the other hand, *were* specifically interested in production and the products that resulted from it. Indeed, they took production to be the most basic and distinctive of human activities. But like Aristotle, their interest was limited by the overall project they were pursuing—in this case, a theory of economics. For instance, although Marx emphasizes in *Capital* that a commodity must have a use value undergirding its exchange value, the focus of his analysis is on exchange value. So once again, the focus is not material culture in general, but a dedicated account of material perspective dictated by other concerns. The history of Western philosophy is, thus, almost a dead loss as far as a dedicated account of material culture for its own sake goes.

This phenomenon is also apparent in some strands of contemporary philosophy—the recent literature on the metaphysics of ordinary objects, for instance. Ordinary objects include artifacts; naturally occurring objects such as rivers or stones; and sometimes, even living objects such as plants, animals, and persons. Such objects have been ignored or disparaged by metaphysicians throughout the ages, culminating in a contemporary trend toward treating only elementary particles as real objects and ordinary objects as merely aggregates thereof. Opponents of this trend do expend some serious effort on artifacts, which must be rehabilitated along with the rest. But here again, the attention to artifacts is a sideline. The main focus remains on the broader category of ordinary objects and on the narrower issue of its metaphysics.[4]

There are branches of philosophy that do focus on material culture, the two obvious candidates being the historically well-represented field of aesthetics and the much newer field of philosophy of technology. The problem with aesthetics is that it is again not focused broadly on material culture, but narrowly on works of art. In addition, there is the problem of how this narrow focus is related to material culture in the wider sense. If works of art are a unique aspect of material culture, as many aestheticians have claimed, aesthetics may not tell us much about material culture in general. On the other hand, if works of art are *not* unique in the sense claimed by these aestheticians (as I myself believe), then it seems a mistake to treat them in isolation.

Philosophy of technology appears more promising in this respect, since in principle its investigations range over all aspects of material culture. In practice, though, philosophers of technology have had a much narrower focus. First, they have defined their project as the complement of aesthetics; that is, as focusing on 'practical' as opposed to 'contemplative' cultural objects. Frederick Ferré (1988), for instance, defines technology as 'practical implementations of intelligence' (26), and thus as excluding 'aesthetic or religious artifacts' (27). Implicitly or explicitly, the overwhelming majority of philosophers of technology have accepted this delimitation of their field.[5] Second, philosophy of technology has focused almost exclusively on what might better be called 'high tech,' that is, on the recent, sophisticated technologies of the industrialized West, such as computers and nuclear power plants. There are two reasons for this. Some philosophers of technology, especially those in the founding generation, such as Heidegger and Hans Jonas, claim that these modern technologies are essentially different from traditional technologies, and so give rise to distinctive ethical and social problems (Heidegger 1993b; Jonas 1984). So they talk about traditional technologies only as a foil for their 'high tech' quarry. Similarly, more recent philosophers of technology, especially those working in the Anglo-American (analytic) philosophical tradition, are heavily influenced by philosophy of science, and their concern about technology is at the core a concern about the relationship between science and technology. So again, traditional technologies appear only as a foil for 'high tech.'[6]

This dual narrowing of the focus of philosophy of technology is problematic: first, because the distinction between art and instrument (or between the practical and the aesthetic/contemplative—however you wish to formulate it) that drives the partitioning of the field between aesthetics and philosophy of technology is widely acknowledged to be specific to recent Western intellectual history. It was all *techne* to the ancient Greeks, for instance, and the distinction is absent from non-Western cultures, as well.[7] Similarly, the claims that modern, sophisticated technologies are essentially different from traditional technologies are based on arguments that are, at least, uninformed about the nature and use of traditional technologies, and sometimes reflect a romantic mythologizing of them (Ihde 1993). The more recent fascination with science is mostly just that, as opposed to a principled restriction of a field of investigation.

But more importantly for my purposes, the dual narrowing of focus in philosophy of technology makes hash out of the general question about material culture. It is admitted on all fronts, for instance, that artifacts typically have *both* practical and aesthetic aspects simultaneously. Works of art have practical uses (e.g., as financial investments) and instruments typically are decorative as well as useful (e.g., fashion in clothes). Moreover, these practical and aesthetic aspects are not necessarily instantiated in distinct properties of things. The red of a stop sign is aesthetically pleasing *and* useful, for instance. Similarly, ancient technologies (e.g., spoons, needles, hammers) continue in use cheek by jowl with more sophisticated technologies. The problem, then, is that the partitioning of the field between aesthetics and philosophy of technology is at least artificial and quite possibly distorting with regard to the experience and interaction of human beings with their material culture. What is needed in addition to these traditional areas, then, is an area of philosophy that addresses the full range of material culture, and that takes items of material culture whole rather than trying to isolate particular aspects.

But there is one more problem. People use naturally occurring objects—often for the very same purposes subserved by artifacts. They build stone walls and brick walls; they throw sticks, as well as balls, for their dogs; they mulch their vegetable patches with leaves even more often than with black plastic; and so on. So, in terms of an account of use, it would also be artificial and perhaps distorting to limit the investigation to artifacts, if by 'artifact' is meant something made by human beings. This is one respect in which the 'ordinary objects' terminology suggests a helpful corrective. So what is needed, I ended up thinking, is a general account of the making *and/or* using of things.

TERMS AND CONDITIONS

Philosophizing about things people make and/or use in the course of their everyday activities calls for a general term to refer to the things in the domain of interest, but there are no entirely unproblematic candidates. Terms such as 'thing' or 'object' are too broad. 'Tool' is too narrow, because it is usually understood as referring to medium-sized objects that are manipulated by hand. But houses, clothing, beverages, and songs, which are all within the domain of interest, are not tools in this sense (Shumaker, Walkup, and Beck

2011; Preston 1998a). 'Technology' is problematic in light of the narrowly instrumental sense in which philosophers of technology and other folks normally deploy the term. Heidegger's term 'equipment' (*Zeug*) is, well, too Heideggerian, since the line we will be pursuing is not a Heideggerian one.

'Artifact' is perhaps the most obvious choice, but it might easily be the worst. Even its etymology—something made by craft—is problematic. As we noted above, some of the things we use are not made but occur naturally and are simply put to use, often without modification. Moreover, some of the things we make are not made by craft, or even with specific intention. Paths, for example, often grow by the passage of many feet, not necessarily all bent upon the same errand or even all of the same species. Similarly, footprints are used by forensic scientists and trackers, but are the unintended traces of other activities. And then there are the ubiquitous by-products of craft, such as sawdust or buttermilk, which may be used as-is for various purposes or as raw material to make other products. Compounding this problem is the practice in recent philosophy of using 'artifact' to refer exclusively to things that are intentionally made by individual human beings (Dipert 1993; Hilpinen 2011).[8]

This practice is not necessarily shared by other disciplines. In anthropology and archaeology, 'artifact' may refer to any thing that is the result of, and/or used in, human activity. It may thus include naturally occurring use objects, sometimes referred to more specifically as 'ecofacts,' as well as things that are not produced intentionally but do reflect important patterns of individual or collective behavior, such as debitage (waste material produced during the production of stone tools). So at first blush, 'artifact' in this anthropological sense *does* seem appropriate for our purposes. But there is another problem with the anthropological usage stemming from its particular association with archaeology. When we think of artifacts, we think of the medium-sized, durable things we find in museums. But very large artifacts such as roadways, canals, fences, and plowed fields do not appear in most museums. More importantly for our purposes, many artifacts are not durable enough to leave traces in the archaeological record, and so do not make it into museums. Food, cosmetics, body art, and textiles are rarely preserved. Songs, dances, and religious rituals are never preserved, and even contemporary records of such performances on film or compact disc are unlikely to survive for very long under archaeological deposition conditions.[9] This is especially problematic for us, because we will be using the music domain extensively as a source of examples and data. Thus, a term with less baggage than 'artifact' is needed.

The last, best hope is the anthropological term 'material culture.' This has the stylistic problem of forcing the writer to resort to phrases such as 'item of material culture' in order to refer to single things in the domain of interest. But because it is not in regular use in philosophy, it does not bring with it the unfortunate connotations of 'artifact.' In anthropology and archaeology, its use is of long standing (Buchli 2002). Recently, it has become the core term for a more interdisciplinary area of research, usually called material culture studies, which is still centered on anthropology and archaeology but also includes sociology, geography, design studies, history of technology, and the like, and has had its own journal (the *Journal of Material Culture*) for the last decade or so.

A recent and compendious handbook introduces material culture studies this way:

> Empirically material culture studies involve the analysis of a domain of things or objects, which are endlessly diverse: anything from a packet of fast food to a house to an entire landscape, and either in the past or in the present, within contemporary urban and industrial cultures in the United States and Europe to small-scale societies in Africa, Asia or the Pacific. Contemporary material culture studies may take as their principal concern, and starting point for analysis, particular properties of objects or things: things as material matter, as found or made, as static or mobile, rare or ubiquitous, local or exotic, new or old, ordinary or special, small or monumental, traditional or modern, simple or complex.
>
> Alternatively, material culture studies may take the human subject or the social as their starting point: the manner in which people think through themselves, and their lives and identities through the medium of different kinds of things. Material culture studies in various ways inevitably have to emphasize the dialectical and recursive relationship between persons and things: that persons make and use things and that the things make persons. (Tilley et al. 2006, 3–4)

This sounds like exactly what we want. It is clear that the focus is on things—this is the 'material' bit—but that these things are considered from the perspective of their involvement in human activities—the 'culture' bit. In addition, there is an explicit effort to avoid artificially restricting the domain of interest in advance. Indeed, the editors of the handbook go on to say that 'the terms "materiality" and "material culture" defy any strict definitions' (Tilley et al. 2006, 4), so that what is or is not included in the domain of interest is entirely fluid and potentially contestable (Miller 2010).

This open-ended approach is likely to make some philosophers nervous and others scornful, given the traditional disciplinary insistence on defining one's terms. So here is an argument for the probity and value of adopting this approach. In any discipline or subdiscipline, it can be observed that it is precisely the central and most important concepts that resist definition and occasion the most controversy. Thus, mathematicians argue about what numbers are, anthropologists about what culture is, psychologists about what intelligence is, aestheticians and art historians about what a work of art is, epistemologists about what knowledge is, and so on. There is a reason for this. These concepts orient the more specific questions and problems in the field. So a psychologist, for instance, might ask how to measure intelligence or whether non-human animals are intelligent, an epistemologist might ask how we justify our knowledge claims or whether nonhuman animals know things, and so on. Now the problem with strict definitions of these central concepts is that they can invalidate some interesting and significant questions and/or foreclose the possibility of certain answers to them. Thus, you could easily define intelligence or knowledge in such a way that questions about nonhuman animals being intelligent or having knowledge could be answered only one way or would not even make sense. This is not a desirable way of conducting an inquiry if what you want is the best and most fruitful results, as opposed to the validation of some pretheoretical assumptions. What 'material culture' provides, then, is not a strict definition but the delineation of a focus. In the first instance, the focus is on the things made and/or used, and secondarily on the making and/or using of them.

OVERVIEW

There are two parts to this project. Since material culture involves activities of production and use, an action-theoretic foundation is requisite for a philosophy of material culture. Part I provides this through a critique, revision, and extension of existing philosophical theories of action. These adjustments are necessitated not by special features of action involving material culture, but by difficulties endemic to traditional action theory. Part II investigates a salient feature of material culture itself—its functionality. A basic account of function in material culture is constructed by revising and extending existing theories of biological function to fit the cultural case. Here, the adjustments are for the most part necessitated by special features of function in material culture.

   These two parts of the project are held together by a trio of overarching themes. First, a particular view of the relationship between individual and society is supported. On this view, which I call sociogenerism, the individual is not *sui generis* (literally, 'of its own kind'), but is formed by society in important ways. This is not a new idea, of course, and it is widely acknowledged in the abstract. But it is equally widely ignored when getting down to particulars. Specifically, it is typically ignored by traditional Anglo-American action theory, which starts with an essentially independent individual agent and tries to build up collaborative and social agency on this basis (Part I). And it is typically ignored in contemporary accounts of artifact function, which start with the intentions of independent individual agents and try to build up the panoply of function in material culture on this basis (Part II). I show that neither of these individualistic approaches works well, and that a better alternative is instead to start with social and collaborative structures as always already in place and to understand individual action and intention on that basis. In short, whether you start your inquiry into material culture from the side of human production and use (Part I), or from the side of the things produced and used (Part II), you end up with a sociogeneric view of the relationship between individual and society.

A second and related overarching theme concerns what I call the problem of centralized control. When the individual is regarded as *sui generis,* there is a tendency to regard the individual as controlling her output, whether that output is actions (Part I) or material products (Part II). In action theory this model shows up in the form of planning-based theories, where the control of action is analyzed in terms of the construction and execution of plans. In Part I, I offer a critique of planning theories of action and an alternative in the form of an account of action as fundamentally improvisatory. In function theory, the centralized control problem shows up in the form of intentionalist accounts, where the establishment of functions in material culture is attributed to designer's intentions. In Part II, I offer a critique of such intentionalist theories, and an alternative in the form of a more biologically inspired account of function in material culture that acknowledges the complexity of the role of individual intentions in the establishment of functions, while insisting on their subsidiary character.

The third overarching theme is creativity. This is important as a counterpoise to the view that emerges on the basis of the first two themes, which could be seen as denying any real creative leeway to individuals formed by their society and subject to its practices and authority structures. My view, on the contrary, is that all human action is what you might call small-c creative (as opposed to the big-C Creativity you get with scientific discovery, art, or social innovation). Small-c creativity is a necessary characteristic of human action because we have to cope with dynamic environments using limited cognitive, physical, and material resources. The question in Part I is where this creativity lies in human action. Planning theories of action relegate it entirely to the mental creativity involved in constructing a plan. My account of action as fundamentally improvisatory, on the other hand, distributes the creativity throughout the action itself, as agents respond in an ongoing way to opportunities and problems. In Part II, the issue of creativity emerges from the account of function in material culture. The established, proper functions of items of material culture constrain us to use them in accordance with society's practices and values. But people can, and constantly do, use their material culture in ways that do not follow established custom, for example, using a coffee mug as a pencil holder or a chair as a step ladder. So function in material culture reproduces established functions, but on the other hand, provides us with resources for creative use.

The purpose of Chapter 1 is to show why traditional Anglo-American action theory does not provide an adequate foundation for a philosophy of material culture. I begin with a historical perspective, arguing that Aristotle, Marx, and Randall Dipert, although widely separated in time and differing in the details of their accounts, all assume that action is to be analyzed in terms of the execution of plans—mental constructs centrally located in the heads of individual agents. Moreover, all three of them apply this model—

which I call centralized control—to the production of material culture, which makes a consideration of their work especially appropriate. The last part of the chapter begins the critique of this model. First, the individualistic assumptions underlying the centralization dimension of the model run afoul of the typically collaborative nature of everyday action. Similarly, the control dimension runs afoul of the typically improvisational character of everyday action.

Chapter 2 continues the critique of the centralized control model by showing that the planning orientation of current (Anglo-American) action theory not only makes improvisation invisible as a distinct phenomenon, but also hinders the development of the action-theoretic resources necessary for analyzing it. There are folk senses of 'plan,' which do leave room for a conception of unplanned (i.e., improvised) action. But the philosophical sense of 'plan' involved in current theories of both intention and intentional action usurps the room left by the folk for a conception of unplanned action so that 'action' and 'planned action' end up seemingly synonymous. I argue that action theorists would be well advised to resurrect the folk distinction and theorize improvisation alongside planning. Finally, I consider whether philosophical action theory currently has the resources for such a theory of improvisation, and conclude that although there is at least one rather remote and unattended corner where a theory of improvisation could conceivably take root, the majority of the resources for the construction of such a theory will have to come from outside action theory.

Chapter 3 does for collaboration what Chapter 2 does for improvisation. And it is here that the theme of individual and society comes into its own. The first part of this chapter considers what, if anything, action theory can tell us about multiple-agent improvisation, as opposed to multiple-agent planning. First, I argue that action theorists have concentrated too exclusively on cooperative multiple-agent action, and urge the reassessment of this trend in light of the need for a philosophy of material culture to encompass non-cooperative action as well. The last part of the chapter concerns the relationship between sociality and collaboration. I argue that action theorists exhibit a reliable tendency to conflate collaboration with sociality, and that a philosophy of material culture, in contrast, will need to distinguish them carefully. In addition, there is a related tendency to assume the view I call suigenerism, in which sociality is taken to derive from the activities of *sui generis* individuals agreeing to collaborate with each other. I argue that this direction of analysis is backward. Sociality actually precedes multiple-agent action, in the sense that it is always already socialized individuals who enter into collaborative relationships. I call this view sociogenerism.

The project in Chapter 4 is to outline a basic account of improvisatory action, both individual and collaborative. The theme of creativity emerges here. The account of improvisation is based largely on actual examples gathered from an interview study of a specific type of improvisatory activity—songwriting. The idea is to ground theory as firmly and explicitly as possible in empirical data of a qualitative sort. This methodology is intended to contrast both with more standard philosophical methodologies based on thought experiments and hypothetical examples, as well as with more standard laboratory-based methodologies in cognitive science and experimental philosophy. First, I explain why songwriting was chosen as the domain and outline how the songwriting data was gathered and analyzed. Then I use this data to identify three improvisation strategies—very general procedures for generating and concatenating actions in an ongoing manner without the benefit of an advance plan. All of these strategies require ongoing creative responses on the part of the individuals involved. The last part of the chapter focuses on practices and habits—procedures for generating and concatenating actions that are specific to particular cultures or subcultures. The main purpose of this section is to sketch the relationship between the constraints of sociality, particularly as they emerge in the discussion of sociogenerism in Chapter 3, and the creative leeway enjoyed by each individual in light of the basically improvisatory structure of the activities carried out under these constraints.

Part II proceeds to an investigation of function in material culture, with the themes of sociogenerism, centralized control, and creativity in hand. Chapter 5 lays the groundwork. The first section describes five central phenomena for which any adequate theory of function in material culture must account—the multiple realizability of function, the multiple utilizability of functional structures, the process of reproduction with (innovative) variation, the possibility of malfunction, and phantom functions (e.g., the function of amulets to ward off the evil eye). Two theories of biological function serve as a starting point: Ruth Millikan's theory of proper function and Robert Cummins's theory of system function (my term for it, not his). I argue that these two theories cannot be unified, but since both are necessary to account for the phenomena, a pluralist theory of function in material culture is the best option. Moreover, while Cummins's notion of system function does transfer fairly unproblematically to material culture, the same is not true for Millikan's notion of proper function, because of its grounding in concepts of selection and fitness that are problematic as applied to material culture. I suggest usefulness as a more appropriate central concept in the case of function in material culture.

Chapter 6 completes the adjustment of the originally biological notion of proper function to the analysis of material culture. Doing so requires dealing with a version of the centralized control problem—the nearly universal tendency to appeal to human intentions as the basis for function in material culture. Such intentionalist approaches come to grief over two phenomena: novel prototypes and phantom functions. Appealing to the intentions of designers to establish proper functions for novel prototypes turns out to cause more function-theoretic problems than it solves. And appealing to the intentions of users to establish the proper-functional status of phantom functions is no more successful, because these intentions do not track the actual history of reproduction and use of phantom-functional items very well at all. The upshot of these two discussions is a further refinement of the central concepts of a theory of proper function in material culture. Usefulness now appears to be too strong a notion. I recommend instead appeal to historical patterns of actual use and reproduction for that use. My theory is thus non-intentionalist, appealing in the first instance to what people do rather than to their intentions.

The primary purpose of Chapter 7 is to deal with two topics that surface as important at the end of Chapter 6—reproduction and use. The themes of sociogenerism and creativity reemerge here. Reproduction in material culture has traditionally been understood as a matter of human agents imposing structure and function on raw material in accordance with their purposes. But this is only half the story. The other half is that those very purposes are themselves the result of children learning—from direct interaction with material culture, facilitated by already competent adults—how to use and/or reproduce a pre-existing material culture, and *acquiring* the purposes relevant to that culture in the process. Thus it is just as correct to say that our purposes are imposed on us by the material culture we inhabit, as that we impose our purposes (functions) on material culture. This supports a sociogeneric view of the interaction of individual and society in the reproduction and use of material culture. But it also problematizes innovation and individual creativity by emphasizing the extent to which agents are products of their culture rather than *sui generis* producers of it. I argue that use in accordance with *proper* function does reflect the influence of a pre-existing material culture on the formation of human agents, but that *system*-functional uses reflect the ability of these same agents to turn existing items of material culture to novel and creative purposes. This conclusion parallels that of Chapter 4, where the ability of individuals to act creatively within the constraints of social practices was highlighted.

Part I
Action

1   The Centralized Control Model

I was central.
I had control.
I lost my head.

—R.E.M., 'Country Feedback,' *Out of Time*
(Warner Bros. 1991)

Perhaps the most obvious fact about material culture is that it is not only largely a result of human activity, but also is put to use in almost every activity. So, understanding material culture means understanding production and use. In contemporary Anglo-American philosophy, there is a specialized area of research called action theory that traces its descent back to Aristotle. Action theorists have not directed their attention specifically to material culture, but they hardly need to, since most human action involves production or use or both. Thus, an obvious way to get a philosophy of material culture off the ground would be to adopt the conceptual framework of action theory as the foundation for a more specific account of production and use. Randall Dipert (1993) did just that in his path-breaking action-theoretic account of artifacts. The burden of this chapter is to explain why, contrary to reasonable expectations, this is actually a bad move. It is a bad move because traditional action theory has two deep-seated problems that undermine its account of action, and thus make it unsuited as a foundation for understanding the specific activities of production and use.

First, action theory has traditionally focused on the actions of individual agents. A body of work on joint intentions and actions has emerged only recently. But items of material culture are not only typically produced collaboratively, they are also typically used collaboratively. No one makes a car by themselves; and while driving, we are constrained to collaborate with other users on public roads and sometimes with passengers in our vehicle. So, the first problem with traditional action theory is the lack of a well-developed account of collaborative action.

Second, action theory has concentrated on the analysis of intentional action, and in recent years has swung rather heavily toward planning as its fundamental analytical concept. Plans do have an important role to play in human action, but not all our activity is planned in the relevant sense. Instead, much of our everyday activity has an improvisational structure. For example, you cannot plan ahead for every action you will perform while driving from one place to another because you cannot know what other cars and pedestrians you will encounter—not to mention detours, downpours, or deer. So the second problem with action theory is the lack of an account of improvisation to complement its already well-developed account of planning.

These features are not due to recent innovation, but have roots in the history of action theory. Following Aristotle, action theory has consistently focused on developing a model of action I shall call the *centralized control model*.[1] The dominant features of this model are the previously described emphases on individual action and planning. The basic problem posed by action theory for a philosophy of material culture is a consequence of the one-sidedness of this model that overemphasizes these aspects of action while marginalizing others (collaboration), or leaving them out of account altogether (improvisation). It should be noted that this problem does not reflect a difficulty in applying action theory to material culture, but rather a difficulty inherent in action theory itself. In this chapter and throughout Part I, I will be talking about action theory in a quite general way, often without specific reference to either the production or the use of material culture. The goal is to end up with a more adequate theory of action, the application of which to the production and use of material culture should be straightforward.

It should be noted that there are other aspects of human activity neglected by action theory but which are of importance for a philosophy of material culture. One such aspect is habit, which is sometimes mentioned but rarely is the focus of discussion or investigation.[2] Another is skilled action. There is a growing body of literature on this topic, stemming from Hubert Dreyfus's search for an alternative to the expert systems model in artificial intelligence (Dreyfus and Dreyfus 1988; Ennen 2003; McDowell 2007; Dreyfus 2007; Montero 2010; Sutton et al. 2011). But again, this literature is not a focus of discussion among the core constituency of action theory.[3] In the long run, it will be essential for a philosophy of material culture to weigh in on these neglected aspects of human activity, as well. But in the short run, I believe it is more important to concentrate on collaboration and improvisation, because these phenomena are more fundamental. Our earliest engagement in activity as infants is in joint, improvisatory activity with caregivers— feeding, changing of diapers, play—long before skill acquisition, the laying down of habits, and other more sophisticated action structures develop. So if action theory is entangled in misunderstandings about collaboration and improvisation, it would be sensible to sort those out first.

It must also be noted that these failings of traditional, Anglo-American action theory are not necessarily shared by theories of action in other disciplines (e.g., sociology or anthropology) or in the Continental tradition in philosophy. So why not simply base a philosophy of material culture on some already more adequate understanding of action from elsewhere? First of all, the work of reorienting Anglo-American action theory must be done anyway. And the best way to do it, I think, is through an internal critique rather than through an external challenge. Although external challenges do sometimes eventually succeed—Hubert Dreyfus's Heidegger-inspired critique of artificial intelligence is a good example—they are harder for the challenger to mount, and easier for the challengee to ignore. So I have elected to address Anglo-American action theory on its own terms. I will make reference along the way to theories of action in other traditions and disciplines that connect with my view, but will not discuss them in detail here.

I will begin this chapter with a brief history of what might be called production theory. Aristotle, Karl Marx, and Randall Dipert all single out the production of items of material culture for particular attention. And all of them understand production in terms of the centralized control model predominating in action theory. So examining these accounts of production will serve the dual purpose of explicating the development of the centralized control model and simultaneously providing representative historical examples of the application of action theory to material culture. The second half of this chapter will then begin the critique of the centralized control model by examining the role of collaboration and improvisation in everyday action.

ARISTOTLE

For Aristotle, production consists in impressing a form on matter. We produce neither the form nor the matter, but only the union of the two (*Metaphysics* 1033a20–1034b5). This requires thinking about how to bring the desired form into union with suitable matter:

> Every craft is concerned with coming to be; and the exercise of the craft is the study of how something that admits of being and not being comes to be, something whose origin is in the producer and not in the product. For a craft is not concerned with things that are or come to be by necessity; or with things that are by nature, since these have their origin in themselves. (*Nicomachean Ethics* 1140a10–15)

> [F]rom art proceed the things of which the form is in the soul . . . The healthy subject, then, is produced as the result of the following train of thought; since *this* is health, if the subject is to be healthy *this* must first be present, e.g., a uniform state of body, and if this is to be present, there must be heat; and the physician goes on thinking thus until he brings the matter to a final step which he himself can take. Then the process from this point onward, i.e. the process towards health, is called a 'making'. Therefore it follows that in a sense health comes from health and house from house, that with matter from that without matter; for the medical art and the building art are the form of health and of the house; and I call

the essence substance without matter. Of productions and movements one part is called thinking and the other making—that which proceeds from the starting-point and the form is thinking, and that which proceeds from the final step of the thinking is making. (*Metaphysics* 1032b1–20)

The first thing to notice here is that the process starts with a specification of the thing to be produced (the form in the mind of the producer), and the ensuing deliberation or thinking concerns the specification of the steps by which this form may be realized in matter. So, at the end of the thinking process, the producer has in her mind a mental design for the product, complete with step-by-step instructions for constructing it. Second, Aristotle suggests that this mental design is finished prior to the production proper, the actual construction. So, for Aristotle, there are two clearly demarcated phases in the overall production process—an antecedent design phase and a subsequent construction phase. Moreover, since all of the thinking is relegated to the design phase, the construction phase must be a matter of unintelligent execution of the step-by-step instructions. Thus, for Aristotle, the real interest of production lies in the mental process of design, not the actual construction process.

Aristotle also has something important to say about the thinking that goes into the design phase. Art (*techne*), he says, is a state (*hexis*) involving (*meta*) true reason; lack of art (*atechnia*) is a state involving false reason (*Nicomachean Ethics* 1140a5–25). *Hexis* can also be translated as 'habit.' So, for Aristotle, the thinking involved in production is habitual, and need not be explicitly articulated on every occasion. This may also suggest that the specification of the steps in construction does not have to be complete, but may call up action sequences as integral units. For example, in thinking about building a house, the designer does not have to specify step-by-step instructions for using a hammer or putting up drywall. The builder can be relied upon to have the right habits of thinking required to accomplish such things. Thus, Aristotle's view is not simplistically rationalistic. A deliberatively generated design may contain elements that are not themselves deliberatively generated on that occasion.

It is also important to note something Aristotle does *not* discuss—the typically collaborative nature of production. As the passages quoted above from the *Metaphysics* and the *Nicomachean Ethics* show, Aristotle routinely speaks of *the* producer, usually a skilled artisan or expert, such as a potter or a physician, working alone. Aristotle's account of production is at least implicitly individualistic. This might be an expository device, but it is not without philosophical consequences. In real life, as opposed to philosophical reconstruction, people typically collaborate in producing material culture, and they do so in a number of importantly different ways. For example, the designer is often not the same individual as the constructor of an item. Similarly, either the construction phase or the design phase or both may involve teams of collaborators working together. And the problem is that

Aristotle makes no attempt to show how, if at all, his individualistic account of production and action applies to such collaborative activities.

Finally, the most unusual feature of Aristotle's account of production from a contemporary point of view is his insistence that production is not a subspecies of action, but rather a distinct species of activity in its own right:

> What admits of being otherwise includes what is produced and what is done in action. Production and action are different; about them we rely also on [our] popular discussions. Hence the state involving reason and concerned with action is different from the state involving reason and concerned with production. Nor is one included in the other; for action is not production, and production is not action. (*Nicomachean Ethics* 1140a1–10)

Nevertheless, production and action *are* clearly the same in one respect—both involve a process of deliberation concerning what means we may employ to attain our ends with regard to things we can change (cf. *Nicomachean Ethics* 1112b25–1113a5, 1140a10–15). Where production and action differ is with regard to the relationship between the end and the process of attaining it:

> For production has its end beyond it; but action does not, since its end is doing well itself. (*Nicomachean Ethics* 1140b5–10)

Thus, the end of production is something external to, and independent of, the production process, whereas the end of action is internal to it. This distinction is also connected to a parallel distinction between motion (*kinesis*) and energic activities (*energeia*) (*Metaphysics* 1048b15–35). Examples of motions are knitting a sweater or going on a diet. The goal you wish to achieve is achieved only when the process terminates. For example, you do not lose weight for the sake of losing weight, but for the sake of being thin in the end. In contrast, examples of energic activities are seeing or flute playing. Here the goal you wish to achieve is in effect already achieved the minute you start the activity. Flute playing or seeing are, thus, activities you can engage in for their own sake and not for the sake of some result that will occur only at the end of the activity. Energic activities may, of course, simultaneously be practical activities with further ends. For example, seeing usually has further ends, such as finding your keys, and flute playing might also be for the sake of earning a fee. But Aristotle's point here is that activities such as seeing or playing the flute *can* be done simply for the sake of doing them, whereas it would make no sense to say that you were losing weight just for the sake of losing it and not for some further end.[4]

In proposing these distinctions, Aristotle is not just pursuing a descriptive project, but an evaluative one. His purpose is not only to understand what different kinds of activities people engage in, but also to rank activities with regard to their worthiness and contribution to the good life. As he explains at the beginning of the *Nicomachean Ethics* (1094a1–1094b10), the principle of this ranking is the extent to which we engage in an activity for its own sake. And by this criterion, production is clearly inferior to action, because the process of producing is undertaken only for the sake of the product, which is, therefore, superior to the process (*Nicomachean Ethics* 1094a5–10). So we cannot achieve human excellence by producing, because productive activity only aims at the excellence of the product, not at the excellence of the activity itself. But actions, to the extent that they are undertaken for their own sake, aim at their own excellence and are thus constitutive of human excellence. Perhaps Aristotle's most telling pronouncement on the inferiority of production is his remark that productive activity must be missing entirely from the divine life of the gods (*Nicomachean Ethics* 1178b20)—certainly a sharp contrast with the Judeo-Christian view of production as a prerogative of the divine that humans usurp at their peril.

Aristotle's distinction between production and action has disappeared without a trace from contemporary Anglo-American action theory. Action theorists assume without discussion that production is simply a subspecies of action. For instance, Myles Brand (1970, 3) lists building a bridge as a paradigm case of action right alongside raising your arm and buying a loaf of bread. I think the reason for the disappearance of the distinction is that the basis on which Aristotle proposes it, the status of the end with regard to the process, does not have any valence for contemporary Anglo-American action theorists. Descriptively, their concern is exclusively with the nature of the process by which intentional activity is generated; as we noted above, Aristotle takes this process to be the same in the case of both production and action. Moreover, although contemporary action theorists are often concerned with specific moral issues, such as the assignment of moral blame, this is not the same sort of concern Aristotle had for the overall character of a person's life that motivated his thinking about the difference between action and production.

In the Continental tradition of political theory, on the contrary, heroic attempts have been made to counteract any such assimilation of production to action, and to reestablish the Aristotelian distinction, complete with its original evaluative force, on a new basis. Such a project lies at the heart of Jürgen Habermas's longstanding critique of Marx's production paradigm, and his own theory of communicative action (Grumley 1992). It also underwrites Hannah Arendt's (1958) influential analysis of the *vita activa,* in which she argues for a rigorous three-fold distinction between labor, work (fabrication), and action. This rehabilitation of Aristotle's distinction between production and action by Continental political theorists reflects their retention of broadly Aristotelian concerns about the good life, transposed to the contemporary political context.

This raises the question of what role, if any, Aristotle's production-action distinction should play in a philosophy of material culture. It is a significant part of the history of philosophical thinking about material culture, so it should not simply be passed over in silence. On the other hand, accepting it at face value as part of the basic conceptual framework for the analysis of material culture would be a much bigger mistake. This is because the phenomena of material culture cut across Aristotle's distinction in a number of ways. First, a theory of material culture must consider not just the creation of items of material culture, but also their use. And clearly the use of material culture occurs in both productions and actions in Aristotle's sense. Second, and more importantly, Aristotle's distinction categorizes activities in an abstract way that is not aimed at capturing anything about their role in creating material culture. Thus, many activities we would not regard as creating material culture fall on the production side of the distinction—losing weight, or curing an illness, for example. On the other hand, some activities we might well regard as creating material culture fall on the action side— music or dance, for example. Last but not least, the evaluative dimension of Aristotle's distinction should give us pause. For Aristotle, improvising a song is not just descriptively different from painting a painting—it is a *better* and more praiseworthy kind of activity. It would certainly be tendentious to build such value judgments into the basic conceptual framework of a philosophy of material culture. So Aristotle's production-action distinction must be relegated to a purely historical role for our purposes.

MARX

For Marx, production is the most fundamental form of human activity:

> Man can be distinguished from the animal by consciousness, religion, or anything else you please. He begins to distinguish himself from the animal the moment he begins to *produce* his means of subsistence, a step required by his physical organization . . . This mode of production must not be viewed simply as reproduction of the physical existence of individuals. Rather it is a definite form of their activity, a definite way of expressing their life, a definite *mode of life*. (Marx and Engels 1994, 107)

Marx does not mean to deny that other animals produce things; rather it is *how* we produce that distinguishes us from them:

> The animal is immediately one with its life activity, not distinct from it . . . Man makes his life activity itself [i.e., production] into an object of will and consciousness. He has conscious life activity. It is not a determination with which he immediately identifies. Conscious life activity distinguishes man immediately from the life activity of the animal . . . Only on that account is his activity free activity. (Marx 1997, 294)

As Marx goes on to explain, this means, first, that while nonhuman animals produce only to satisfy their physical needs, we produce largely in freedom from basic physical needs; and second, while nonhuman animals produce according to species-specific standards, we produce according to freely variable standards of our own devising, and in particular according to aesthetic standards (Marx 1997, 294–95). Although Marx does not say so explicitly, it seems clear that these standards are for the most part cultural standards, not individual standards. Thus, production takes on different forms under historically local conditions, and the history of these changing forms is the history of what Marx calls 'modes of production.' In short, Marx's view is that human beings, unlike other animals, do not just produce a few things for their immediate personal use, but produce material cultures that subserve social institutions and are passed down from generation to generation. This is possible because human production is under conscious, rational control and thus free, rather than under the control of instinct.

In a famous passage, Marx goes on to suggest that this conscious, rational control has a core structure that is species-specific and universal:

> We presuppose labour in a form in which it is an exclusively human characteristic. A spider conducts operations which resemble those of the weaver, and a bee would put many a human architect to shame by the construction of its honeycomb cells. But what distinguishes the worst architect from the best of bees is that the architect builds the cell in his mind before he constructs it in wax. At the end of every labour process, a result emerges which had already been conceived by the worker at the beginning, hence already existed ideally. Man not only effects a change of form in the materials of nature; he also realizes [*verwirklicht*] his own purpose in those materials. And this is a purpose he is conscious of, it determines the mode of his activity with the rigidity of a law, and he must subordinate his will to it. (Marx 1976, 283–84)

The account of production here is strikingly similar to Aristotle's. Marx distinguishes an antecedent, mental design phase from a subsequent construction phase. The design phase includes not only a representation of the thing to be made but also a step-by-step specification of how to make it in the form of a mental rehearsal of the construction process. The construction phase must, then, be an unintelligent execution of the design, which is fully laid out in advance in the mind of the producer. Marx does not specifically describe the procedure by which the design is formed as a matter of deliberating about the means for achieving a given end. But he does say that the end, or purpose, determines the activity of the producer, and that this determination is accomplished through consciousness of the end. So we may reasonably suppose that, like Aristotle, Marx had in mind the conscious purpose of the producer, guiding her thinking about the steps necessary to accomplish her end.

There is one important departure from Aristotle's view here, though. Rather than being a realization of an independent, pre-existing form, the product is expressive of the producer's own needs and purposes. This marks

Marx's account as a modern conception of the role of production in human life. More specifically, it is an interested, economic conception rather than a disinterested, aesthetic one. For Aristotle, the producer is merely a calculator who takes pre-existing elements—the form and the matter—and figures out how to realize the one in the other. For Marx, when you make something, you do not merely change the form of the material you work on, you also endow it with a use-value expressive of your own socially and historically conditioned needs and purposes. Marx's laborer thus creates material culture in a way that Aristotle's artisan does not, because on Marx's view it is production in the first instance that is responsive to changing conditions in a society and is, thus, the driving force behind cultural innovation. Changes in social institutions and ways of thinking are dependent on these changes in the mode of production:

> Conceiving, thinking, and the intellectual relationships of men appear here as the direct result of their material behavior. The same applies to intellectual production as manifested in a people's language of politics, law, morality, religion, metaphysics, etc. Men are the producers of their conceptions, ideas, etc., but these are real, active men, as they are conditioned by a definite development of their productive forces and of the relationships corresponding to these up to their highest forms. (Marx and Engels 1994, 111)

Moreover, as this passage also shows, Marx does not recognize Aristotle's distinction between production and action. Instead, he characterizes all human activity as production, but sees the production of material culture as fundamental, and all other kinds of production as dependent. This also has the effect of reversing Aristotle's evaluation of production and action. Not only is production for Marx the most significant and valued human activity—it has effectively swallowed up all other kinds of activity, which are now just secondary forms of it.

Marx, like Aristotle, routinely speaks of the producer as a single individual. But in Marx's case, there is some reason for thinking this is more than an expository device. There is a difference between conceiving of production as inherently social—which Marx does—and conceiving of it as inherently collaborative, about which he is at best ambivalent. For Marx, production is inherently social, first, because the individuals who engage in it are the individuals they are only in virtue of the social conditions that have informed their development; and second, because the mode of production in which individuals engage is specific to historically local social conditions. But you are fully social in this sense even when *not* collaborating in the literal sense of working together face-to-face:

> To be avoided above all is establishing 'society' once again as an abstraction over against the individual. The individual *is* the *social being*. The expression of his life—even if it does not appear immediately in the form

of a *communal* expression carried out together with others—is therefore an expression and assertion of *social life*. (Marx 1997, 306)

In his early work, Marx explicitly valorizes individual production as the ideal form of production, and, thus, implicitly devalues collaborative production at the same time. This comes out in his brief discussion of what he calls 'free human production'—the form production would take in the ideal communist society:

> Suppose we had produced things as human beings: in his production each of us would have *twice affirmed* himself and the other. (1) In my *production* I would have objectified my *individuality* and its *particularity,* and in the course of the activity I would have enjoyed an individual *life;* in viewing the object I would have experienced the individual joy of knowing my personality as an *objective, sensuously perceptible,* and *indubitable* power. (2) In your satisfaction and your use of my product I would have had the *direct* and conscious satisfaction that my work satisfied a *human* need, that it objectified *human* nature, and that it created an object appropriate to the need of another *human* being. (3) I would have been the *mediator* between you and the species and you would have experienced me as a redintegration of your own nature and a necessary part of your self; I would have been affirmed in your thought as well as your love. (4) In my individual life I would have directly created your life; in my individual activity I would have immediately *confirmed* and *realized* my true *human* and *social* nature. (Marx 1997, 281)

This passage glorifies the social aspects of production and the relationship between the producer and the consumer. But if a product is to be the expression of an individual's particularity, then the production process, or at least the design phase, must be an individual activity rather than a collaborative one. To the extent that I collaborate with you in the design of a product, it will not be an expression of *my* individuality, but at best a compromise that does not express the individuality of either one of us. Thus, the point at which others enter the picture here is necessarily as consumers of my product, not as co-producers. And although the individual producer both exemplifies social characteristics and uses his product to promote social bonding, his productive activity itself is presented as solitary.

Marx's later views are more complex. He came to realize the importance of collaboration—particularly the division of labor in industrial manufacturing contexts—in increasing productivity and, thus, underwriting economic and technological progress:

> When the worker co-operates in a planned way with others, he strips off the fetters of his individuality, and develops the capabilities of his species. (Marx 1976, 447)

But at the same time, Marx criticizes all historical forms of cooperation for restricting the freedom of action of the individual. There are passages in both earlier and later works that point to the unavoidable division of labor in cooperative endeavors as the underlying cause of this curtailment of individual freedom:

> [T]he division of labor offers us the first example for the fact that man's own act becomes an alien power opposed to him and enslaving him instead of being controlled by him—as long as man remains in natural society, as long as a split exists between the particular and the common interest, and as long as the activity is not voluntarily but naturally divided. For as soon as labor is distributed, each person has a particular, exclusive area of activity which is imposed on him and from which he cannot escape. (Marx and Engels 1994, 119)

This applies to collaboration at any scale—from small face-to-face task groups, to large capitalist manufacturing plants, to work specialization in society as a whole. In all historically attested collaborative situations, the individual is subject to an external power directing her activity. This is not necessarily the opposing power of another individual, but the institutional power inhering in the distinctive social structures of the collaborative interaction. This situation is aggravated in the division of labor in large-scale manufacturing under capitalism, which dehumanizes the worker by relegating her to the machine-like repetition of unskilled operations.[5] Marx calls this contemporary form of cooperation 'purely despotic' (Marx 1976, 450):

> Moreover, the co-operation of wage-labourers is entirely brought about by the capital that employs them. Their unification into one single productive body, and the establishment of a connection between their individual functions, lies outside their competence. These things are not their own act, but the act of the capital that brings them together and maintains them in that situation. Hence the interconnection between their various labours confronts them, in the realm of ideas, as a plan drawn up by the capitalist, and, in practice, as his authority, as the powerful will of a being outside them, who subjects their activity to his purpose. (Marx 1976, 449–50)

Thus far, it seems that loss of individual freedom of action is an ineluctable side effect of collaboration in production, especially in industrial manufacturing.

But Marx has a vision. He believes that in the ideal communist society the advantages of cooperation will be maintained, but the freedom of the individual will not be curtailed by collaborative structures. Rather it will be preserved in a free association of workers.

> In communist society, however, where nobody has an exclusive area of activity and each can train himself in any branch he wishes, society

regulates the general production, making it possible for me to do one thing today and another tomorrow, to hunt in the morning, fish in the afternoon, breed cattle in the evening, criticize after dinner, just as I like, without ever becoming a hunter, a fisherman, a herdsman, or a critic. (Marx and Engels 1994, 119)

In place of the old bourgeois society, with its classes and class antagonism, we shall have an association, in which the free development of each is the condition for the free development of all. (Marx and Engels 1999, 85)

Marx was notoriously vague about how this free association of producers would work, and equally vague about how the goods and services produced would be distributed to those who needed them. But he was very clear that the possibility of such a free association depended on the abolition of private property and the institution of collective ownership of the means of production. As he explains in chapter 32 of *Capital,* in the bad old days, individual producers owned their own means of production and they were free producers in that respect. But the fragmentation and isolation of resources attendant on this dispersed individual ownership stifled productivity and technological development. At the next major stage, capitalism concentrated ownership of the means of production in a few hands, and turned the vast majority of individual producers into wage slaves. But at the same time, capitalist manufacturing systems pooled resources and organized cooperation on a vast scale, thus promoting higher productivity and technological progress. Marx predicts that the next stage, the transition to communism, will return ownership of the means of production to the producers, but this time as collective rather than individual property. Thus, individual workers will both own the means of production *and* have the organizational knowledge for large-scale cooperation gained over the course of the industrial revolution (Marx 1976, 927–30). Ultimately, when the transition to communism is complete, the whole idea of ownership will drop out, and will no longer govern our relationships to our material culture, to nature, or to each other. In particular, the exploitation of others through the expropriation of the means of production will become literally inconceivable. This will render individual producers truly free for the first time in history, since for the first time they will be able to collaborate with each other, unconstrained by imposed social roles or limitations on their access to the means of production.[6]

What Marx is envisioning here is a sort of Hegelian synthesis, combining maximum individual freedom of activity (from the bad old feudal days) with maximum social cooperation (from bad old contemporary capitalism). In the communist future, the cooperating producer will nevertheless be able to produce in complete independence, that is, *as if* working alone. Thus, individual production as an *ideal* is still upheld here by Marx (Elster 1985). Indeed, it is *aufgehoben* in this synthesis, because it is not only preserved but enhanced by its embedding in cooperation. So, the twist here is that in the ideal communist society, Marx thinks it will be possible to have the individualistic cake and eat it. too. The individual will be completely free to produce as and when she wishes, and yet society will still reap the benefits of cooperation, thanks to some vaguely specified social arrangements for coordinating productive activity and distributing products. Thus, even in his later work, after having recognized the importance of collaboration in human production, Marx still holds on to individual production and the freedom of activity inherent in it as the ideal to be achieved, and so strengthens Aristotle's implicit individualism. But unlike Aristotle—and, indeed, unlike most action theorists in philosophy, ancient or modern—Marx thinks very seriously about collaboration in production in general, and has important things to say about its organization in large-scale manufacturing settings in particular. Where he falls short is in his understanding of the relationship between individual and collaborative productive activity.

DIPERT

Contemporary action theory has not taken up production as a subject matter in its own right. But Randall Dipert's (1993) 'artifact theory' applies contemporary action theory to the study of artifacts, thus generating an action-theoretic account of production. Dipert's leading idea is that artifacts must be understood in terms of the intentions of their creators:

> A correct description of an artifact as an artifact describes the artifact in the way that its creator conceived of it—at least as much as is now possible. Specifically, an object is contemplated by an agent, and some of its properties are intentionally modified (or perhaps, intentionally left alone); the production of an artifact is the goal of some intentional activity. (Dipert 1993, 15–16)

Dipert goes on to distinguish between instruments, tools, and artifacts. Instruments are naturally occurring objects that have been intentionally *used* for a purpose, for example, a stone used as a hammer. A tool is an instrument that has been intentionally *modified* for a purpose, for example, a flint nodule that has been flaked to a sharp edge for use as a hand axe. An artifact is a tool that is intended to be *recognized* as a tool with a specific purpose. This category, somewhat counterintuitively, includes objects we would normally call tools, such as carpenter's hammers and axes, as well as books, works of art, and so on. It also includes performances, which, Dipert argues, are artifacts fair and square by his definition, even if not commonly thought of as such. Dipert's account of production is meant to apply only to artifacts in this technical sense, but some easy modifications would generate parallel accounts of the production of tools and the adoption of instruments.

On Dipert's view, the intentions of the creator of an artifact are the outcome of a 'deliberative history,' in the course of which the creator contemplates the overall function of the artifact as her end and the possible alternative means for achieving this end, and then forms a complex set of intentions in the form of a construction plan:

> Of the many elements of the deliberative history, perhaps most important is the means-ends hierarchy, or plan, according to which the artifactual features were imposed on the object. Elsewhere, I have distinguished among the high-, middle-, and low-level intentions within the plan for an artifact. Roughly, these reflect goals or intentions increasingly subordinated, as means to ends, to the purpose or purposes of the artifact. (Dipert 1993, 54)

> My intentions, in making a screwdriver, to have another person come to believe it is a tool for turning screws, or actually come to use it easily for turning screws, are high-level intentions. My intention that the handle be out of stable plastic and that it have a certain shape, that the blade be metal, and so on, are middle-level intentions. They are conceived as means to my high-level intentions as ends. Finally, my intentions that I must use a lathe to create this shape, a drill press to place the hole in the handle for the blade, and so on, are low-level intentions. (Dipert 1993, 151)

Like Aristotle, Dipert emphasizes the role of habit. The plan, which consists of fully conscious, explicit intentions, is supported in execution by a network of not fully conscious 'half-intentional' habits (Dipert 1993, 49–51). For example, my choice of wood as opposed to plastic for the handle of the screwdriver would be a fully conscious intention, but my manipulation of the lathe in shaping it would be a half-intentional habit.

Dipert's account of production reproduces the main features we found in both Aristotle's account and Marx's account. There is a design phase in which a mental plan for producing the artifact is devised, and then a construction phase in which this plan is carried out. The design phase involves an elaborate hierarchy of intentions, the lower levels of which spell out the steps and conditions necessary for achieving the desired results at the higher levels. This hierarchy of intentions is the result of deliberation about the means for achieving the desired overall end and any intermediate ends that may be required. The most important advance Dipert makes here is to characterize this mental design as a plan. This reflects the influence of action theory, which in the last few decades has developed a planning theory of intention (Goldman 1970; Brand 1986; Bratman 1999b; Mele 1992). Aristotle's conception of production as involving a mental means-end analysis is already well on the way to a plan-based account of production, but the direct appeal to planning theory makes available a much more precise and sophisticated conceptual framework, as we shall see in the next chapter.

Finally, since on Dipert's view the features of the artifact are imposed on it in accordance with a mental plan, construction would seem to be unintelligent execution. But Dipert introduces an apparently countervailing consideration with regard to plan execution in the case of performance artifacts. The performer is, in effect, the constructor of the artifact. But she is not necessarily its creator, that is, the original author of the work; and this is particularly true in the case of Western classical music, the domain from which Dipert draws most of his examples. Dipert's (1993, 206) theory of performance suggests that the performer is an agent whose intention is to carry out the intentions of another agent, the creator. But typically, the intentions of the creator of the work are not fully known. So in practice, the performer is forced into a creative role, fleshing out the author's known intentions with some of her own. Thus, a performance is to some extent a matter of *intelligent* execution.

The important point is that Dipert *does* uphold the idea of unintelligent execution as an ideal, although one that can rarely be fully achieved in practice. On his view, if the creator's intentions were completely known, the performer would—and should—be an unintelligent executor. So the intelligent execution Dipert allows for is merely *faute de mieux*. Thus, Dipert clings to unintelligent execution as an ideal even while recognizing the importance of intelligent execution in practice, just as Marx clings to individual production as an ideal even while recognizing the importance of collaboration in practice.

Unlike either Aristotle or Marx, Dipert is explicit about the individualism of his view:

> What I call 'art works' are necessarily experienced as artifacts, and what I call 'artifacts' are necessarily conceived in terms of an individual agent, deliberative history, act of creation, and so on. This account of artifacts, and thus of art works, is highly biased toward 'individualistic' accounts of agency, thought, and action. I think it is useful to have such an account of idealized individual agency, even if one ultimately ends up rejecting that there are many such examples in actual human behavior. I happen to think the idea is also necessary for making sense of many of our institutions and thoughts about ourselves and that the theory is, to some extent, of some people, and on some occasions, true. (Dipert 1993, 194–95)

Dipert goes so far as to suggest that the deliberative history of all artifacts, even those known to have been created collaboratively, should be reconstructed as if it were the work of a single individual. He mentions that one motivation for this is to give an account of the unity of the artifact in terms of the unity of the producer's intentions as directed towards an end. Thus for Dipert, individual production functions as a sort of ideal type in accordance with which actual production activities and their results can be understood

(Dipert 1986, 406 and 1993, 32–37). But this leaves his account open to the same worries that Aristotle's account raised, since however useful these reconstructions may be for some limited purposes, they direct attention away from the study of collaborative production. Thus, while acknowledging that individual production is an ideal not always instantiated in practice, Dipert does not make any significant effort to understand collaborative production or its relationship to individual production, as Marx at least tried to do. On the other hand, Dipert's forthright individualism with regard to production is an important confirmation of the historical tendency toward individualism we detected in less clear forms in both Aristotle and Marx.

THE CENTRALIZED CONTROL MODEL

All three accounts of production we have considered share the following features:

- An antecedent, mental design phase is distinguished from a subsequent construction phase;
- The mental design is formed by an individual deliberating about the means for constructing a given product;
- The design specifies the features of the product and gives step-by-step instructions for constructing it;
- The construction phase is an unintelligent execution of these instructions carried out either by the designer or by some other individual or individuals.

These four features can be collectively characterized in terms of centralized control. The common sense of 'control' is that of a directive or determining force. But etymologically 'control' is an accounting term derived from the French *contre-roller,* which refers to the practice of keeping a copy of a ledger for purposes of account verification. The etymological and common senses of 'control' are unified by the idea that in *faithful* copying, the features of the original determine all the relevant features of the copy through the transcription process. Faithful copying involves two distinct phases—an antecedent phase in which an original is devised or identified, and a subsequent copying phase in which the features of the original are transcribed. These are the design and construction phases of the account of production we have been considering. The design (original) specifies all the relevant features of the product (copy).

In the case of simple copying procedures, the copier can be assumed to know how to transcribe these relevant features. But where this assumption cannot be made, the original must also include instructions for how the copying is to be done. These instructions are the construction plan in the accounts of production we have been considering. The actual construction (copying), then, is a process that faithfully follows the instructions of the construction plan, and by so doing reproduces in a material medium the features of the product specified in the design. This faithful copying relationship between the design and construction phases of production is the *control* aspect of the model.

The main idea behind the *centralization* aspect of the model is that the design—and, thus, control—typically resides, or ideally should reside, in the mind of a single individual. This idea incorporates two related assumptions. First, even if the construction is carried out by a group of collaborating individuals, control of the construction process is implicitly understood to be exercised centrally by the designer. And second, the designer is implicitly understood to be a single individual. A common variation of this second assumption is to admit that design is often the work of a team or group of people, but to insist, as Dipert does, that it can be better understood by reconstructing it as the work of a single individual. The centralization aspect of the model thus embodies the assumption that the paradigm case of production is the individual skilled artisan working in solitary splendor.

This individualism with regard to the activity of production is the most important sense of centralization for our purposes here. But there is also a secondary sense of centralization found in many contexts. In the centralized control model, the design is regarded as a mental plan devised through deliberation. This implies centralization *within* the mind of the individual designer. Specifically, it implies a central planning function that takes as input all the available information about the desired product, processes it, and outputs a plan, or design.

I said at the outset of this chapter that the two main problems with action theory are its lack of attention to collaboration on the one hand, and to improvisation on the other. The historical review of Aristotle, Marx, and Dipert suggests that these *lacunae* are long-standing in the history of action theory, and that they are the consequences of a historical commitment to the centralized control model. My project in the rest of this chapter is to give some indication of how wide and deep these *lacunae* really are, and in consequence how inadequate the centralized control model really is.

It might seem strange that the existence of these *lacunae* has not been recognized, or when recognized has not been considered problematic for the centralized control model. But I think the implicit assumption has been that collaboration and improvisation are strictly secondary phenomena, and that once individual action and planning are well understood, accounts of collaborative action and improvisation will just fall out, or, at worst, require only a bit of tweaking and the reapplication of available theoretical resources. I fear this is unlikely to prove true.

First of all, the assumption that collaboration and joint action generally can be understood on the basis of a prior understanding of individual action and very little more, involves a commitment to some form of methodological individualism—the idea that social structures and group activities can be fully explained in terms of the intentional states and actions of the individuals making up the social group. Methodological individualism has been repeatedly challenged on the grounds that the individual is developmentally the product of social processes involving interactions with others, that individuals routinely carry out many of their activities in concert with others, and that even solitary action is continuously oriented to locally established practices and social norms. Thus individual action cannot be properly understood without a prior understanding of the relevant social practices and interactional structures (Joas 1996; Kincaid 1986). On some interpretations, this is taken to mean that individual action is the secondary phenomenon and that joint action is primary. On the interpretation I favor, however, it means that joint action and individual action are equiprimordial modes of human activity that must be investigated side by side and in interrelation with each other from the start. In any case, if the critics of methodological individualism are correct, an adequate account of collaboration is not going to just fall out of a prior, adequate account of individual action. It will require a separate and parallel effort.

Unfortunately, it is not clear that the centralized control model renders an adequate account of individual action, either. The focus on control through planning as the sole structuring principle of human action betrays an implicit assumption that improvisation can be understood as a diluted or degraded form of planning, and that all the resources for understanding improvisation are thus in principle already available to the planning theorist. This assumption has not been as widely challenged as methodological individualism has been, although some challenges to it have surfaced in anthropology (Suchman 2007) and artificial intelligence (Brooks 1999; Agre and Chapman 1990). But this work is rarely cited in the philosophical literature, and no similar critique of planning has arisen indigenously in action theory. Indeed, improvisation is not even a topic of conversation among action theorists. But if the relevant work outside philosophy is on the right track, it indicates that the structure of improvised activity has distinctive features that set it apart from the structure of planned activity. Thus, in this case, too, a separate and parallel effort is needed to understand improvisation and its relationship to planning. In the next two sections, I will lay the groundwork for investigating these issues by briefly describing some of the more distinctive general features of collaboration and improvisation.

CENTRALIZATION AND COLLABORATION

Collaborative activity in the production of material culture is ubiquitous. Sometimes it is necessitated by the nature of the task and the agents involved. For example, collaboration is often necessary because no single individual possesses the physical strength and/or the time to accomplish the construction task alone. Any item of material culture that is large (e.g., buildings, roads) or involves simultaneous performance (e.g., most plays and many musical pieces) thus requires collaborative construction. Many construction projects are also impossible to accomplish alone, because no one individual possesses all the necessary knowledge or skills. Technically sophisticated items (e.g., computers, cars) are of this sort, but even in the case of buildings as relatively unsophisticated as residences, specialization to specific skilled tasks is standard. The carpenter, the plumber, the electrician, the mason, and the roofer are typically all different individuals. Collaboration among designers is also often necessitated by such natural limitations of individual knowledge and skill. This is perhaps most evident in the case of technically and socially sophisticated items of material culture, such as photocopiers or electric guitars. Companies that make such things usually employ design teams. Typically, some team members are responsible for the technical side, with further specialization for specific technical aspects; other team members are responsible for the aesthetic side and the marketing-related aspects. An important variation on this last type of collaboration, and one that does not usually involve face-to-face contact between individuals, is the use of parts or materials that have been designed and constructed separately by other people. Cooks do not make their own butter or grind their own flour, and luthiers buy rather than make strings and electric pickups for their instruments.

I want to stress the necessity of collaborative production under certain commonly encountered conditions in order to highlight the inevitability of collaboration in everyday activity. But it is important to note that, for the most part, collaboration is not strictly necessitated. One reason for this is that even where it is possible for an individual to manage the physical requirements or learn all the necessary skills for a task, there is often a clear advantage in relying on collaboration. Making your own butter is not all that difficult, but it takes time and equipment, so the most efficient thing is to get it from the dairy farmer instead. And then you have time and energy left over to make fancy pastries. This is precisely Marx's (1976) point when he says that the collaborating individual 'strips off the fetters of his individuality and develops the capabilities of his species' (447). In addition, traditional divisions of labor and work specialization in human societies promote collaboration beyond what is either necessitated by the nature of the task, or recommended for reasons of efficiency. And last but not least, collaboration may be prompted not by hard and fast limits on what individuals can reasonably know or do by themselves, but by sheer differences of interest. For example, you might offer to make the salad for dinner because that is something you particularly enjoy doing, even though the main cook might be a fine salad maker and have plenty of time to do it.

Some important and especially interesting forms of collaboration arise because the designer and the constructor are often different individuals. Here, too, collaboration is frequently necessary. You would not expect a composer or an architect to have either the physical capacity or all the requisite skills to realize their designs on their own. On the other hand, collaboration between designer and constructor is often in principle voluntary. Songwriters are typically quite capable of performing their own songs as solo pieces, and it would be an odd recipe deviser who could not prepare the dish herself. But in both of these cases, the proliferation of the item through collaboration between designers and constructors is integral to the social practices involved in the production and use of the items of material culture in question.

The centralized control model understands design and construction as distinct phases of production, with all the thinking relegated to the design phase and construction construed in consequence as merely unintelligent execution. This puts a particular slant on the nature of the collaborative relationship between designers and constructors—constructors collaborate by doing what designers tell them to do. But the discussion of Dipert's theory of performance already pointed to a problem with this slant. Although Dipert adheres to the idea of unintelligent execution as an ideal, he rightly stresses that it is rarely realized in practice, because the performer is usually not in a position to know the intentions of the designer. And this means that the performer must be an intelligent executor to one extent or another. This is not specific to performance theory, but has general application to any case where the collaborative relationship bridges design and construction. We will return to this point, but for now it should simply be noted that the constructor, as a more or less intelligent executor, is a full-fledged collaborator in the sense that some of the deliberation and creative decision making is actually vested in them.

In addition, collaboration between designers and constructors is important because it calls attention to the fact that collaboration can be a more or less distant relationship. The designer and the constructor need not work face-to-face, know each other as individuals, or even communicate directly. Indeed, the designer may be long dead, as is often the case with the performance of musical pieces or plays. This kind of distant relationship between collaborators occurs in a slightly different form within both the design phase and the construction phase. As we noted above, component parts of items of material culture are often separately constructed and simply incorporated into the item presently under construction. These component parts often are also separately designed, and either specified as integral components by the designer, or decided upon by the constructor. For example, a recipe writer might include sherry in the list of ingredients, but the recipe for the sherry and the making of it are entirely the work of other people.

A particularly interesting variant I shall call creative appropriation combines distant collaboration between designers and constructors with execution that is not merely intelligent but overtly creative. Songwriting, which we will look at in detail in Chapter 4, yields paradigmatic examples, such as writing new lyrics to an existing tune. The Beach Boys' 'Surfin' USA,' for instance, is Chuck Berry's 'Sweet Little Sixteen' with new lyrics written (probably) by Brian Wilson. More interesting cases involve the interpretive appropriation of a song in such a way that the music as well is substantially redesigned. Led Zeppelin did this brilliantly with Memphis Minnie's 'When the Levee Breaks,' for example, changing the tempo and the key, abandoning most of the original verses, rewriting some lines of the verses they kept, changing the melody substantially, and writing a bridge verse with a different melody and lyrics.[7]

Creative appropriation may very well be more common in material culture domains that involve performances or items that are consumed during use, such as food and drink or medication. Such items of material culture must be constructed anew for every occasion of use, and this means there is a permanent possibility of constructing them differently each time—changing the recipe a bit, or varying some aspect of the performance, for instance. But even more durable items of material culture require maintenance, repair, and refurbishing, and may be voluntarily rebuilt or remodeled. Thus, they, too, are subject to creative appropriation—barns or churches are sometimes remodeled for use as residences, for example.

At this point, we must refine the distinction we made between the social and the collaborative when we examined Marx's theory of production. Collaborators may be geographically separated, temporally separated, communicatively isolated, or socially isolated in the sense that they do not know each other personally as individuals. So there is a continuum between the social and the collaborative, with clear cases at both extremes, but no sharp dividing line anywhere in between. A clear case of collaboration would be members of an extended family spending the afternoon in the kitchen putting up tomatoes. Here there is face-to-face contact between individuals in a single spatiotemporal location with ample use of direct communication. A clear case of sociality would be Big Joe Williams's creative appropriation of a traditional field holler as the basis for his now ubiquitous 'Baby, Please Don't Go.' It is not clear exactly which traditional holler inspired Williams—different sources make different speculations. What is clear is that the traditional variants of this tune stretch back into the mists of time, and no one really knows who originated any of them. So Williams was relying on what may be fairly characterized as a social resource.[8]

When we consider this last example more closely, though, we can see that it is best described as a case of *individual* action, but with a social dimension. As the anthropologist Peter Reynolds puts it:

> Although human beings can and often do work alone, even solitary labor is almost always a social activity because it is typically directed towards social ends, requires materials conveyed through social exchange, is typically one step of a larger, cooperative endeavor, and uses skills developed as a member of society. (Reynolds 1993, 412)

But, of course, collaborative activities have this inherent social dimension as well. So although collaboration is overtly social in that it involves interaction among individuals, all human action is covertly social, in that it depends on social practices, products, norms, and so on. Thus, the social does not first enter the arena of human action in overt forms of collaboration, but pre-exists both individual and collaborative action as a sustaining medium for human activity. There is no sharp dividing line between individual action and collaborative action, because the relationships and interactions between people that might be thought to constitute collaboration exist in varying degrees, from face-to-face interactions with persons known to you, to more distant interactions with strangers, or even, through their works, with people long dead and perhaps unknown even to history as named individuals.

Individual Action • Attenuated Forms of Collaboration • Face-to-Face Collaboration

$\leftarrow$ Sociality $\rightarrow$

Collaboration as a distinct species of sociality has a special significance for a philosophy of material culture. First, to the extent that action theory inquires into the social at all, the domain of the investigation has been collaborative action. Second, and more importantly, collaboration is the most concrete manifestation of human sociality. And as sociality at work in the world, collaborative activity is the growing point of human sociality in general, and of specific cultures in particular. Even more specifically, it is the primary locus of both the reproduction of material culture traditions and innovation within them.

This claim might be rejected by some on the grounds that individuals acting alone are at least equally responsible for the reproduction of culture; and perhaps even more responsible for cultural innovation than are collaborators, since innovation is the province of the lone artistic genius or solitary inventor. We have already stressed the ubiquity of design phase collaboration. But a more comprehensive answer to this objection is provided by Peter Reynolds (1993). He argues that the perception of individual action as central or especially typical of human activity in production contexts is a culturally specific bias, promoted as much by the scientific community as by anyone else, but not supported by the anthropological evidence. Reynolds compared videotapes of archaeologists demonstrating the construction and use of stone tools, in which the archaeologist is virtually without exception represented as an individual working alone, with field videotapes of Australian Aborigines making and using stone tools for everyday purposes, in which most of the activity is collaborative. He concludes that:

> In industrial societies, 'tool use' is defined as something that is done with the hands by an individual working alone . . . and in popular books in Western culture, such as Jean Auel's novels about the Paleolithic . . . the heroine discovers fire, invents the bow and arrow, tames the horse, and so on. Although this view of human history is dismissed by anthropologists as simplistic, it is not as far from canonical scientific theory as many archaeologists would like to believe. Indeed, evolutionary notions

of tool use are permeated with Eurocentric assumptions that cannot be reconciled with the activities of children in a preschool, much less survive cross-cultural comparison. (Reynolds 1993, 410)

Moreover, solitary labor is the exception in the human species rather than the rule, and in all societies work is typically performed by face-to-face task groups of people cooperating to accomplish a common goal. Even in the manufacture of stone tools, which can in fact be done by a single individual working alone (as indeed has been proven by the archaeologist turned flint-knapper), people such as the Australian Aborigines who depend on this technology for their livelihood nonetheless produce stone tools as a collective enterprise, as for example when one person molds the knife handles, while another attaches them to the blades. (Reynolds 1993, 412–13)

Reynolds's main argument focuses on the twin claims that what is distinctive about human tool use is the social organization of activity in technical contexts; and that this social organization centers on collaborative face-to-face task groups engaging in what he calls 'heterotechnic cooperation.' In support of the first point, he analyzed cross-species and cross-cultural videotapes, including videotapes of children playing at making things. The most striking difference he observed was that nonhuman primates invariably make and use tools individually, whereas human beings normally make and use them in collaboratively organized groups. Other differences do exist. For example, human products tend to have a complex structure consisting of separable but interrelated parts; and human skill in manufacturing and manipulating these tools outstrips that of other primates. However, neither of these differences is particularly evident in children, whose skills and products are often well within the competence of nonhuman primates. On the other hand, children do typically exhibit full-fledged social and collaborative behavior in their play, which aligns them clearly with adult humans rather than with nonhuman primates. Reynolds does not deny that nonhuman primates do engage in social and collaborative behavior such as mutual grooming and group play. His point is, rather, that in their case sociality and collaboration are *not* integrated into their technical activity, as is the case with humans. Collaborative production and use of material culture is, thus, not just typical of human beings as a matter of fact, but has deep phylogenetic roots.

Reynolds also has something to say about the exact nature of the collaborative organization introduced by the integration of the social and the technical:

I call this process *heterotechnic* cooperation ('different crafts') to emphasize the complementarity of social roles. Heterotechnic cooperation may be contrasted with *symmetric* cooperation, in which all the participants do the same thing at the same time in order to facilitate a common goal . . . Thus human technology is not just 'tool use,' and not just 'cooperative' tool use, but tool use combined with a social organization for heterotechnic cooperation. This heterotechnic aspect of human tool use, characterized by complementary technical roles among the participants, is manifested in all human societies by a distinct form of social organization that I call the *face-to-face task group*—a social structure defined by *the shared intention to transform matter and energy through the cooperative and complementary use of tools and tool-using skills by a group of people in face-to-face contact.* (Reynolds 1993, 412)

The complementarity of social and technical roles brings with it a number of other features, such as communication among task group members. Reynolds also holds, somewhat controversially, that this entire complex of features rooted in the basic structure of heterotechnic cooperation is not only distinctively human, but characteristic of all human societies, from the less technologically sophisticated to the industrial.

Reynolds introduces significant difficulties for the centralized control model. First, if he is right, individualist approaches miss precisely what is most characteristic and distinctive about the production and use of material culture by human beings. Moreover, Reynolds casts suspicion on the idea, explicitly endorsed by Dipert, that individualist reconstruction of what are in fact collaborative activities constitutes an appropriate methodology for the study of production. This methodology conceals collaborative structures of interaction as a matter of principle, and so is at best simplistic and at worst ideological.

Second, it follows from Reynolds's analysis that individualist accounts will not provide adequate resources for the understanding of collaboration, because the central phenomena involved in collaborative activity, such as task specialization, complementarity of roles, and symbolic communication, simply do not show up in solitary individual activity. Sociality is common to the individual and the collaborative case. For example, a solitary thinker and a group might both use the same language. The problem is that the individual and the group do not necessarily use language in the same way or to accomplish the same things. For example, group deliberation—say, by a group of designers deliberating about the features of a new product—exhibits phenomena not found in individual deliberation. It is possible for the members of the group to surprise each other, either by bringing in novel information, or by presenting a novel line of reasoning. Similarly, when group members disagree with each other, some standard ways of resolving disagreements include a senior member of the group having final say or veto power, majority rule implemented by voting, or agreement to disagree, perhaps with some members of the group splitting off to form a new group with a divergent project. Such phenomena indicate dimensions of group deliberation for which there are no good analogues in individual deliberation.

Finally, Reynolds's view raises questions about where the mental design would be in the case of a collaborating group. Task specialization and role complementarity ensure that it is vastly unlikely to be present in its entirety in any member of the group. One possibility would be to understand the collaborative design process as distributed cognition *à la* Hutchins (1995). On this view, groups, not individuals, are taken as the unit of analysis, and cognitive processes are regarded as distributed across agents and their cultural environment, including public representations and material culture. This would require giving up on the idea that the design is a monolithically mental construct, since in distributed cognition, mental representations have no privileged status and are typically only elements in a dynamic propagation of representations through individual, social, and material contexts. A somewhat more exotic option would be to understand the collaborating group as a group mind. Although there were stirrings earlier (Gilbert 1989, 1996), in the wake of the proposal by Andy Clark and David Chalmers (1998) that minds extend outside the bounds of skin and skull, there have been a number of serious attempts to work out an account of socially extended minds (Pettit 2003; Tollefsen 2006; Huebner 2008). This option would allow the mental status of the design to be preserved. I favor the first option myself. But in either case, the important point at this juncture is that individualistic accounts of production committed to the centralized control model routinely ignore these and many similar issues about group production, regardless of whether the individualism is a matter of principle or a mere expository convenience.

CONTROL AND IMPROVISATION

The control ideal of the faithful copy calls for all relevant features of the product to be specified in the design along with a set of instructions for construction. In other words, the design is ideally supposed to be an algorithm (effective procedure) for realizing both the construction process and the product. Not surprisingly, this ideal is not an accurate description of everyday processes of production. The most recent thinking characterizes designs as plans,[9] and plans are sometimes thought of as recipes.[10] So in this section, I will use the example of cooking with a recipe to demonstrate and categorize the divergences of everyday production processes from what would be expected based on the control ideal. The examples on which I will focus involve written recipes, which may be conveniently regarded as externalized versions of the originating cook's mental design, for the purpose of communicating the design from the designer (the originating cook) to potential constructors (other cooks).

At first blush, recipes do seem to conform to the control model, since they normally include a description of the dish and instructions for combining the listed ingredients in order to achieve the result specified. But a closer look reveals an important divergence from control as an ideal—recipes typically leave many details open. Some of these involve features of the product. For example, a recipe may suggest either sour cream or yogurt as a thinner for cucumber soup, or a cake recipe may simply tell the cook to 'frost with a butter frosting.' Many recipes also list some ingredients as optional altogether—chopped nuts are often optional in cookie recipes, for example. Indeed, this is such a common practice that some cookbooks have a convention for indicating optional ingredients, such as enclosing them in parentheses. In addition, recipes frequently specify ingredients generically. A recipe might call for a cup of shortening, for instance, and then you have to decide between butter, margarine, vegetable oil, and so on.

The construction instructions also leave details open. Consider the following (highly recommended) cookie recipe.

Rolled Pecan Cookies

4 tablespoons powdered sugar	1 tablespoon ice water
7 oz. butter (scant cup)	2 cups flour
2 cups pecans (small pieces)	1/8 teaspoon salt
1 teaspoon vanilla	

Cream butter and sugar, add the rest. Roll with palms of hands into finger lengths. Bake 45 minutes (325°F). Roll in powdered sugar while warm, or shake in bag with ½ cup powdered sugar. (Kander 1947, 477)

Notice, first, that the order in which to mix ingredients is not completely specified—you are on your own after creaming the butter and sugar. Even where recipes do specify this order more completely, it is largely conventional. In making cookies and cakes, it rarely matters whether you first sift the dry ingredients, then mix the wet ingredients, or *vice versa*. The only essential thing is that the dry and the wet ingredients be mixed separately before combining them. The instructions, thus, at best constitute a partial order on the steps in the construction process. Second, some crucial steps are not specified. Even a novice cook will know to put these cookies on a baking sheet before baking them, but the recipe does not actually tell you to do this. In addition, there is an open question about whether to grease the baking sheet or not. More experienced cooks will realize that this is unnecessary, because these cookies have so much butter in them they could not stick to anything if they tried. Finally, the last instruction explicitly requires the cook to decide between two options for coating the cookies with powdered sugar, and if the bag option is chosen, the cook must further decide between paper and plastic.

Whether it is the details of the product or of the construction instructions that are left open, the result is an incomplete specification of what the cook is to do. In some cases, the cook is expected to supply the requisite details on the basis of habits she has acquired (e.g., putting the cookies on a baking sheet). In other cases, the cook is implicitly expected to make a decision based on background knowledge she may be presumed to have (e.g., greasing the baking sheet). This already indicates that some of the thinking necessary for making the product takes place in the construction phase. But in addition, recipes often explicitly prompt cooks to make decisions that will affect what features the product will have, or how those features will be achieved (e.g., listing optional ingredients or offering alternative construction procedures). This confirms that cooking practices do not regard construction as unintelligent execution. Rather, they assign to the construction phase some of the deliberation and decision making regarded under the control ideal as the prerogative of the design phase.

This observation is confirmed and extended by looking at how cooks actually use recipes. The expectation generated by the control model is that cooks faithfully follow recipes. But, in fact, cooks typically use recipes as a basis for improvisations of various sorts.[11] Improvisation is normally a response to local conditions. Sometimes, these are difficulties encountered in the construction process. When you do not have an ingredient called for by a recipe, you can often substitute something else—cocoa and butter can be used in place of baking chocolate, for instance. On the other hand, sometimes, local conditions serendipitously make available resources you can exploit. A cook with a walnut tree in his backyard might substitute walnuts for pecans in the recipe above. A third type of condition involves the special needs or desires of the cook and/or her clientele. In the cookie recipe above, a vegan cook would substitute a vegetable shortening for the butter.

Cooks sometimes arrive at a stable customization of a recipe after a period of improvisatory experimentation. For example, because my oven runs a little hot, I tried out a number of different combinations of oven temperatures and baking times for the cookie recipe above, and finally settled on 325°F for 40 minutes, plus turning the cookie sheet at the 20-minute mark for more even browning. On the other hand, recipes represent a permanent possibility of doing something different on the next occasion, perhaps even just on a whim rather than because of some specific difficulty or opportunity. A cook might just try rolling these pecan cookies in colored sprinkles or shaved chocolate instead of powdered sugar.

So recipes diverge from the control ideal in two ways. They explicitly or implicitly require the construction phase cook to do some of the actual design work. Additionally, they are routinely used by cooks as a basis for further improvisational alterations of the design rather than faithfully followed. This means that the constructor is not regarded as an unintelligent executor for the most part; and even to the extent that the constructor is so regarded on the face of it, the regular practice of cooks is to execute intelligently by revising recipes as need or opportunity arises. These two characteristics of recipes and their use have been recognized in the action theory literature as characteristics of plans in general. Michael Bratman (1999a, 1999b), in particular, has emphasized the partial nature of plans, which requires us to fill them in and revise them, both before and during execution.

Thus, it appears that the divergence of everyday designs and plans from the control ideal is commonly acknowledged.

The reasons for this divergence are clear. The full-fledged control ideal embodies a number of clearly false assumptions about what kind of world we live in and/or what kind of agents we are. Some of these assumptions were close to explicit in early artificial intelligence work on planning, as Martha Pollack describes it:

> The agent is given a goal, it computes a plan for achieving it, and then, at least in principle, it executes that plan. The environment is quiescent; the agent is the only force acting on it. So nothing of significance happens while the agent is forming its plan. And nothing happens while the agent is executing that plan, except what the agent itself causes to happen. (Pollack 1992, 45)

This quiescence of the environment is the assumption that makes detailed advance planning and unintelligent execution even intelligible as options. There is also an implicit correlative assumption here that the world is homogeneous across agents, such that if one agent devises a plan, another agent can in principle always execute it.

But as Pollack goes on to explain:

> Real environments are dynamic. They are populated by multiple agents that can and do effect change. Because they are dynamic, real environments may change while an agent is reasoning about how to achieve some goal, and these changes may undermine the assumptions upon which the agent's reasoning is based . . . Real environments may also change while an agent is executing a plan, and again they may change in ways that make the plan invalid . . . As if this were not enough, real environments may change in ways that do not invalidate a current plan, but instead offer new possibilities for action. (Pollack 1992, 46)

There is one possibility that Pollack does not mention that would make it possible to deal with such dynamic environments and still live up to the control ideal. If agents were omniscient, then the dynamic nature of the real environment would not matter, because all possible changes could be predicted and prepared for in advance in the planning phase. But this assumption also is clearly false. We must reckon with limited knowledge and cognitive capacities. So a serious commitment to the control ideal would commit us to false assumptions about the real nature of the world in which we live and about the kind of agents we are. Of course, no one actually does make these false assumptions. Even planning theorists in early AI work on action only assumed quiescent environments for heuristic purposes.

But the implications of rejecting the false assumptions underlying the control ideal have not been fully appreciated. It is not just a matter of the control ideal being unattainable in practice. Rather, it is a false ideal. Given the actual nature of our environment and of our agency, if we really lived up to it, our actions would routinely fail because our essential flexibility to accommodate problematic contingencies and exploit serendipitous opportunities would be compromised. If this is so, why are we not urged to be better improvisers, rather than constantly prompted to do more and better planning in every area of endeavor from the personal to the public? As individuals and small groups going about our daily lives, we are already consummate improvisers.[12] Improvisation is, thus, normally transparent to us in the same way breathing is. The exception is improvisation in performance arts, such as music or theater, where there are severe constraints on what the improvisers can do and when they must do it. So, these difficult exceptions are what we notice and think about first when someone mentions improvisation. Similarly, planning is relatively difficult for us, since it requires gathering up and organizing information and then monitoring execution. So it, too, is something we notice and struggle to improve. But there is a normative edge to these observations. If improvisation is, as I shall argue in the next chapter, our most fundamental and important *modus operandi,* perhaps we *should* pay more attention to becoming better improvisers rather than better planners.

In any case, for the most part, there has been no turn away from control as an ideal, or, more specifically, away from planning as the foundation for the theory of action in philosophy. The widespread acknowledgement that plans are necessarily partial and subject to revision ought to have generated an interest in *how* we go about filling in, adjusting, and revising our plans—or at least, so you would think. But this has not happened, and the reasons for it lie within action theory itself. The way the planning paradigm has developed has made it seem as though once planning is thoroughly understood, any aspects of action that might seem to fall under the heading of improvisation will already have been explained, and there will, therefore, be nothing for a separate theory of improvisation to do.

Chapter 2 investigates the current understanding of planning in action theory in order to show how this perception has developed, and why it is incorrect. This will further the critique of the centralized control model by showing that the planning orientation of traditional action theory not only makes improvisation invisible as a distinct phenomenon, but also hinders the development of the action-theoretic resources necessary for analyzing it. Then in Chapter 3 we will return to the issue of collaboration and investigate the understanding of multiple-agent action in current action theory. As we shall see, this understanding is also off the mark in important respects, not least because it takes individual action as foundational and attempts to derive the structure of multiple-agent action from it. These chapters lay the groundwork for Chapter 4, which sketches an account of improvisatory action with collaboration built in from the outset.

2   Taking Improvisation Seriously

Listen! Wasn't that the bell? Damn! the day and the dance begin and we
don't know the schedule! We have to improvise—all the world impro-
vises its day. Let us proceed today as all the world does!
—Friedrich Nietzsche,
The Gay Science, Book One, §22

Planning has recently become central to action theory as the foundation for
theories of intention and intentional action. But since almost everything we
do that is considered to be an action, properly speaking, is also considered
to be an intentional action, this development leaves little or no room in
action theory for a conception of improvisation—that is, *unplanned* action.
Improvisation is, thus, rendered invisible as a phenomenon of action, and
something close to inconceivable as a concern of theory. What conception of
planning has led to this understanding of all action as planned action? In this
chapter, we will address action theory in general, without specific reference
to production or use of material culture. The first section explores several
folk senses of 'plan,' which do leave room for a conception of unplanned
action. The second section takes up the philosophical sense of 'plan' involved
in current theories of both intention and intentional action, and shows how
it usurps the room left by the folk for a conception of unplanned action,
so that 'action' and 'planned action' end up seemingly synonymous. The
third section returns to the folk distinction between planned and unplanned
action, and argues that action theorists would be well advised to resurrect
this distinction and theorize improvisation alongside planning in the service
of a more accurate understanding of human life and action. Finally, the
fourth section returns to philosophical action theory to explore the resources
currently available for such a theory of improvisation. The conclusion is that
although there is at least one rather remote and unattended corner where
a theory of improvisation could conceivably take root, the majority of the
resources for the construction of such a theory will have to come from outside action theory.

SOUNDS LIKE A PLAN

There are clear cases of planning. For example: At breakfast on Thursday morning, I think to myself: 'I would really like to make lentil soup for lunch on Saturday. I'd better check the recipe now and put the ingredients I need on the grocery list so I can do the shopping on the way home from work tomorrow.' The salient features of such clear cases are these:

- there is a specified end;
- there are specified steps (means) for achieving that end;
- the end and the steps are formulated in advance of any action being taken; and
- the formulation is conscious and explicit, and involves deliberation about available options.

Cases having these features may be termed *prototypical plans*. They correspond to the lead definition of 'plan' typically found in dictionary entries. More importantly, its features align it clearly with the control aspect of the centralized control model of production. Here we have a mental planning phase distinguished from a later execution phase. This corresponds to the distinction between the design phase and the construction phase in production, except that here the execution *is* the product, that is, an action. Finally, the formulation of a plan, like the formulation of a product design, involves conscious deliberation. So just as a design is faithfully copied into a material medium in production, here a plan is faithfully executed in action. In short, the *control* aspect of the centralized control model of production generalizes to the explanation of action through the concept of planning.

The folk, however, use 'plan' in at least two senses that diverge from this prototype. The first of these is the use of 'plan' in situations where there is a specified end but no specified steps for achieving it. This is the sense in which we may plan *to* do something without having any plan *for* doing it. For example:

- We're planning to take a *real* vacation next year!
- The department plans to replace faculty members who retire.
- I am planning to read more of Foucault's work.

This folk sense of 'plan' diverges from the prototypical sense in that it takes the specification of an end action to be performed as a limiting case of having a plan. This preserves some of the features of the prototype, while dropping others. Specifically, the end is still formulated in advance, and in a conscious and explicit way. But it is not accompanied by a similar formulation of steps for achieving it, nor does it necessarily involve deliberation. The examples above give us some idea of why using 'plan' in this way makes sense from the folk point of view. First, while explicit, the end may be relatively undetailed. You cannot really start devising a detailed plan for a vacation until you have at least decided to take one. Second, your end may be such that you cannot now know much about the circumstances under which you will be setting out to achieve it. The department will have to wait until one of its members does retire before devising a full-fledged plan for recruiting a replacement. And finally, in many cases, the details of a plan can wait until the last minute because you already know in the abstract what you will need to do. I can find out very quickly what other books Foucault has written, whether the library has them, and so on. In short, just specifying an end is next door to having a plan for the folk, because the advance specification of the end is the crucial bit, and devising the means for achieving it is often either not possible at the moment, or is not problematic.

The second divergent use of 'plan' by the folk looks more like a prototypical plan at first blush because it involves the advance specification of a series of actions. For example:

> My plan for today includes beginning the day by preparing my lecture for my afternoon class, turning to some work on this paper, meeting Howard at the Faculty Club for lunch, giving my lecture, talking with John if he is in his office and, finally, picking up a manuscript at the computer center on the way home. (Bratman 1983, 271)

But this is *not* a prototypical plan. It is a list of separate ends, not a series of steps or subgoals for the achievement of an overall end. In this example, there is, in fact, a prototypical plan embedded in the list—preparing the lecture is a necessary step toward giving the lecture—but in principle, such a list may consist only of unrelated ends. What holds this sort of 'to do' list together is not overall means-end organization, as in the case of a prototypical plan, but rather a stated interval of time, in the course of which all the listed items are to be accomplished. This means that the list is typically not order sensitive, and that failing to accomplish one item on it has no effect on the accomplishment of the others. If I serendipitously run into John before lunch, I might talk to him then instead; or if he is not in his office that day, this end may be held over till tomorrow without affecting anything else on the 'to do' list. In this second folk sense of 'plan,' then, the specification of a *series* of ends is taken as a special case of a plan. This meaning, too, makes sense from the folk point of view because it shares with prototypical plans the feature of specifying explicitly in advance what is to be done.

What *both* these divergent folk senses of 'plan' share with prototypical plans is the idea of explicitly specifying in advance the action to be taken or the end to be achieved, even if only very schematically. This is extremely important for present purposes, because it means that the folk leave conceptual room for unplanned activity—activity that is *not* arranged in advance, but is literally improvised (not seen beforehand). Here are some examples of actions that would count as unplanned on the folk understanding.

- I see olives on sale at the supermarket, and grab a jar, although olives are not on my grocery list.
- I am driving to the grocery store on Saturday morning when I suddenly catch sight of a yard sale underway in a church parking lot. I hit the brakes and the turn signal and turn abruptly into the lot.
- I turn my head in response to noises coming from the hallway.

These are all cases where the use of the term 'plan' would be strange from the folk point of view. If asked why I bought the olives, given that they were not on the list, for instance, a typical response would be: 'Well, I didn't plan to get them, but they were on sale.' If, instead, I replied: 'Oh, I *planned* to get them—they were on sale!' I would be regarded as offering a lame excuse for impulse buying, or perhaps making a mild joke. Similarly, I did not plan to stop at the yard sale because I did not know it was going on until I caught sight of it; and I did not plan to turn my head because it was a response to unexpected noises. But as we shall see in the next section, these are all cases that are included in the meaning of 'plan' as many philosophical action theorists use this term. Thus, unlike the folk, action theorists leave little or no room for anything that might reasonably be called unplanned action.

PLANNER TAKES ALL

Planning has assumed a position of centrality in recent action theory as the basis for leading theories of both intention and intentional action. But the relationship between intention and intentional action has, at the same time, been problematized in certain respects. So, we will first look at how planning underwrites current theories of intention, and then examine separately how it underwrites theories of intentional action, where it plays a somewhat more complicated role.

It is generally accepted that intentions have, on the one hand, a motivational (or volitional) component that explains how they move us to act, and on the other hand, a representational (or cognitive) component that explains how the intention relates to specific resulting actions. It used to be generally accepted that intentions are reducible to configurations of beliefs and desires—an initially plausible view, since the desires supply the motivational component and the beliefs the representational component (Audi 1973; Churchland 1970; Davis 1984). But having a desire does not necessarily imply a commitment to fulfilling it the way that having an intention implies a commitment to achieving some end. And having beliefs relevant to an end does not necessarily involve any organization of intermediate actions toward the achievement of that end as having an intention seems to do.

Concerns such as these have prompted an appeal to planning as a central notion in the explanation of what it is to have an intention.

Having a plan prototypically involves the specification of an end and a series of steps for achieving it. And executing, or being prepared to execute, such a plan involves commitment to a course of action and to the achievement of the specified end.[1] Thus, the most straightforward view of the role of plans in having an intention is that the representational component of the intention is a plan and the motivational component is an executive attitude toward that plan. As Alfred Mele puts it:

> Intentions are executive states whose primary function is to bring the world into conformity with intention-embedded plans. (Mele 1992, 162)

This view must be further refined, however, because, as noted in our discussion of the folk senses of 'plan,' we often say we intend *to* do something without having a full-fledged plan *for* doing it:

> The representational element [of an intention] incorporates what we may call an *action plan,* or simply a *plan*. Plans need not be complex, detailed, or explicitly entertained. In the limiting case, an agent's plan for acting is a simple representation of his performing a basic action of a certain type. In other cases, the agent's plan is a representation of his prospective A-ing and of the route to A-ing that he intends to take. (Mele 1992, 109)

A basic action is an action an agent can just do, without any consideration of how to do it (Goldman 1970). Standard examples are simple movements, such as raising your arm or turning your head. But basic actions are relative to developmental level and skill—walking is a basic action for most adults, but not for infants; and playing an A minor chord is a basic action for skilled guitarists, but not for novices. Mele's point, then, can be spelled out in terms of the general relationship between an overall action and the steps needed to accomplish it. When the steps either do not need to be, or cannot be, explicitly contemplated by the agent at the time of intention formation, the agent may be considered to have a plan just in virtue of representing the overall action as her end. But when spelled out this way, the point can be seen to generalize far beyond basic actions. For instance, in the case of highly habituated activities—walking a familiar route to work, for example, or playing a familiar song on the guitar—the steps need not be contemplated at the time of intention formation. At the opposite end of the scale, in the case of actions where the terrain is unfamiliar or highly uncertain—following someone's lead in playing an unfamiliar song, for example, or following instructions for assembling a new appliance or item of furniture—the steps *cannot* be contemplated in advance by the agent, because they are to be supplied by someone or something else. If this is the right way to understand

and extend Mele's point, then it looks like action theorists are converging on the same understanding of 'plan' that we already noticed among the folk—a conception that in the limiting case allows the mere specification of an end to count as a plan.

Michael Bratman extends the view that plans are the representational component of intentions in another direction. At first blush, it seems that Bratman has quite a different idea about the role of planning in intention, since rather than characterizing plans as components of intentions, as Mele does, he characterizes intentions as components of plans:

> We form future-directed intentions as parts of larger plans, plans which play characteristic roles in coordination and ongoing practical reasoning; plans which allow us to extend the influence of present deliberation to the future. Intentions are, so to speak, the building blocks of such plans; and plans are intentions writ large. (Bratman 1999b, 8)

The last phrase here suggests that although intentions may be components of larger plans, plans are simultaneously components of intentions. This is borne out by Bratman's analysis of intentions in terms of a 'volitional' dimension and a 'reasoning-centered' dimension. The reasoning-centered dimension points to the role that intentions play in guiding the ongoing practical reasoning that results in the formation of further intentions and overarching plans (Bratman 1999b, 108–9). But intentions can hardly play this role unless their reasoning-centered dimension contains at least a representation of what the agent is committed to doing. So the best interpretation of Bratman's view is that it agrees with the more straightforward view set forth by Mele, but extends this view to include the important point that while plans or plan elements are embedded in intentions, intentions are simultaneously embedded in larger plans. The general point is that action typically involves complex hierarchies of intentions and associated plans. Thus, intentions are plan-based in two ways. First, they *incorporate* plans, and this explains the internal representational feature of intentions. Second, they play an essential role in the *formation of further* plans, and this explains the character of the external relations intentions have with other intentions, psychological states, and processes.

Planning theories of intention must posit a plan everywhere an intention is detected. But even spontaneous or impulsive actions are typically characterized as involving an intention on the part of the agent. The three examples of erstwhile unplanned action we looked at above—an impulse purchase, an on-the-spot decision to stop at a yard sale, and the spontaneous basic action of turning your head in response to noises—all would normally be characterized as intentional actions, and thus as involving an intention on the part of the agent. Action theorists committed to a planning theory of intention are thus committed to characterizing such actions as planned. The problem, of course, is that it seems the intentions in such cases must be formed and acted upon instantaneously, for all practical intents and purposes. So, they cannot have two of the main features of prototypical plans—advance specification of the plan, and conscious deliberation. This apparent difficulty has not deterred planning-oriented action theorists.

> Calling something an 'action-plan' is not intended to suggest that the agent spends time deliberating or reviewing the projected acts in his mind. Action-plans do not require meditation or reflection. The wants and beliefs that constitute action-plans sometimes crop up suddenly and forthwith precipitate corresponding acts. Thus, even impulsive acts may result from action-plans. (Goldman 1970, 57)

> There is no minimum time, other than the speed of thought, required for plan formation. It is not necessary that we ponder our plans; plans can be formed rapidly. Rapid plan formation often proceeds by combining well-rehearsed subroutines. As I see the detour sign, I quickly form a new, ad hoc plan. This utilizes well-rehearsed subroutines for safe driving. (Brand 1986, 226)

> A driver might straightaway hit her brakes upon seeing a dog dart into her car's path; and a man angered by *an insult may immediately and impulsively strike the offending party—in both cases, intentionally.* The suddenness of the relevant reactions might suggest that the agents lacked sufficient time to *form* an intention to hit (respectively) the brakes or the offending person. If forming an intention is an *action*, however, an agent can *acquire* an intention without forming one. Some intentions are *passively* acquired, as are many beliefs and desires. If intention-acquisition can occur at something approaching the speed of thought, the problem dissolves. In that case, sudden and impulsive intentional actions are plausibly viewed as products of suddenly or impulsively acquired intentions—or more precisely, as products of the *acquisition* of such intentions. (Mele and Moser 1997, 231)

These passages are supposed to make rapid planning and intention formation plausible for some specific modes of thought. For Brand, the idea is that you have a library of stored plans or plan components that you can simply retrieve—plausibly much faster than formation from scratch. Mele and Moser's reference to passive acquisition suggests a similar idea, although in this case the intention and its embedded plan are apparently acquired *de novo*. This claim is plausible because the limiting case of plans, consisting only of a general representation of the action to be performed, might indeed be acquired as quickly as a simple perceptual belief, say, or a desire. But the plausibility of what we may call the Speed of Thought (SOT) hypothesis is not the main issue here. Rather it is the very appeal to SOT to underwrite the idea that spontaneous actions do involve intentions that is important, because this appeal is in the service of a characterization of all spontaneous actions as planned actions—what is acquired at the speed of thought is a commitment to a plan.

It is also clear from these passages that intention formation—and, thus, planning—need not involve conscious attention, let alone deliberation. Mele (1992, 220) intentionally leaves open the question of whether the plan component of an intention is conscious or even accessible to consciousness. Goldman (1970, 57), on the other hand, defines 'intentional action' as action caused in 'a certain characteristic way' by an action plan. And in a later discussion, he says that the representations constituting action plans may be wholly or partly unconscious, and that it is the pattern of causation that is really important (Goldman 1970, 121–25). This accommodates the common idea that an agent may have and act on intentions she is not conscious of having or acting on. On the other hand, it raises the question of how to draw a distinction between an action involving an intention on the part of an agent, and a mere reflex movement. Goldman (1970, 166–67) speculates that it can be drawn in terms of the difference between the central nervous system on the one hand, and the autonomic nervous system on the other. But regardless of these unresolved issues, the point is that, as understood by many action theorists, plans may not only be formed instantly, they may be formed and executed without conscious attention.

It is important to understand that this view is a natural consequence of a planning theory of intention. Because this theory posits a plan everywhere it intuits an intention, and because many actions that are held to involve an intention on the part of the agent are undertaken on the spur of the moment, plans in the technical, action-theoretic sense cannot have the features of prototypical plans. They are not necessarily formed through deliberative processes. They may be abbreviated to a schematic representation of an action to be performed and may not specify any steps toward that end. They need not be formulated in advance of the action, but may instead be acquired or retrieved at the speed of thought. And neither their formation nor their execution necessarily requires conscious attention. As we saw, the folk are willing to go part way down this path. They do not insist on deliberation or on the specification of steps toward the specified end. But the folk do insist on conscious, explicit, advance formulation of the end or action to be performed. As we noted at the end of the last section, the insistence on retaining conscious, advance specification of an end allows the folk to retain a clear notion of *un*planned action as action *not* explicitly formulated in advance. Thus, the folk are able to retain a clear distinction between planned and improvised action. We can now see how action theory has lost this distinction. Under the planning theory of intention, virtually any representational structure involved in the generation and guidance of action, no matter how abbreviated with regard to the elaborate means-end representational structure of prototypical plans, or how unattended by or inaccessible to the agent, is a plan.

If all intentional action is plan-based, the very idea of unplanned or improvised action seems conceptually incoherent. Perhaps reflex actions, such as blinking, and unintended side effects, such as leaving a footprint in the mud on the way to the mailbox, might in some sense still be regarded as unplanned. But reflexes and side effects are not the domain of improvisation any more than they are the domain of planning. If improvisation is an interesting or important phenomenon it is so because it inhabits the same domain as intentional actions—most likely because it *is* a kind of intentional action. But there is really no conceptually coherent way of talking about such a phenomenon in the context of planning theories of intention and intentional action, so if it exists, it is effectively invisible to action theory. If it is thought about at all, the implicit assumption is that whatever improvisation might be, it will be caught in the wide sweep of the net that is the planning theory of intention and intentional action, and will be analyzable in terms of the conceptual resources already available to action theorists within that theoretical framework.

So we are left with two questions. First, is there a philosophically significant phenomenon, appropriately described as improvisation or unplanned action? Second, if there is such a phenomenon, does action theory already have the conceptual and theoretical resources to deal with it?

TO IMPROVISE OR NOT TO IMPROVISE

Perhaps the most obvious place to start looking for phenomena that might qualify as improvisation is in the domain of spontaneous action. As we saw in the previous section, action theorists often characterize even spontaneous actions as involving plans—plans acquired or formed almost instantly—in order to preserve the intentional character of such actions under a planning theory of intention. But, as we shall see in a moment, there is actually some disagreement among action theorists of the planning persuasion as to whether this is really the right way to handle spontaneous action. Perhaps this is an indication that the phenomena associated with spontaneous action are open to an interpretation in terms of improvisation rather than planning.

In his discussion of the intentional status of spontaneous actions, Michael Bratman (1999b, 126–27) offers two alternative suggestions that might have a bearing on this question. Spontaneous actions like catching a ball unexpectedly thrown at you (Bratman's example) do seem to be intentional, since they are goal-directed and involve options that are under your control—you can either dodge the ball or catch it, for instance. But, Bratman says, the fast and unreflective nature of such spontaneous actions casts doubt on the idea that we are forming and executing intentions in such cases, and if no intentions are involved it is hard to see how spontaneous actions can be intentional.

One of the suggestions Bratman makes is that spontaneous actions are not backed by intentions formed at the time of action, but by general, standing intentions he calls 'personal policies,' for example, a policy of protecting yourself from thrown objects. This would be a version of retrieval of stored intentions, and would make at least some spontaneous actions—the ones that are covered by some stored personal policy—fully intentional. But many spontaneous actions are not covered by personal policies, either because the agent does not have a relevant policy, or because the action performed is in fact a spontaneous violation of a policy the agent does have.[2] For example, it is unlikely that an agent would have a policy of uttering an expletive when an object is unexpectedly thrown at her. On the other hand, even an agent who has a policy of *not* uttering expletives might nevertheless utter one if she is in a particularly foul mood, for instance. So personal policies do not cover all spontaneous actions, and thus do not constitute a general solution to the problem of underwriting their intentional status.

Bratman's alternative suggestion is that spontaneous actions may best be construed as *neither* intentional nor unintentional, but merely *purposive*— that is, goal-directed and under our guidance to some extent, but involving no full-fledged intentions. This view is still compatible with the idea that some spontaneous actions are intentional, in virtue of falling within the motivational and/or cognitive potential of larger patterns of planful, intentional action. But it holds that spontaneous action is never intentional in its own right; it must inherit intentional status from somewhere if it is to have any. This view thus abandons the project of underwriting the intentional status of spontaneous actions in all cases where we might folkishly want to characterize them as intentional.

Let us take stock of the discussion of spontaneous action so far. It is clear at this point that there is no standard account of spontaneous action, and that intuitions about how such an account should go are variable. The central problem is whether the mental representations responsible for the generation of spontaneous actions should be regarded as constituting the required plan component of an intention or not. At one end of the spectrum, there are thinkers such as Goldman, who are happy to call any action-mediating representation a plan, provided it has the right structure and causal effects—thus making all action planned action, in effect. At the other end of the spectrum, there are thinkers such as Bratman, who are hesitant to call the representations mediating spontaneous actions plans because of the rapidity, automaticity, and lack of conscious attention involved in their formation and execution, and who are ready to consider spontaneous actions as a distinct category of purposeful but non-planful—and so non-intentional—actions. This disagreement raises the possibility that improvisation is to be identified with spontaneous action, and that some action theorists have, in fact, recognized its special character, if only in passing.

But a facile identification of improvisation with spontaneous action would miss the nature and significance of improvised activity. To see this, let us return to our folk examples of erstwhile unplanned action—an impulse purchase of olives, an unanticipated stop at a yard sale, and turning your head in response to noises. The important point about such actions—the point that is missed by action theorists—is how they are connected to other actions. Consider turning your head in response to noises from the hall, for instance. One possibility is that you might immediately turn back to your reading, in which case the action of turning your head is a momentary interruption to your plan to finish the reading for your seminar before going to lunch. On the other hand, you might listen, become increasingly alarmed, get up and open your door, find a couple of workers in the hallway tearing up the flooring, have a conversation with them about the nature and length of their project, go down to the department office to complain to the office manager about not having been warned that this work was going to start, return to your office to collect your book, and decamp to the library to resume your reading. This whole sequence of actions also constitutes an interruption to your reading plan, but a temporally extended and complex one. It is not a sequence of actions for which you have an advance plan. But it is, nevertheless, a coherent sequence of actions describable in a unified way, as 'dealing with distracting noises from the hallway,' for instance. The other two examples give rise to similar scenarios. In the case of the yard sale, a concatenation of further actions is the overwhelmingly likely scenario, because the purpose of turning off the road into the parking lot is precisely to spend some time at the yard sale—looking over the items for sale, perhaps asking a few questions of the yard sale personnel, chatting with the other customers, or buying some things. Similarly, the impulse purchase of olives may lead to other actions, such as buying some good cheese to go with the olives, and then a nice bottle of wine to go with both. And then, perhaps, to calling some friends on your cell phone to see if they want to stop by for snacks and a drink before dinner. *Now* you have a plan for a social event, but it grew by accretion through concrete activity, rather than being constructed in advance through armchair deliberation.

The problem such examples pose for action theory is that, from the planning perspective, such sequences of coordinated actions are effectively invisible *as* extended, structured wholes. Rather, the actions that make up such sequences are analyzable only as separate actions, many of which are spontaneous, and each of which is driven, on most accounts, by a separate, rapidly formed planful intention. In other words, action theory has had a lot to say about the coordination of extended stretches of activity through long-term, advance plans, and it has had something (although a lot less) to say about isolated spontaneous actions structured by short-term, mini-plans concocted or retrieved on the spot. But it has had nothing to say about extended stretches of activity that appear to be coherent, well-coordinated concatenations of largely spontaneous actions. To put the point another way, action theory's exclusive focus on planning as a structuring principle for actions has resulted, on the one hand, in the stretching of the term 'plan' to include just about any action-related representation the agent has, and on the other hand, in tacitly discouraging action theorists from looking for action-structuring principles of any other kind. Thus, the only way action theory now has of understanding extended activities not structured by advance plans is to understand them as structured by planning done in very short, isolated increments. But this analysis is not adequate to the phenomenology of many daily activities, because it gives us no grasp on how the increments are coordinated into larger action chunks that are recognized by agents as integral wholes.

Up to this point, we have been talking about spontaneous actions that are relatively isolated interruptions of planned activity. But we also need to look at stretches of activity that are part of planned activity, although not specified in the plan itself. It is accepted that plans are necessarily partial or sketchy, due to limitations of our knowledge and ability to predict future conditions and/or the inefficiency of bothering to predict them ahead of time. So plans must be filled in. Some of this filling in can be done ahead of time. For example, you might make plane and hotel reservations for a vacation months in advance, but put off reading the guidebook and planning which sights to see until the week before you leave. On the other hand, a lot of filling in, such as wending your way through security at the airport, must be done on the spot as the plan is being executed because it is not until then that you have the relevant information. Similarly, advance plans often must be revised. Sometimes, the revision can be carried out ahead of time, when the unexpected opportunity or problem prompting the revision is foreseen. This is usually thought of as replanning, and is not essentially different from initial planning. But other times, revisions are made on the spot as the plan is being executed, as when you miss your plane because of the length of time you spent wending your way through security and have to rebook.

Filling in and revision are sometimes single, isolated actions. But much more often, they, too, involve sequences of actions. For example, you may plan which streets to walk down on your way to the mailbox, but you do not plan how many steps to take, how long to wait at intersections before crossing, whether and when to take opportunities to pick up dropped coins or examine interesting plants in gardens you pass, or what puddles, potholes, or piles of dog poop to avoid. These unplanned filling-in actions form a concatenated and interdependent sequence—the number of steps you take will be influenced by how many puddles you encounter, for instance, and whether you walk around them or jump over them, as well as by whether you stroll, jog, or run. The same is true of revisions. Take following a detour when a planned route is blocked. This might involve a sequence of responses to detour signs posted by the highway department, or a sequence of decisions about what turns to make as you deftly wend your way around the traffic jam through back streets. Thus, filling in and revision both often involve extended, highly structured sequences of actions.

It is important to note that filling in and revision are not determined by the initial plan, although they are clearly constrained by it. We can get a handle on this question by going back to the discussion of recipes from Chapter 1.

Recipes, like plans, leave a lot unspecified. But these unspecified actions typically are *not* determined indirectly by the explicit specifications of the recipe. Rather, the cook is an intelligent executor possessing background knowledge and decision-making abilities, and with a range of options open to her. The range is constrained by the recipe, but no particular option is uniquely determined as the only possible one. The same is true in the case of intermediate steps left open by plans in general. Take the next step in your trek to the mailbox. It could just as well be a hop, a skip, or a jump. And it need not be in the direction of the mailbox, either. It might be a step to the right to get out of the way of another pedestrian coming in the opposite direction; or even a step back when you think better of crossing the street in light of the speed of an oncoming vehicle. In short, your plan to walk to the mailbox to mail your letter only constrains the *overall* mode and direction of locomotion—it does not uniquely determine the mode and direction of loco-motion at any particular point. Furthermore, intermediate steps are often sequences of actions with their own internal and situational constraints. So the sequence of actions you take on your way to the mailbox, for example, is indeed constrained in some respects by your advance plan, but it is also subject to a whole host of other constraints, among them the local circum-stances (e.g., traffic at intersections), opportunities (e.g., a dropped coin), problems (e.g., a large puddle), and your own propensities (e.g., for hopping through the hopscotch boxes chalked on the sidewalk rather than walking sedately over them). Last but not least, it is worth reiterating that these are *constraints*—they delimit a range of relevant options rather than uniquely determining a next step.

   Similar points apply in the case of revisions. A revision may even depend solely on the agent just preferring to do something other than what she originally planned. Such preferences are unlikely to be uniquely determined by any single factor. For example, you may plan to go to a particular restau-rant for lunch, but then just decide when you get there that you really would rather eat somewhere else today, and consider several options or even walk around a bit looking at sidewalk menu boards before settling on an alterna-tive. Revisions are also often sequences of actions rather than single actions. If the highway department, for example, sets up a detour, the sequence of actions that detour involves is certainly not structured by your plan, but rather primarily by the plan the highway department has for routing traffic around a construction zone. But suppose the detour is your idea—you are stuck in traffic, say, and decide to try another way around. Now you might sit in traffic and plan a new route that you then follow at the first available opportunity. On the other hand, you might notice a side street and say to yourself: 'Okay, I've never been down that way before, but there must be some way around, so here goes,' and commence wending your way through the back streets, assessing your position periodically as you go. In a case like this, your original destination does constrain your route to some extent, but it leaves many choices open, such as whether to take a left at this intersection or the next one; and other constraints analogous to those encountered in the case of the walk to the mailbox are operative, as well. Thus, just as in the case of filling-in actions, the structure of sequences of revisions substituted for planned actions does not flow primarily from the original plan but from other sources. In short, these are improvised sequences of actions rather than indirectly planned sequences.

Now we can see that because of the necessarily partial and revisable nature of plans, planned activities include improvised stretches of activity as filling-in or revised components. Thus, except in some very exceptional circumstances, the execution of plans actually consists of the carrying out of pre-specified actions interleaved with episodes of improvisation. But the more important point we have uncovered here is that improvised action is not to be simply identified with spontaneous action. The main reason for this is that action theorists tend to understand spontaneous action in terms of isolated single actions. Such actions may well belong under the rubric of improvisation as one category of unplanned actions. But improvisation is interesting and significant primarily because it involves alternative, non-plan-based ways of structuring *extended sequences* of actions.

We now have a rough idea of what improvisation might be, and of the place it might occupy in the domain of human action. But how important a factor is improvisation in our everyday lives and activities? There are at least three points to be made here. First, there are some activities that *require* improvisation. The most obvious example is informal conversation. A large percentage of the conversations in which we engage on a daily basis are struck up opportunistically—the conversations with the workers in the hallway and the other yard sale customers in the examples above, for instance—and these are improvisatory in origin as well as in conduct. We do sometimes plan to have a conversation with some particular person, perhaps at some particular time or place, perhaps even about some specific topic—Bratman's plan to talk with his colleague, John, if he is in his office, for instance. But even in such cases, the actual conduct of the conversation cannot be prepared in advance in any detail. We plan *to* have such conversations, but we do not normally have plans *for* them. Thus, conversations and other unscripted linguistic exchanges are pervasively improvisational. The reason improvisation is required in the case of conversation is that there is no way to predict what your interlocutors are going to say with any certainty or in any detail. So, to carry on a conversation you have to be able to respond to your interlocutor's utterances without preparation. Thus, improvisation will be required for action of any kind that is pervasively unpredictable in this way. Good examples include sports and games, especially those where the action is very fast, such as basketball or sparring in martial arts; improvisational art forms, such as most musical and some theater traditions (Sawyer 1997a; Sudnow 2001); and pretend play on the part of both children and adults (Sawyer 1997b).

The second point to be made about the role of improvisation in human activity is that the same ends that can be achieved through planning usually can be, and frequently are, achieved through improvised activity instead. For example, suppose your goal is dinner. You can plan out ahead of time what you are going to eat and how you are going to procure it or prepare it. On the other hand, you can just go home and open the refrigerator to see what you have in the way of leftovers and raw materials, and devise dinner on the spot. Similarly, you can shop from a list prepared in advance, or you can see what is available and good first, and then buy whatever else you need to go with it. Sometimes, the alternative between planning and improvising is institutionalized in some way. For example, the difference between a lecture course and a seminar is pretty much the difference between a class where the instructor has prepared what to say in advance and a class where she has not.

The third point to be made about the role of improvisation begins with the observation that there are indeed some activities where advance planning is required if the end in question is to be achieved at all. These tend to be activities involving a large number of people, relatively long-term projects, and/or relatively sophisticated technology. Spaceflight, long terrestrial trips, and mass production of consumer goods are obvious examples. But this observation about the necessity of planning for some kinds of goals must be tempered by an acknowledgement of the role of improvisation in the execution of plans. As we have seen, the inherently partial and revisable nature of plans means that planned activity is normally interspersed with intervals of improvised activity representing unplanned intermediate steps or revisions. In addition, planned activity is often interrupted by episodes of improvised activity. So where there is planning there is improvisation, but not necessarily *vice versa*.

Improvisation is, thus, an important and characteristic aspect of all human activity. First, it is necessary for carrying out some kinds of activities; second, it is a reliable and frequently employed alternative to planning for carrying out most other kinds of activities; and finally, interleaved episodes of improvisation are necessary for the execution of plans. These observations contrast sharply with the tenor of the recent literature in action theory, which implicitly or explicitly takes planning to be the most characteristic and only important and interesting aspect of human activity. This view is expressed most clearly by Michael Bratman:

> [S]tructures of planning agency of the sort I am trying to describe are basic and, perhaps, distinctive aspects of our agency. Many animals, human and non-human, are purposive agents—agents who pursue goals in light of their representations of the world. But we—normal adult human agents in a modern world—are not merely purposive agents in this generic sense. (Bratman 1999a, 5)

> We are planning agents. Our purposive activity is typically embedded in multiple, interwoven quilts of partial, future-directed plans of action. (Bratman 1999a, 1)

These passages indicate that on Bratman's view, human agents do at least sometimes act 'merely' purposively, since human agency is said to be typically, but by this very token not exclusively, planning agency. However, Bratman clearly gives pride of place to the planning aspect of human agency. In later passages, he gives some reasons for this view:

> [S]uch planning structures are universal means: useful in the pursuit of a wide range of ends whose complexity requires levels of organization and coordination made possible by planning agency. (Bratman 1999a, 5)

He adds in a footnote to this passage:

> When I say planning capacities are universal means I am not only trying to convince a nonplanning agent to become a planning agent. I am also, in part, trying to contribute to what, following T.M. Scanlon, we can call a planning agent's 'enterprise . . . of self understanding.' I am trying to highlight ways in which a planning agent's planning capacities contribute to her ends, for a very wide range of ends and including ends whose very specification presupposes such capacities. (Bratman 1999a, 5)

Taken together with the previous passages, the picture that emerges is of planning as not just *a* basic feature of human agency, but as *the* most important feature of it. At least four reasons for this can be extracted from these passages. First, Bratman says planning is a 'universal means' for attaining our ends, that is, it is a means for attaining all our ends, or at least all that are of any great complexity or significance. Second, if, as Bratman says, characterizing planning as a universal means is intended to persuade non-planning agents to plan, it appears that planning agency must also be the *best* and most suitable means of attaining our ends. Third, Bratman says planning capacities are actually constitutive of some of the ends we can adopt, rather than being merely a means for achieving ends we would have in any case. This agrees with the observation we made that some human activities, such as space flight or mass production, require advance planning. And finally, he suggests that the ends for which planning is thus constitutive are more characteristic of human beings than other ends we have. In short, planning is the most important feature of our agency, because it is the best means of attaining all our ends, and because it is outright constitutive of our most complex—and, thus, arguably most significant—ends.

Unpacked in this way, this is a substantive set of claims about the nature of human agency. It is possible that Bratman would not want to defend all of them exactly as formulated here. However, it is important to identify such claims, because they embody underlying assumptions about the nature of human agency that in one way or another inform the thinking of contemporary action theorists. However, in light of what we have said above about the role and importance of improvisation in human action, these claims embody a view of human agency that is at best one-sided, as well as incorrect in some respects. First of all, we noted that improvisation is necessary for some activities that are pervasively unpredictable, like informal conversations, and some games and art forms. So planning is not a universal means for attaining our ends. Second, planning is not always the best means of attaining our ends. It is often too time consuming, given the constraints of action in real-time, real-life situations. And even when there is plenty of time, it is sometimes an inefficient use of that time with regard to the cognitive resources required. You would be ill advised to spend your evenings trying to predict who you might meet the next day and scripting conversations to have with them, for instance. On the other hand, we can agree with the important point Bratman makes about our planning ability being constitutive of some of the ends that we can have, rather than merely a means of attaining ends we would have had in any case. But this agreement must be tempered by the corresponding observation about improvisation, which is equally constitutive of some ends, such as being a good conversationalist or a proficient boxer. Finally, many of these ends for which improvisation is constitutive are among the most complex and significant ends we have as human beings—linguistic communication and performance art being obvious examples.

The alternative picture of human agency that emerges here is one in which planning and improvising are (to borrow a term from Heidegger) equiprimordial human capacities, with neither being more important or more distinctively human than the other. What makes our agency different from other animals is not that we are planning agents as opposed to 'merely' purposive agents; we may well share these capacities with nonhuman animals. But in human beings, *both* these capacities have evolved to a higher level—we are better improvisers as well as better planners—and have thus opened up domains of activity not available to nonhuman animal agents. Thus, when we act purposively in improvisatory ways, we are not failing to plan; rather, we are exercising a different but equally essential capacity involved in our special kind of agency. So the enterprise of self-understanding of which Bratman speaks will be extremely one-sided if it is oriented exclusively toward an understanding of human beings as planning agents.

But improvisation has not been a topic of discussion in action theory. Let us review the reasons for this lack of attention. Having set out to understand what intentions are and what makes actions intentional, action theorists fastened on planning as the key explanatory concept. This led them to posit a plan wherever there was, intuitively speaking, an intentional action. And this, in turn, required the very notion of what counts as a plan to be expanded well beyond anything that counts as a plan in the folk sense, let alone the dictionary sense. The end result is that any action in which action theorists take an interest is now understood as planned action in an expanded, technical sense. In short, under the planning theory of intention and intentional action, preserving the folk categorization of intentional actions has meant simultaneously destroying the folk distinction between planned and unplanned (improvised) actions. In this section, we have discussed the problems the loss of this distinction raises. The main difficulty is that action theory does not have any way of identifying or explaining the overall structure of extended activity that is not specified in advance in a plan. Instead, it is constrained to analyze such stretches of activity as incremental, short-term planning, and this chunks the activity much too finely, discouraging investigation of more coarsely grained structuring of the activity. Exploring alternatives for the structuring of extended sequences of actions that are not plan-based is the business of a theory of improvisation. The next question we must ask, then, is to what extent the resources for such a theory are already available in action theory, and correlatively, to what extent we must look for them elsewhere.

DOING THINGS ON PURPOSE

Of the action theorists we have considered, Michael Bratman is the least wedded to the idea that all actions right down to the spontaneous and impulsive must be categorized as intentional, and therefore planful. Instead, he suggests that spontaneous actions might better be characterized as purposive (Bratman 1999b, 126). He does not develop this distinction between planfulness and purposiveness as part of his theory of action, and has very little to say about what purposiveness is. But what he does say shows us where a theory of improvisation might take root in the otherwise exclusively planning-oriented field of current action theory because, like the folk, Bratman leaves room for a conception of unplanned, improvised action. Bratman says purposive action is voluntary and under the agent's control (1999b, 126)[3] and involves the pursuit of goals in light of representations of the world (1999a, 5). But planning clearly shares these features. So what distinguishes purposiveness and planning? Simply that planning agents are purposive agents with the special capacity to use their representations of the world to construct advance plans.

This sketchy but intriguing picture raises two important questions. First, what ways other than planning *are* there of using representations of the world in the pursuit of goals? In other words, how does a 'merely' purposive agent—or a planning agent operating in 'merely' purposive mode—go about her business? Bratman is completely silent on this score. But this is an important question, because whatever improvisation is as a species of purposiveness, it must involve the use of representations of the world to do something other than construct and execute plans. Second, there is a conceptual question here regarding where to draw the line between 'mere' purposiveness and planning. This is an important question, because distinguishing purposiveness in general from planning is the first step in making the more specific distinction between planning and improvisation.

Moreover, this question is particularly acute, because as we have seen, both the folk and the philosophers have a tendency to regard commitment to a goal as a limiting case of a plan. This is the folk sense in which an agent may have a plan *to* do something without having a plan *for* doing it, for instance. But this makes it look as though purposiveness, which does involve having a goal, is just a limiting case of planning. And then we are right back on the garden path to the view that all action is really planned action. If, as we are now surmising, improvisation and planning are both purposive, then they are bound to share some characteristics. But if operating in 'merely' purposive mode is to be *distinct* from operating in planning mode, a line must be drawn somewhere.

Let us consider the conceptual question first. One possibility would be to follow the folk, who usually use the term 'plan' only when there is a commitment to a goal well in advance of the initiation of action aimed at achieving it. So, for example, you might plan to go grocery shopping next Thursday without having any plan yet for where to shop or what to get. On the other hand, when you see olives on sale at the grocery store, you acquire the goal of buying a jar on the spot, and that is why it seems odd to say that you planned to get the olives. But this is not a workable solution, because the goals that govern improvised action are often entertained well in advance. For example, you may commit yourself in the morning to the goal of having dinner as soon as you get home after work, but the process of deciding what to eat and preparing it may be entirely improvisatory. Thus it seems that the folkish 'plan to' is ambiguous. It may eventuate in a full-fledged plan for achieving the adopted goal, or it may eventuate in improvisatory activity. Moreover, in the case of improvised action that fills in a plan or substitutes for a planned step, the goal of the original plan is still in force. For example, if you improvise an alternate route around a traffic jam, the destination that governed the construction of the plan for your original route still governs the improvisation. You have not given up your commitment to meet Sonya for lunch at The Grit—you are just trying to get there by a different route. So it does not seem that the distinction between planning and improvisation can hinge on whether the goal of the activity is adopted in advance or on the spot.

Bratman also says that purposive action is voluntary. But this is clearly a feature that planning and improvisation share, and so cannot be used to distinguish them. The other two features Bratman mentions are more promising, though. He says that purposive action is under the control (guidance) of the agent, and that the agent's representations of the world are employed in the pursuit of her goals. Stated very generally in this way, these features, too, seem to be shared by improvisation and planning. But distinctions might easily be found at more specific levels of description, because there might be different ways of guiding action, and different ways of employing representations of the world in pursuit of goals. We have a pretty good idea at this point of how these features are construed in the context of planning. Planned action is under the control of the agent in the technical sense embodied in the control ideal—that is, the agent constructs a mental plan, and then controls her subsequent actions by (ideally) executing that plan step by step. The agent's representations of the world are brought into play primarily in the construction of the plan, which reflects her knowledge of the current state of the world and her predictions about its future states; and secondarily in monitoring the execution of the plan. So the question is: what other ways might there be of guiding action other than by executing a previously constructed plan? And how else might an agent employ her representations of the world, other than in the construction of plans and the monitoring of their execution?

This brings us right back to the first question we had for Bratman—how does a 'merely' purposive agent operate, as opposed to how a planning agent operates? It now seems that the difference must lie in the way the agent guides her actions toward the achievement of her goals; and most particularly, perhaps, in the way representations of the world are employed by the agent in this process. Here we are met by silence from action theorists. This is just not a matter they have considered. More specifically, the dominance of the planning paradigm has generated the background assumption that any use—or, at least, any interesting use—of representations of the world in the pursuit of goals counts as planning, so the question of how else representations of the world might be employed by human agents just does not arise. Moreover, the dominance of the planning paradigm means that there are at present no real resources within action theory for answering this question, since, as we noted above, there are no resources for understanding extended, coherent sequences of actions that are not planned.

Where might we find such resources outside philosophical action theory? There are, in fact, many options, and we will make use of some of them in Chapter 4 to help lay the foundations for a philosophical account of improvisation. But to end this chapter, I would like to answer a related and prior question—are there available accounts of improvisation that the action theorist might simply adopt and adapt to philosophical needs? With only one possible exception that I have been able to identify (of which more in Chapter 4), the answer seems to be 'no,' if improvisation is taken in the sense we have been using it here, namely, as the coordination and concatenation of actions over time by means other than planning. What might at first seem like accounts of improvisation turn out to miss this phenomenon, either because they focus on cognition rather than action, or because they focus on action in general rather than on the distinction between planned and unplanned action that we have outlined here.

Let us start with accounts that focus on cognition. There is a constellation of recent theories coming under headings such as embodied, embedded, enacted, extended, situated, or distributed cognition. What they have in common is a view of cognition not as a purely interior process, but rather as a process that loops through the body and the world. A pioneering example was Edwin Hutchins's *Cognition in the Wild* (1995), in which he proposed that cognition takes place not in individuals, primarily, but in systems composed of individuals, artifacts, and environmental structures. Accepting the view of cognition as computation, he traced the flow of representations in one such cognitive system, the navigation deck of a Navy ship, as these representations circulated through instruments, crew members, and charting operations. Andy Clark's *Being There* (1997) followed up with a wide-ranging synthesis of work in artificial intelligence and cognitive science that sought to understand the brain as only one element in a tightly coupled assemblage of bodily activity, language, and artifacts collectively configured to cognitive ends. Clark expanded this position recently to an even more radical view of cognition as actually constituted in part by processes taking place outside the bounds of the skull. The brain does not merely use the environment with which it is coupled for cognitive purposes; rather, cognition takes place as much outside the brain as inside, so that the mind must be understood as extending beyond the bounds of the skull (Clark and Chalmers 1998; Clark 2008).

These theories and the many others in the same vein (Robbins and Aydede 2008) are clearly an important resource for constructing an account of improvisation. If anything is clear in advance about improvisation, it is that it requires a more intimate, moment-by-moment engagement of the agent with her environment. Moreover, how representations and other cognitive resources might be deployed in such ongoing interaction is an important issue. But however closely these theories take cognition to be entwined with action, they are still focused on what action does for cognition, not what cognition might do for action. And most importantly, however especially appropriate this view of cognition might be for accounts of improvisation, as a general thesis it is intended to apply to both planned and unplanned action. So these theories are not accounts of improvisation.

The account of absorbed coping first broached by Hubert Dreyfus (Dreyfus and Dreyfus 1988; Dreyfus 2007) and a similarly Heidegger-inspired view elaborated more recently by Michael Wheeler (2005) might at first blush look more promising. Inspired by Heidegger's (1962) distinction between the ready-to-hand and the present-at-hand, Dreyfus drew a distinction between skilled action, which unfolds fluidly without explicit attention, and novice action, which requires explicit attention and constant readjustment in order to succeed (Dreyfus and Dreyfus 1988). More recently, Dreyfus reformulated this as a distinction between absorbed coping with the world and a distanced, reflection on the world. He claims that absorbed coping has 'a kind of content which is non-conceptual, non-propositional, non-rational . . . and non-linguistic' (Dreyfus 2007, 360), and which consists of responding in a bodily way to the 'solicitations' of the affordances of the world (Dreyfus 2007, 357). In reflective mode, on the other hand, we wield conceptual and rational deliberation in order to understand the world rather than to deal with it. Wheeler accepts this basic framework, but massages it to fit with current trends and results in cognitive science. In particular, Wheeler argues, instances of absorbed coping as Dreyfus describes them are vanishingly rare, as are instances of pure reflection. The vast middle ground, Wheeler (2005, 12) thinks, is occupied by what he calls online intelligence, in which the cognitive apparatus Dreyfus excludes from absorbed coping is indeed deployed, but only as implemented in 'action-oriented representa-tions' that are tailored to specific actions, context-dependent, and egocentric (Wheeler 2005, 195–200).

Are absorbed coping or online intelligence accounts of improvisation as opposed to planning? A first clue that they are not is the focus on the issue of mental representation. There may well be different kinds of mental represen-tations, as Wheeler claims, or no representation at all in some cases, as both Wheeler and Dreyfus are inclined to think. But the distinction Dreyfus and Wheeler are both after crosscuts the distinction between planned and impro-visatory action we have drawn here. Our question is: how do agents struc-ture and coordinate their action over time in the absence of a plan? At first blush, it might seem that planning lines up with both the distanced, reflec-tive mode Dreyfus opposes to absorbed coping, and the offline intelligence Wheeler opposes to online intelligence. But this is a mistake. Concocting a plan may well line up; but the important aspect of planning with regard to action is execution. And the execution of a plan must for the most part con-sist in absorbed coping or online intelligence, because otherwise it will not have the required result of getting things done in the world. Nor does impro-visation line up with absorbed coping and online intelligence. If improvisa-tory action is just action that does not rely on a plan for structure, then we might expect improvisers to make use of *either* reflection or absorbed cop-ing, *either* online or offline intelligence, depending on the situation. So here again, although the Heidegger-inspired frameworks of Dreyfus and Wheeler may well serve as resources for an account of improvisation, they do not provide—and are not aimed at providing—such an account.

Let us now turn to theories that do emphasize action as opposed to cogni-tion. We may begin with the companion view to situated cognition—situated action. The *locus classicus* is Lucy Suchman's *Plans and Situated Actions,* first published in 1987, and now in a new, expanded, and retitled edition (Suchman 2007). Suchman argues for an understanding of purposeful action as invariably unfolding in concrete circumstances. But the intelligibility of these circumstances, and thus of the action itself, is achieved by the agents involved, especially through language. Here we have an easy case, for Such-man (2007, 16) herself characterizes the identification of situated action with 'spontaneous or improvisational' action as a misreading, insisting that 'the essential nature of action, however planned or unplanned, is situated' (27). So clearly, accounts of situated action are not aimed at providing an account of improvised action as distinct from planned action.

The recent work of Tim Ingold and his associates on cultural improvisa-tion (Hallam and Ingold 2007) is also aimed at an account of the nature of action in general. In their introduction, Hallam and Ingold propose that all human action is creative and improvisational. Improvisation in their sense has four characteristics: it is generative of forms of culture, relational in its responsiveness to the actions of others, temporally structured, and the way we work in both everyday life and reflection on it. The generativity of improvisation, they say, is due to the fact that design requires execution, but that execution cannot be faithful copying, because it must be responsive to a world that is in constant motion. This obviously echoes our discussion of the vicissitudes of planning, as well as the point, accepted on all hands even in action theory, that plans require filling in during execution. But Hallam and Ingold go further. They claim that, in spite of the existence of designs, plans, instructions, and the like, action is not just unscripted, 'but more fundamentally . . . it is unscriptable' (Hallam and Ingold 2007, 12). In other words, improvisation in their sense is the fundamental nature of all action—the way we work across the board. This elides the distinction between planned and unplanned action as surely as the planning theorists do, but from the other direction. So here, again, we do not see the kind of account we are envisioning of improvised action as distinct from planned action.

A different divergence from our project is exhibited in Michel de Certeau's *The Practice of Everyday Life* (1984). In the wake of the monumental studies by Pierre Bourdieu (1977) and Michel Foucault (1977) of the operations of social power in the formation of individuals and their daily activity, Certeau felt the need to redress the balance with an analysis of the subversion of this power by ordinary individuals going about their ordinary lives. The operations of social power produce the environment in which individuals are constrained to live, says Certeau, but the uses of this environment are not fully determined by it. Thus the weak can subvert the 'strategies' of power through 'tactics'—ruses, deceptions, diversions, and the like, which take advantage of opportunities and make do with what is available for contrary purposes. For example, Certeau describes a practice known as *la perruque,* in which workers divert some of their time and the equipment available at work to their own ends, such as a secretary sending email on their company account to apply for another position or make vacation reservations. Certeau (1984) does often describe tactics in a way entirely consonant with improvisation, as when he characterizes them as operating 'in isolated actions, blow by blow' (37). But in the very same paragraph, he defines a tactic as 'a calculated action determined by the absence of a proper locus' (36–37). And this is the tipoff that the distinction between strategies of power and tactics of weakness is orthogonal to our distinction between planned and unplanned action. For a worker practicing *la perruque,* for instance, might well need to plan her diversion in great detail so as to escape detection.

The claim we have been working on in this chapter is that, at a certain level of analysis, a distinction between planned and unplanned action is requisite to make sense of the phenomena. The proof of this pudding will

only emerge in Chapter 4, with our attempt to say explicitly how improvising agents proceed, so that the distinction between improvisation and
planning may appear more clearly. But the work we have touched on in the
preceding paragraphs is not trying to exhibit this distinction, and, in some
cases, actively rejects it. So it does not provide an account of improvisation,
however great its value as a resource for constructing one.

In this chapter, we have completed our critique of the centralized control
model as it manifests itself in action theory. When we get to Part II, we will
find a version of the centralized control model manifesting itself in function theory, as well. But first we must attend to a related difficulty raised
by contemporary action theory—its treatment of multiple-agent action as
derivative of individual action. The planning theory picture of the centralization of control in the head of the planner already shows an individualist
bias. But this has become even clearer as action theorists have branched out
to the investigation of what is variously termed joint action or collective
action. The tendency is to try to account for such multiple-agent actions as
deriving from individual action. What tends to be ignored in the process is
the always already social nature of the individuals engaging in the multiple-
agent action. Chapter 3 will thus do for collaboration what this chapter has
done for improvisation—provide a critique of the individualist assumptions
embodied in current accounts of multiple-agent action, an approach I call
suigenerism, and suggest an alternative, sociogeneric approach. Then, in
Chapter 4, the critiques of Chapters 2 and 3 will be offset by a positive
account of the basic structuring processes of improvisatory action, with a
collaborative aspect built in from the start.

3 Coming to Terms with Collaboration

It is often said that the model of a society that has individuals as its constituent elements is borrowed from the abstract juridical forms of contract and exchange. Mercantile society, according to this view, is represented as a contractual association of isolated juridical subjects. Perhaps . . . But it should not be forgotten that there existed at the same period a technique for constituting individuals as correlative elements of power and knowledge. The individual is no doubt the fictitious atom of an 'ideological' representation of society; but he is also a reality fabricated by this specific technology of power that I have called 'discipline'.

—Michel Foucault, *Discipline and Punish:*
The Birth of the Prison, III, 2

Unlike improvisation, which has not come up as a topic of discussion in action theory, multiple-agent action (to use as neutral a designation as possible) has come up as a subsidiary topic in recent action theory. It has come up under a variety of headings, such as shared, joint, collective, cooperative, or social action, and it has been slowly but steadily gaining market share, so to speak. The body of philosophical literature in this area is, thus, neither very large nor particularly prominent, but it is well-established enough for definite tendencies to emerge. We must assess some of these tendencies in terms of their implications for a theory of multiple-agent improvisation and a philosophy of material culture.

There are four main topics to be addressed. First, we must consider what resources, if any, action theory has for analyzing multiple-agent improvisation. Second, action theorists have tended to focus quite narrowly on cooperative multiple-agent action. This tendency must be assessed in terms of the need for a theory of multiple-agent action appropriate for the study of material culture to encompass non-cooperative types of action as well. Third, action theorists exhibit a reliable tendency to conflate multiple-agent action with sociality *per se*. This tendency must be assessed in light of the need we discovered in Chapter 1 to distinguish sociality from collaboration. Finally, there is a related tendency of action theorists to assume that sociality emerges from multiple-agent action. We shall argue that this direction of analysis is backwards. Sociality precedes multiple-agent action in the sense that it is already socialized individuals that enter into collaborative relationships. This will supply crucial background for our analysis of collaborative improvisation in Chapter 4 and of reproduction and use in Chapter 7.

'WE HAVE TO IMPROVISE'

In the epigraph to the previous chapter, Nietzsche recommends improvisation as a *modus operandi*. But what he recommends, specifically, is that *we* improvise. As the examples we have already looked at show, much improvisatory activity is indeed carried out in concert with other people. Unscripted conversations are necessarily both collaborative and improvisatory, for instance, and most other activities involve some degree of collaborative improvisation, due largely to the impossibility or inefficiency of trying to predict exactly what other people will do. Navigating populated places, for example, we constantly encounter other people; and we negotiate the details of these encounters with them on the spot. So any adequate theory of improvisation must account for collaborative as well as individual improvisatory activity.

The recent focus on planning theories of intention and intentional action leads naturally to planning theories of shared intention and multiple-agent action. In particular, shared intentions can be construed in terms of shared plans. This view is explicit in Bratman's (1999a) work on shared intentions and shared cooperative activity, for example. It is also explicit in Gilbert (2008) and close to explicit in Tuomela's (1995, 2000) work on cooperation and joint action, as well as the related work of Velleman (1997). Planning theories of multiple-agent action are subject to the critique of planning theories of individual action, *mutatis mutandis*. This can be left as an exercise for the reader. But a brief examination of the planning-oriented account of cooperation offered by Michael Bratman will reveal that Bratman opens up a space where a theory of multiple-agent improvisation could take root, even though he makes no attempt to nurture such a theory himself.

In a series of articles, Bratman offers an account of cooperation in small groups ostensibly lacking relations of authority.[1]

> The basic idea was that at the heart of these phenomena is *shared intention . . . Shared intentional activity*, in the basic case, is activity suitably explainable by a shared intention and associated forms of mutual responsiveness. *Shared cooperative activity* requires, further, the absence of certain kinds of coercion and commitments to mutual support in the pursuit of the joint activity. (Bratman 1999a, 142; emphases added)

Thus, shared cooperative activity is a subspecies of shared intentional activity. As Bratman (1999a, 122) notes, the other major subspecies of shared intentional activity is shared competitive activity. Thus, what we really need to understand is shared intentional activity, which encompasses both competition and cooperation. On Bratman's view, it has two components—shared intention, and forms of mutual responsiveness.

For Bratman, sharing an intention is not as simple as having the same plan. Rather, what is required is individual subplans that mesh.

> [I]t would be too strong to require that the subplans of our intentions . . . completely match, for there can be features of your subplan that I do not even know or care about, and vice versa . . . Still, it seems that we will each want them in the end to *mesh:* Our individual subplans concerning our *J*-ing *mesh* just in case there is some way we could *J* that would not violate either of our subplans but would, rather, involve the successful execution of those subplans. (Bratman 1999a, 120)

This definition of 'mesh' stipulatively excludes the subplans of competitive activities, since these are designed to 'thwart' each other rather than to be jointly achievable (Bratman 1999a, 107). But thwarting requires meshing subplans no less than cooperating does—it is just that the meshing has a different character and outcome in each case. Bratman (1999a, 122) does acknowledge this in a later essay, but declines to pursue the requisite revisions to his definition. We will assume they would be relatively unproblematic and that a full account of shared intentional activity in terms of meshing subplans would encompass both competition and cooperation.

Shared intentional activity also requires mutual responsiveness. Because of the partial nature of plans, agents can share an intention and even undertake shared intentional activity without having complete or fully meshing subplans already in hand:

> What is required is that each of us *intends* that we *J* by way of meshing subplans. Perhaps you and I have not yet filled in our subplans. Or perhaps we have filled in each of our subplans, they do not yet mesh, but we each intend to seek revisions that allow them to mesh. We may even have conflicting preferences concerning subplans and be involved in negotiations about how to fill in our plans. We may be involved in such negotiations even while we have already begun to *J*. (Bratman 1999a, 121)

Bratman distinguishes two forms of mutual responsiveness. First, there is *mutual responsiveness of intention*, which operates during the planning phase when the participants are forming their subplans. Second, there is *mutual responsiveness in action*, which kicks in after the action is already underway and underwrites further filling in and revising of the subplans. In the passage just cited, Bratman describes both forms of responsiveness as involving full-fledged bargaining or negotiation; but in earlier passages, he makes clear that they may merely involve mutual awareness and appropriate adjustment of plans and/or actions without discussion (Bratman 1999a, 106).

Bratman does not have much more than this to say about mutual responsiveness. But clearly, mutual responsiveness in action points in the direction of improvisation. As we characterized it in Chapter 2, improvisation involves spontaneous actions, often concatenated into extended action structures. In the case of shared intentional activity, Bratman's point is that a special kind of spontaneous action is involved, namely actions that are responsive to the other agents participating in the same activity. This is an excellent point as far as it goes. But on the one hand, it needs to be developed into an explicit account of varieties of mutual responsiveness among agents in shared intentional action; for Bratman has in effect only pointed to an important phenomenon, not given an analysis of it. And on the other hand, the account must be extended to include other interactions between agents that arise in the course of action. For example, consider people walking or driving on a busy street. There is certainly mutual responsiveness involved here, but the activity does not fit Bratman's definition of shared intentional activity, because there is no common project involving meshing subplans, except in a very minimal sense. Everyone is going about her or his own business, but is nevertheless interacting with other agents in a mutually responsive way. Similarly, even in the case of shared intentional activities in Bratman's sense, responsiveness to agents other than the official participants is often called for. Consider the phenomena of joining in or interrupting, for instance. Joining or interrupting agents are responded to and respond in turn, but except in the case of successful joining they are not participating in the intentional activity already underway.

In addition, the account should be extended to include responsiveness to aspects of the action situation that are *not* other agents. In acting, we respond not only to other human agents, but to nonhuman animals, items of material culture, and natural features of our environment. The responsiveness is not mutual in all of these cases, of course. It might be regarded as mutual in the case of nonhuman animals, who may not be full-fledged agents in the human sense—or planning agents, in Bratman's sense—but who are nevertheless capable of purposive responsiveness in action. For example, your cat may sit by the door staring fixedly at the doorknob when she wants to go outside, and respond to your response of opening the door by scooting out. There might also be a sort of mutual responsiveness in the case of some items of material culture. For example, when your computer says you have mail, you respond by clicking on the appropriate button and reading the mail. You may then click on the 'reply' button, to which your computer responds with a composition box, and so on. Your computer may not be a purposive agent, but it does embody an automated form of planning and purposiveness, including certain automated kinds of responsiveness. Other items of material culture and natural objects might better be said to react than to respond. For example, when you turn the heat on under a pot of water for tea, the pot reacts by heating up, and the water eventually boils. And then you respond to the boiling water by pouring it into the teapot and turning off the heat.[2]

Bratman's mutual responsiveness in action is, thus, only the tip of a much more general and important phenomenon. Responsiveness is foundational for collaborative and individual improvisatory activity alike. But most importantly for us at this stage, Bratman's introduction of responsiveness in action is important because it shows why a theory of multiple-agent improvisation is called for, as well as where it would fit in the analysis of multiple-agent action already underway in action theory.

COLLABORATING WITH THE ENEMY

Bratman's analysis of shared cooperative activity also foregrounds the marked tendency in recent work on multiple-agent action to limit the discussion to cooperative action. Should our inquiry into multiple-agent activity in material culture contexts do the same? The answer is clearly 'no.' We need a theory of multiple-agent action not for its own sake, but as part of the foundation for a theory of the production and use of material culture. But it is surely the case that the production and use of material culture involves both cooperation and competition. So we need a more encompassing account. Moreover, there are more general reasons to be concerned about the narrowing of the focus in action theory to cooperative action. Some of these concerns are methodological, centering on the advisability of separating discussions of cooperation and competition. And some concerns question the feasibility of such a separation in the first place.

'Cooperation' is the term usually used generically to designate the kinds of activity central to the action theory literature on multiple-agent action. It is understood to refer specifically to actions that are *not* competitive, aggressive, selfish, and so on (Tuomela 2000; Bratman 1999a). An acknowledged difficulty with isolating cooperative activity in this way is that much multiple-agent activity is simultaneously competitive and cooperative. Competitive activities from spelling bees to armed warfare have rules and standard practices that the participants cooperatively follow. Similarly, highly cooperative activities such as participating in a personnel group (an academic department, to give just one example) often involve aggressive or competitive interactions with other participants in the same group. Action theorists usually deal with this difficulty by stipulating that their analyses apply only to the cooperative aspects of these activities, which they assume can be relatively neatly carved off from the competitive aspects. Bratman (1999a), for example, says that an activity 'can be cooperative down to a certain level and yet competitive beyond that' (107), as if these aspects were clearly distinguishable.

Annette Baier lists several methodological concerns about the advisability of separating cooperative and competitive aspects of action in this way:

> If we want eventually to get an understanding of all the intentional multi-person actions and activities, then we need to keep in the view the

unplanned as well as the planned intentional activities, and the competitive, mutually interfering and even hostile activities as well as the harmonious and non-competitive ones. (Baier 1997, 27)

It is because contradiction, disputation, even resigning or opting out on grounds of principle (internal emigration) have positive roles to play in reasoning and discourse that I want to include more than the smoothly cooperative variants of what we do in common. I want to include the harsh and abrasive versions of common activities, as well as the 'sweet, smooth, tender and agreeable' forms, so that they all get their due, and so that their relation to other common activities be recognized. (Baier 1997, 37)

Baier identifies two main reasons why an adequate theory of multiple-agent activity will be compromised by dividing up the subject matter and theorizing the divisions separately. First, this approach may overestimate or underestimate the importance of specific aspects of human action; and second, it may conceal important connections between these different aspects. The ultimate risk is that reuniting the separately theorized parts in a comprehensive theory might then prove outright impossible.

These methodological worries are real and important. But we should also worry about the *feasibility* of separating cooperative and competitive aspects of action in the first place. To understand why, we must go back to the observation that everyday activities typically exhibit mixed features of competition and cooperation. Indeed, examples of absolutely pure competition or cooperation are vanishingly rare in real life. So, separating out competition and cooperation is not just a matter of categorizing whole activities under one or the other of these two headings. Instead, it requires either the dismembering of whole activities into cooperative and competitive components, or else the theoretical reconstruction of these activities into 'as if' purely cooperative or purely competitive activities. But the relationship between cooperation and competition may well be too intimate to allow either of these operations to be carried out, even in theory. As we have mentioned, in competitive activities like board games, warfare, or stock market trading, there are rules and practices participants cooperatively follow which both set up and maintain the competitive activity. In other words, the very nature of the competition and how it works depends on the specific cooperative elements involved. Similarly, cooperative activities such as teamwork, military operations, or playing in a musical ensemble are set up and maintained by competitive interactions of various sorts, including hiring, training, disciplinary action, intimidation, politicking, and so on. So in these cases, the very nature of the cooperation and how it works depends on the specific competitive elements involved.[3] Thus, competition and cooperation are not just cobbled together in action, but are mutually constituting. So trying to theorize them separately is not really possible without wholesale misunderstanding of the character of the action under consideration.

Finally, this whole discussion prompts a renewed look at the terminology action theory currently uses in its discussions of multiple-agent action. To talk of shared intentions, joint actions, and the like embodies a cooperation-oriented perspective. In order to circumvent this, we will instead use the term 'collaboration' to talk about multiple-agent action. The etymology of this term implies working together, specifically, rather than acting together in an entirely general sense. This is a drawback, since the general sense is the one we want. But what recommends this term is that action theorists do not currently use this term, and it is relatively free of the distracting connotations of cooperativeness we have been discussing. In particular, because 'collaborate' is used idiomatically in the phrase 'collaborating with the enemy,' it captures the ambiguously cooperative/competitive nature of action in a way that 'cooperate' cannot. So, 'collaboration' may serve to counteract the narrowing of focus in action theory to cooperative actions, insofar as that can be managed through choice of terminology alone.

SORTING OUT THE SOCIAL

In addition to the tendency to focus exclusively on cooperation, action theorists have a tendency to conflate the social and the collaborative. The task of this section is to explicate this conflation, and explain exactly why it is problematic for an understanding of action. To begin, we noted in Chapter 1 that Marx makes a distinction between the social, on the one hand, and the collaborative or group agency, on the other hand. On his view, even individual action is always already social, because it depends on the social practices, norms, products, and so on of the culture in terms of which the individual developed her competencies as an agent in the first place. Thus, the social is not first generated by full-fledged individuals forming themselves into groups for the purpose of acting jointly in some common enterprise. Rather it pre-exists both individuals and groups, because it is essential for the development of infants into competent, individual agents, and because it continues to inform and delimit the specific activities in which these individuals engage. Sociality in this sense is a cultural medium in which all human activities take place, much as the activities of fish take place in water. Second, we noted that individual action and collaborative action exist on a continuum, since collaborative activity can involve more or less close contact with others. The more attenuated the relationships with identifiable others become, the closer you are to individual action.

Acknowledging the social nature of all activity and bringing it under the purview of theory is absolutely essential for a philosophy of material culture. In the first place, material culture—the products of a society—constitute a crucial dimension of social structure. Second, material culture plays a major role in enabling and sometimes enforcing the practices and norms that constitute other dimensions of social structure. You cannot play a game of basketball without the requisite number of players. But you also cannot play without a suitable ball, hoops, and a court, however crudely marked off. Similarly, phone booths both enable and enforce certain norms of privacy (interestingly violated by the recent introduction of cell phones), automatic door closers enforce norms about keeping the door shut (Latour 1992), software products that block access to pornography web sites enforce sexual *mores,* and so on. Thus, understanding material culture and its role in human activity requires not only acknowledging, but also theorizing the social medium of action. Unfortunately, contemporary action theorists typically abstract from this social medium in describing the phenomena they wish to consider and in constructing their examples. As a result, there is an initial failure to recognize sociality as distinct from multiple-agent action itself. This is where the conflation begins, but we must take a closer look at how it has become entrenched.

As we discovered in the last chapter, the analysis of individual action revolves around the nature of intentions and their relation to intentional action. Thus, when action theorists turn their attention to multiple-agent action they naturally think of such actions in terms of shared intentions.[4] But if the nature of individual intentions is mysterious, the nature of shared intentions is infinitely more so; and at this point there are a considerable number of accounts among which to choose.[5] They lie on a continuum ranging from accounts that understand shared intentions as reducible to appropriately interrelated individual intentions, to accounts that lean toward the idea that there is something special and irreducible about group intentions over and above the aggregation of individual intentions. Bratman's account of shared intentions as meshing subplans lies more to the aggregated-individual-intentions end of the spectrum. In this section, we will focus on Margaret Gilbert's plural subject theory, which occupies a place more toward the irreducible-group-intentions end of the spectrum. Doing so will help us see more clearly how action theory tends to conflate sociality and collaboration.

On Gilbert's view, a plural subject is a union of individuals characterized by a joint commitment to doing something as a body, such as two people agreeing to walk together.[6] Gilbert believes the phenomenon of plural subjecthood is paradigmatically social, and the source of other social phenomena:

> The range of uses of the predicate 'social' that people find comfortable suggests that sociality is a very broad category. At the same time, there is reason to judge plural subjects to be the most highly social phenomena. They involve a strong, symmetrical type of mental connectedness, producing what one can see as a real unity between distinct persons. It is not implausible to conjecture that plural subjects are implicitly understood to be the social phenomena proper, while other so-called social things are so-called by virtue of their various relations—some quite distant—to plural subjects. (Gilbert 1997, 31)

On Gilbert's view, the core of sociality, ontologically speaking, is to be found in the small-scale, personal relationships set up by individuals among themselves. In effect then, sociality has its source in multiple-agent action.

Although their position on shared intentions lies more toward the aggregated-individual-intentions end of the spectrum, a remarkably similar view is expressed by Raimo Tuomela and Kaarlo Miller (1988) in an early and influential article. The main business of the article is an analysis of 'we-intentions'—their term for shared intentions. A we-intention consists of the intention of an individual to do her or his part in some prospective action of a group, along with some beliefs about the we-intentions of the other members of the group and about the opportunities for action. These we-intentions make intentional joint action possible. Tuomela and Miller add:

> While this is not the place to go into details, let us point out that, given an adequate notion of we-intention (involving the notion of mutual belief) the notion of an intentional joint action can be formulated, we remember. With the help of we-intentions, mutual beliefs, and (intentional) joint actions, one can characterize social norms. Given the notion of social norm, social roles can be analyzed. Next, with the help of roles and we-intentions, one can define a strong, normative notion of a social group. From social groups, one can proceed to social organizations, institutions, and finally to the notion of a social community without adding any holistic social notions (or—if you prefer to call our we-intentions holistic—any supraindividual notions) to the conceptual basis of the analysis. (Tuomela and Miller 1988, 372)

Tuomela and Miller are here tracing the trajectory of analysis, which on their view must start with the we-intentions of small groups of jointly acting individuals to arrive at other social notions, such as norms, roles, institutions, and the like. In this respect, their view is indistinguishable from Gilbert's, although expressed in epistemic rather than ontological terms.

This indicates that there is agreement that group agency is the source of sociality among action theorists with very different views of what the nature of group agency itself is. Thus, when they disagree about the nature of group agency, they are in effect disagreeing about the nature of sociality *per se*. Consequently, all discussion of sociality is absorbed into debates about the nature of group agency. This gives us a more precise sense in which the social and the collaborative are conflated in action theory. This conflation would, of course, be entirely unproblematic if group agency were indubitably the ultimate source of sociality. But this view has been repeatedly challenged, although more commonly outside the ambit of action theory proper.

In order to understand the challenges, we must look more closely at exactly what action theorists commit themselves to when they locate the source of sociality in group agency. If sociality is created entirely through the actions of full-fledged, competent individuals forming themselves into groups of various kinds, then full-fledged, competent individuals must be essentially *non-social*. In other words, the behavior, dispositions, mental states, and other relevant characteristics individuals bring to group formation must be regarded as *sui generis,* not requiring for their existence or for our understanding of them anything itself already social in nature. Gilbert, for one, explicitly endorses this view:

> [T]he concept of an individual person with his own goals, and so on, does not require for *its* analysis a concept of a collectivity itself unanalysable in terms of persons and their noncollectivity-involving properties. (Gilbert 1989, 435)

Although it is a rather clunky term, I will call this view 'suigeneric individualism,' or 'suigenerism' for short. The rival position I will call 'sociogeneric individualism,' or 'sociogenerism' for short. This rival view holds that the vast majority of the characteristics of individuals that are of importance or interest to philosophers and social scientists (as opposed to biologists, for instance) require for their analysis an appeal to the social conditions into which those individuals were born, brought up, and/or now live. Action theorists have in effect regarded the issue as settled in favor of suigenerism. However, challenges to suigenerism from a sociogeneric standpoint have emerged in some recent critical assessments of action theory from relative outsiders to the field.

In a perceptive essay, Annette Baier points out that action theorists have traditionally started with individual action and gone on later to group action, as if the latter were somehow less basic and/or more difficult to understand than the former. But, Baier says, this approach ignores the fact that fully formed, competent individuals are not born; they are made through a developmental process that relies on what she calls the 'mental commons':

> Because this commons exists, individuals can use it to do all sorts of things which without it would not be possible for them. A child's mental maturation consists in learning to enjoy the commons, to speak, reason, sing with others, keep in tune, play card games and checkers, respond to others' expressed feelings, and in all sorts of other ways to draw from the common wellsprings of the human mind. She also learns to show proper respect for these common resources, learns not to pollute the wells nor erode the commons. Learning honesty in speech, learning when to look others in the eye, when to take another's hand, learning how to walk and talk together, is part of this maturation. (Baier 1997, 15)

Baier adds that this maturation process is not, for the most part, something the child does for herself on her own. It is initiated, managed, or facilitated by others who are already competent in the relevant skills. Thus, even the activities we usually carry out in solitary splendor as adults, such as bathing, reading, or driving, we first did—and learned to do—in the company of others (Baier 1997, 42–43). From the developmental point of view, then, it looks very much as though group action is more basic. At the very least, it is chronologically first in the life and formative experiences of every individual. Acting alone is actually the competency that has to be slowly, and sometimes painfully, acquired. Thus, Baier concludes:

> It is our separateness, not our togetherness, that originally needed initiative and assistance from others. The question 'How is individuality and individual action possible?' is just as good a question as the more usual one, 'How is collective action possible?' (Baier 1997, 43)

In conclusion, Baier makes three fundamental points. First, in taking individual action as somehow more basic than group action, action theory in effect ignores the fact that competent individuals are made, not born. Second, the development of individual competencies is dependent on the pre-existence of both a set of social practices and other individuals already competently exercising them. And third, the actions of competent individuals, whether undertaken alone or in association with others, are continuously informed by these social practices. These points constitute an empirically informed, developmental argument for a sociogeneric understanding of the individual.

We can now see the fundamental differences between sociogenerism and suigenerism. First, they differ in their understanding of the *nature of the individual*. On the suigeneric view, the theoretically significant facts about individuals are facts only about them, owing nothing essential to the social or collective aspects of human life. On the sociogeneric view, the theoretically significant facts about individuals are always already social facts, because they reflect the internalization or (as I would prefer to say) instantiation of pre-existing social practices. Second, they differ in their understanding of the *source of sociality*. On the suigeneric view, sociality has its source in the formation of groups and the exercise of group agency by putatively non-social, contemporary individuals. This understanding of sociality is present-directed—we are ourselves the source of our own sociality. On the sociogeneric view, sociality has its primary source in the social practices established by previous generations and reproduced by us in our own lives. We do have some creative input as to the specifics of our own sociality, since we can—and routinely do—revise these practices even as we reproduce them. But sociality precedes and constrains any such revisionary creativity on our part. Indeed, it is a precondition for it. Similarly, sociality is a precondition for groups and group agency rather than an effect of them. Thus, on the sociogeneric view, contemporary individuals are simultaneously created by the social environment in which they develop and acquire their competencies, even as they recreate this social environment for the next generation. This understanding of sociality is past-directed—our ancestors are the primary source of our sociality.

This distinction is crucial for a philosophy of material culture. Whatever else material culture may be, it is clearly a dimension of the social. So, any debate about the nature and source of sociality will be central to a philosophy of material culture. In particular, if the suigeneric view is on the right track, then the social nature of material culture should be analyzed as only an *effect* of the sociality generated by the group agency of contemporary individuals. But if, on the contrary, the sociogeneric view is on the right track, then material culture should be analyzed as an aspect of the *source* of sociality. It is inherited—often quite literally—along with the social practices involved in its production and use, and a large part of what is involved in the development of full-fledged individuals is training in the use and production of the material culture peculiar to their society. So the sociogenerism–suigenerism distinction has implications for the approach philosophers take to the investigation of material culture. What is most important at this juncture, then, is to foreground the suigeneric–sociogeneric distinction and to present it as embodying open questions about the nature of individuals and the source of sociality. In the next section, we will lay the groundwork for a philosophy of material culture along these lines by articulating in more detail the difficulties inherent in trying to understand multiple-agent action on suigeneric assumptions.

CORRALLING CRUSOE

If there is nothing essentially social about individuals prior to their engagement with other individuals in group activities, they can be treated for theoretical purposes as if they were what Gilbert (1989, 59) calls 'congenital Crusoes'—individuals who have never come into contact with society and whose language and culture are of their own invention or are an innate endowment. Gilbert's own well-known plural subject theory treats individuals in precisely this way in some crucial respects. Since Gilbert is more explicit about these suigeneric commitments than are most other action theorists, we will focus on her plural subject theory as representative of the wider tendency. By so doing, we may discover the problems inherent in action theory's suigeneric assumptions from the inside, as it were, rather than relying on external critiques.

Why does Gilbert think it makes sense to treat individuals as if they were congenital Crusoes for the purpose of theorizing about sociality? In light of the fact that other action theorists simply bypass the suigenerism–sociogenerism issue, it is to Gilbert's everlasting credit to have provided a lengthy argument for the suigeneric view.[7] The version of the sociogeneric view Gilbert tries to counter is a Wittgensteinian one, and not the empirical, developmental version exemplified by Annette Baier. As we shall see, the stronger arguments—the ones that apply most clearly to Gilbert's plural-subject theory—come from the empirical side. But let us start with Gilbert's counter to the Wittgensteinian view, which will enable us to see better how suigenerism informs her plural subject theory.

Gilbert interprets arguments of the Wittgensteinian type, especially those advanced by Peter Winch in *The Idea of a Social Science* (1958), as seeking to establish the conclusion that it is logically impossible (or perhaps conceptually incoherent—this is not very clear) for an individual human being who had grown up somehow in complete isolation from any society to have intentions, exhibit meaningful behavior, or, perhaps most importantly, make meaningful linguistic utterances. Gilbert's counterargument seeks to establish the conclusion that, on the contrary, these phenomena are logically possible, even in complete isolation from any society. The position she ultimately aims to support is what she calls 'intentionalism'—the view that 'the concept of intention is logically independent of the concept of a social group' (Gilbert 1989, 128) or more concretely that 'thought is logically prior to society' (58). Intentionalism, in turn, is crucial to Gilbert's (1989) later introduction of the plural subject as the centerpiece of her account of sociality, since 'these are intentionalist accounts' (58).

Gilbert (1989, 66) begins by pointing out that the bedrock issue concerns the possession of concepts, understood as rules for the application of terms, emissions of behavior and the like. Could a being entirely without any social contact for its entire life—a congenital Crusoe—have concepts, and consequently full-fledged intentions, language, culture, and the like? On the Wittgensteinian view, the answer is famously, 'no.' Rules require a public standard for assessing their correct application, and that standard is implemented by other people who supply corrections in cases of misapplication. Thus, the possession of concepts is intrinsically a social matter, and a congenital Crusoe consequently could not possess any. Gilbert (1989, 93) agrees that an external standard of correctness is necessary, but argues that it is *not* necessarily located in social norms and practices.

Her explication of this claim begins with five theses that she suggests characterize the intuitive or 'natural' view of what the possession of concepts involves (Gilbert 1989, 93–99):

- *Rule thesis*—to grasp a concept is to grasp a rule or standard for sorting things.
- *Infinity thesis*—a concept already determines for an infinity of possible cases, whether or not it applies to them.
- *Privacy thesis*—grasp of a concept is a property of an individual that can be ascertained without considering anyone else.
- *Subjectivity thesis*—there is a subjective experience associated with using a word in a specific sense (or, presumably, grasping a specific concept).
- *Content certainty thesis*—when an individual grasps a concept or uses a word in a specific sense, the individual knows what concept is grasped or in what sense the word is used.[8]

Gilbert (1989, 116) adds that if this 'natural' view is to be philosophically tenable, it must be combined with a Platonic view of concepts as abstract, objective particulars that provide the alternative, external standard of correctness:

> The concept in question establishes what is correct, and whether or not she [Maude, a hypothetical congenital Crusoe] makes a mistake is not up to her, it is a function of the nature of this concept. It seems, then, that Maude can have a language and this is a function of facts about her considered in isolation from any society . . . If the natural view as characterized above is coherent, the story of Maude and similar stories are coherent also. At the same time, it follows that society is not the only possible source for a standard according to which an individual's linguistic behavior can be judged right or wrong. (Gilbert 1989, 98–99)

Whether there really is a 'natural' view of concept possession and whether a Platonic account of concepts is viable are both eminently debatable questions. More importantly for us, though, Gilbert's argument admittedly only establishes the *coherence* of an alternative to the Wittgensteinian account. It does not establish the *truth* of this alternative account for any being, let alone for human beings as they are born, grow up, and live adult lives. In other words, it does not establish the *existence* of a being either originally endowed with a full complement of innate concepts or capable of inventing them for itself *ad libitum*. Gilbert (1989) does suggest that her view, based as it is on the alleged 'natural' conception of concept possession, may be 'the only view we can live with' (124), and appeals to Kant's transcendental argument for causality as a model for the kind of claim she wants to advance here (Gilbert 1989, 122). But on the one hand, this seems to be just false, since not only Wittgensteinians, but also pretty much the entire community of philosophers on the Continent for the last century or so have lived very happily with a quite different view of concepts. And on the other hand, Gilbert has not given a transcendental argument of the Kantian type for her 'natural' view of concept grasp. So Gilbert's conclusion is pretty much stuck breathing the rarefied air of logical coherence.

Both Gilbert and the Wittgensteinians she criticizes are clearly interested in the application of their conclusions to the actual case of human beings. But although the beings in their thought experiments tend to have names such as Robinson or Maude, the arguments on both sides are in fact made in terms of *a* being—any rational being whatsoever, as Kant might have said—since they are arguments about what is logically possible or conceptually coherent in general, not about what is empirically the case for human beings in particular. Thus, the arguments on both sides do not take into account the laws of nature, the facts of biology, the actual course of individual development, and the like. But Gilbert acknowledges that the empirically established facts do have a bearing on the correct analysis of actual cases:

> The claim that meaningful behaviour, or action, *as such* is social concerns the content of our concept of an action. It is therefore distinct from a number of reasonable and important empirical claims with which it could be confused. For instance, it may be that human infants require the nurturance of other members of their species in order to develop their capacities for more than rudimentary actions. Again, given that adult humans in general live in a social milieu, many if not all of their actions may be expected to bear the stamp of this. For instance, we may expect many human actions to be performed in the light of knowledge that they are considered obligatory or at least permissible in a certain group. (Gilbert 1989, 63)

The question we have before us, then, is how Gilbert's predilection for sui-generism, as supported by her argument for the logical coherence of the idea of congenital Crusoes, affects her analysis of shared intentions and related phenomena. Correlatively, does her analysis give sufficient weight to the empirical facts, the significance of which she acknowledges?

With these questions in mind, let us return to Gilbert's plural subject theory. A plural subject is a union of individuals created through a joint commitment made by them. These joint commitments are described by Gilbert as a 'pooling of wills':

> When a goal has a plural subject, each of a number of persons (two or more) has, in effect, offered his will to be part of a pool of wills that is dedicated, as one, to that goal. It is common knowledge that, when each has done this in conditions of common knowledge, the pool will have been set up. Thus what is achieved is a binding together of a set of individual wills so as to constitute a single, 'plural will' dedicated to a particular goal. (Gilbert 1996, 185)

This binding is accomplished through a special kind of conditional commitment of the 'I will if you will' variety, such that the commitment is not a matter of two or more unilateral commitments, but rather of a single, simultaneous, and interdependent commitment on the part of two or more individuals. What we need to examine here is the connection Gilbert sees between such joint commitments and the sociality of the individuals involved. Gilbert at first says that being a plural subject is, in effect, a necessary and sufficient condition for being a social group:

> On my account of social groups, in order to constitute a social group people must constitute a plural subject *of some kind*. And *any* plural subject is a social group. (Gilbert 1996, 188)

However, in later essays she relaxes this requirement, saying only that plural subject phenomena are 'paradigmatic, or preeminent, social phenomena' (Gilbert 1997, 17), or that they form 'the core of human sociality' (Gilbert 2000, 4), in the sense that all the phenomena we might intuitively think of as social ultimately refer back to plural subject phenomena.

Specifically, Gilbert claims plural subjects give rise to certain rights and obligations that are not necessarily ethical in nature, but are normative and, thus, inherently social. Gilbert's central example of a plural subject is two people who have jointly committed themselves to taking a walk together:

> Thus we can consider that each one's expression of willingness to walk with the other, in conditions of common knowledge, is logically sufficient for them to be plural subjects of the relevant goal, and hence to go for a walk together. If that is right, then once all this has happened, the relevant obligations and entitlements will be in place, and we can expect the parties to know this. (Gilbert 1996, 185)

Gilbert gives the specific example of Jack and Sue, who are walking together in this way as a plural subject. But Jack starts pulling ahead. Gilbert asserts that Jack has an obligation to notice this and correct it, and if he does not, Sue is entitled to rebuke him:

> In other words, it seems that in the circumstances, Sue is *entitled to rebuke* Jack. We would expect both Jack and Sue to understand that she has this entitlement. The existence of this entitlement suggests that Jack has, in effect, an *obligation* to notice and to act (an obligation Sue has also). (Gilbert 1996, 180)

Thus, on Gilbert's view, reciprocal social obligations and entitlements that did not exist before are *created* by the formation of a plural subject, and it is obvious to all the participants from that moment forth what they are.

This is a very clear example. But examining it more closely reveals some stresses and strains. First, since the entitlements and obligations are reciprocal, why does Gilbert say that if Jack is getting ahead *he* is the one with an obligation to notice, and *Sue* is the one with the entitlement to rebuke? It is equally plausible that Sue is obligated to keep up, and Jack is entitled to rebuke her for not doing so. In order to decide between these two options, additional factors must be taken into account. Has Jack drawn ahead because he has longer legs than Sue, whereas she is already walking as fast as she comfortably can? If so, perhaps Jack does have the obligation and Sue the entitlement to rebuke. But what if Jack has drawn ahead because Sue is dawdling, picking wildflowers by the roadside? In that case, perhaps Sue has an obligation to correct the situation, and Jack has an entitlement to rebuke her, given that what they jointly committed themselves to do was take a walk, not pick wildflowers. Thus, even if forming a plural subject does create a situation in which there are some obligations and entitlements, it does *not* settle exactly what those entitlements and obligations are, or who has them. Moreover, the participants may not agree about this. Sue, for example, may feel that in committing herself to taking a walk, she did not *ipso facto* commit herself to passing up all the wildflowers by the roadside, whereas Jack may feel that taking a walk just means going right along without stopping for anything. Typically, such disagreements are settled through a process of mutual clarification of antecedent expectations, followed by negotiations about what to do from that point on.

The important thing to notice is that this process is independent of the plural subject formation process not only temporally, but in structure and content as well. Thus, although there clearly is normativity involved *in* the carrying out of joint commitments, it does not all flow automatically *from* the bare formation of the joint commitment itself. Rather, it frequently requires auxiliary processes that are on the face of it social, but which are separate from and independent of the original plural subject formation process. In other words, just as plans are necessarily partial, so shared intentions formed through joint commitments leave much open with regard to both normative and non-normative factors. Committing yourself to taking a walk with someone is not necessarily committing yourself to walking a specific route with them, for instance. Gilbert acknowledges this in a later article:

> One can expect this spare and basic idea to be filled out in concrete situations by background social conventions or explicit agreements between the parties as to how a walk for two is to proceed. Thus the social conventions to which I am a party dictate that when we go for a walk, we walk alongside each other, unless the terrain requires us to do otherwise. Other such conventions might require the parties to walk in single file, or for parties of one social class or gender to work ahead of those from another social class or gender, and so on. (Gilbert 2008, 504)

But this concession opens up a breach in the tidy scenario presented by Gilbert. For even when the obligations and entitlements *are* clear right from the start, often enough it has to do with the social relations the participants had to each other *before* they made the joint commitment. For example, suppose Sue is elderly, or a member of the royal family. Then, even if she is dawdling along picking wildflowers, Jack's putative entitlement to rebuke her may well be defeated by an overriding obligation to display special courtesies toward the elderly or royalty. Even more radically, suppose Jack and Sue live in a society where a man is expected—perhaps even required by law—to walk several steps ahead of a woman he is accompanying in public. Then, Jack's drawing ahead and Sue's falling behind would not even be cause for comment. Indeed, in such a society it would be walking side-by-side that would constitute a failure on Jack and/or Sue's part to fulfill an obligation, and would entitle one of them to rebuke the other. This also casts a different light on Gilbert's assumption that Jack is obligated to notice he is pulling ahead and to do something about it, and that Sue has an entitlement to rebuke him. If this does go without saying, it is only on the additional, unstated assumption that Jack and Sue are members of a society in which the standard practice for people walking together is to walk side-by-side, even if they are of different genders. Examples such as these show in another way that the normativity *in* plural subject activity does not flow *from* the initial joint commitment. Rather, the source of the obligations and entitlements is in the pre-existing social roles of the participants, and the local social practices and norms to which they conform their activity in fulfilling those roles. It is only because those practices and norms exist and are understood by the participants (although not necessarily explicitly) that it seems clear what the entitlements and obligations are in specific cases where a joint commitment has been formed.[9]

Finally, let us consider some examples of people taking a walk together where entitlements and obligations they antecedently have toward each other constrain the very formation of the plural subject. As Christopher Kutz notes, action theory has focused almost exclusively on small-scale completely egalitarian activities. Kutz (2000) himself is concerned about this, because the resulting understanding of joint intentions insists on a unity between agents that does not obtain in social actions on a larger scale, or actions where some of the agents involved are 'cognitively vague, alienated, or dyspeptic' (26). But the narrow focus he complains about also raises concerns with regard to the normativity of action. Gilbert assumes that Jack and Sue enter into their joint commitment to take a walk on an entirely voluntary and egalitarian basis, in the sense that all that is necessary is that each of them have a readiness or willingness to make the commitment. She does not ask any questions about the genesis of that readiness or willingness. In other words, she treats it as an entirely suigeneric property of the individuals involved.

But suppose Sue is someone to whose requests or suggestions Jack feels—for whatever reason—some degree of obligation to assent; for example, she is his mother-in-law, boss, monarch, or spouse. Under such circumstances, Sue may well feel a reciprocal entitlement to his compliance. Or perhaps the obligation Jack feels is more transient than this. He and Sue are old friends; he has declined to go for a walk with her every day for the past three days; he feels he cannot do so again in light of the general obligations of friendship. In cases such as these, as in the previous set of examples, the obligations and entitlements do not flow *from* the formation of the plural subject, but rather pre-exist and are operative factors *in* the formation process itself. Moreover, as in the previous examples, these obligations and entitlements depend on the pre-existing social roles of the participants and the social practices and norms associated with those roles.

Gilbert might try to avoid this outcome by claiming to be giving an analysis only of joint commitments where the participants *are* on a completely equal social footing, so that nothing about who they already are socially affects the formation of the plural subject.[10] But social and personal factors influencing a person's willingness to assent are legion and one or another of them virtually always obtains and has some influence on assent. How well do you know the other person? How much do you enjoy their company? How safe do you feel with them? What is their relationship to other people you know? How would those other people feel about your going for a walk with this person? How socially acceptable and/or socially desirable would it be for you to take a walk with this person? Indeed, 'Would you care to take a walk?' does not necessarily even *mean* the same thing in all possible social circumstances and for all possible walking partners. In some situations, it is effectively a command, and in others an invitation to a sexual dalliance, for instance. Thus, if forming a true joint commitment requires readiness or willingness entirely uninfluenced by any pre-existing social or personal factors, then true plural subject phenomena must be vanishingly rare. This casts serious doubt on Gilbert's claim that plural subject phenomena are the paradigmatic, foundational social phenomena. On the other hand, if Gilbert acknowledges that such pre-existing social factors influence the initial assent to a joint commitment, then her claim is under even more pressure from another direction. For if pre-existing social factors influence what joint commitments are formed and between whom, then sociality is foundational for plural subject phenomena rather than the reverse.

This conclusion is borne out by the other two sets of examples we considered. The first set showed that, sometimes, joint commitments do not settle what obligations and entitlements the participants have, so that this must be settled afterwards through discussion and negotiation. Thus, the full specification of a joint commitment sometimes depends on auxiliary social processes independent of the formation of the plural subject. The second set of examples showed that in the other cases, where it is clear right from the start what obligations and entitlements the participants have, this clarity obtains only because the participants are situated in a context of social practices, roles and norms that specify in advance what obligations and entitlements are involved in the specific kind of joint commitment they have formed. Thus, the sociality of plural subject phenomena depends on the pre-existing sociality of practices and norms, not the reverse. A joint commitment does not create sociality where none previously existed, but rather implements or instantiates existing social practices and norms in particular concrete situations. So, Gilbert's (1997) claim that plural subject phenomena are 'the social phenomena proper, while other so-called social things are so-called by virtue of their various relationships . . . to plural subjects' (31) cannot be sustained.

The main reason for these difficulties with Gilbert's plural-subject-based construal of human sociality is her suigeneric assumption that the parties to a plural subject can be treated as if they were congenital Crusoes. That is, they can be treated as if all the properties they have when they make their initial joint commitment are suigeneric facts only about them—properties they were born with or invented for themselves out of whole cloth. Consequently, all the facts about their joint commitment, and in particular, facts about their social relationship as exhibited in reciprocal entitlements and obligations, can be treated as facts invented—although this time jointly—out of whole cloth by the parties to the commitment. And this in turn makes it look as though the crucial social aspects of the plural subject are created by the formation of the plural subject itself. But, of course, no individuals forming plural subjects really are congenital Crusoes. They come equipped with all sorts of socially induced knowledge, values, competencies, roles, relationships, and so forth. And what we have shown here is that the social obligations and entitlements that are supposed by Gilbert to flow from the joint commitment founding the plural subject instead depend in crucial ways on these social facts about the individuals involved, so that sociality is in fact imported *into* the plural subject by the individuals forming it, not created by that formation process and then exported. Indeed, it is hard to see how two congenital Crusoes *could* form a plural subject—just for starters, they would not have a common language in which to specify a goal and agree to pursue it. And this suggests that a sociogeneric approach to both individual and multiple-agent action is required. This will have to suffice for now as warrant for proceeding under sociogeneric assumptions in Chapter 4, where we will construct an account of collaborative improvisation. In addition, the sociogeneric approach will be crucial for our account of reproduction and use of material culture in Chapter 7.

Before we proceed to Chapter 4, though, a note about the view I am calling sociogenerism. It is hardly a new view. Elements of it are already apparent in Aristotle's ethics. Plato thought that to become an ethical individual was to acquire a kind of knowledge, something that could be done at any point in one's life on the basis of reason alone. For Aristotle, on the contrary, becoming an ethical individual was a matter of being trained up in the right habits of acting and thinking, starting in childhood. So the Aristotelian ethical individual is the sociogeneric product of long-term social processes, not the suigeneric effect of short-term, logically correct reasoning. Although the more suigeneric Platonic strain has arguably predominated in Western intellectual history, Aristotle's influence ensured a continuous undercurrent of sociogeneric views. We do not need to trace this entire history, but may pick it up in the nineteenth century, when generalized sociogeneric views about the relationship between individual and society surfaced in major thinkers such as Hegel, Nietzsche, and—as we have already noted—Marx.

Contemporary sociogeneric views are common, especially in Continental philosophy and sociology, and come in a variety of flavors. One of its leading theorists among philosophers is Michel Foucault (1977, 1982, 1990), whose later work, especially, focuses on the historically variable social processes through which 'normal' individuals are produced. He characterizes these processes in terms of the circulation of power and knowledge, but is at pains to point out that individual agency is never submerged, because the exercise of power in his sense is only possible with regard to beings capable of resistance. For Foucault, the circulation of power/knowledge essentially involves material culture and the built environment—his best-known example being the (in)famous plans by Jeremy Bentham for the Panopticon prison, where the very design of the building is instrumental in training the incarcerated and normalizing their behavior from the inside out, so that the individual who leaves the prison is no longer the individual who entered it. Among analytic philosophers, Philip Pettit (1996, 1998) has defended a view he calls 'social holism.' Working in a Wittgensteinian vein, he argues that certain aspects of human thought depend non-causally on our social interactions with others. Specifically, our ability to be—and to understand ourselves as being—fallible detectors of properties of the world depends on our ability to follow rules for identifying them. And those rules, in turn, depend on socially inculcated, correctable dispositions. Pettit takes this to be a contingent fact about human beings, if a very deep-seated one. In any case, the upshot is that on Pettit's view, thinkers are made, not born.

Among sociologists, the two leading figures are Pierre Bourdieu and Anthony Giddens, both of whom worked intensively on the relationship between social structure and individual agency. Bourdieu (1977) wends a middle way between objectivism and subjectivism with his conception of habitus, an inculcated set of dispositions to think and act in ways that are consonant with the established practices of the surrounding culture, but are at the same time adaptable to the specific situation of the acting individual. Habitus is embodied, practical knowledge, not discursive knowledge of rules, and so operates primarily below the level of consciousness, both with regard to its acquisition and its operation as an organizing principle for action. Thus, for Bourdieu, the individual incorporates social structures—and like Foucault, Bourdieu stresses the importance of material culture, including the spatial arrangement of living spaces and the like, in this process—only to objectify variants of them in daily activity. Giddens (1984) emphasizes the interactive relationship between structure and agency with his concept of structuration. Structure has a dual role in structuration, because it is both the set of rules and resources relied upon by the individual in order to make sense of her situation, and the outcome of her actions that reproduce these rules and resources in the form of social practices. Although more willing than Bourdieu to grant that the individual agent is conscious of what she is doing and can ordinarily give an account of it, Giddens still insists that the core of agency lies not in intention but in the power of the individual to actually get things done, often with unintended but important consequences that then feed back into the situation of ongoing action. For Giddens, then, agency and structure cannot be understood apart from each other, since the individual is both made by social structures that constrain and enable action, and the maker of these same structures.

The relationship between society and individual agency has also been explored recently in anthropology and archaeology. Ian Hodder and Scott

Hutson (2003) argue that precisely because archaeology deals with material culture, it poses the question of social structure and agency in a unique and pressing form—how is the individual item of material culture, which exists through the agency of an individual or group of individuals, related to the society to which these individuals belong? They deploy the ideas of Bourdieu and Giddens to construct an understanding of agency as a historically variable and local phenomenon. Thus, in studying a material culture, archaeology cannot assume that the individuals who produced it had the same kind of relationship to it, or to their society in general, that contemporary Western individuals do.

Finally, no discussion of sociogeneric views would be complete without mention of actor-network theory. This is a methodology originally developed for studying large technical systems, such as the internet or a public transportation system, but now employed more widely and in a number of variants (Law and Hassard 1999; Latour 2005). The striking feature of this methodology is that it treats both human and nonhuman entities, including items of material culture, as actors, although not necessarily all as actors in exactly the same sense. This approach, thus, agrees with Giddens in understanding agency as a capacity to get things done rather than a matter of intention or even intentional states in general. Most importantly for our purposes, however, an actor is defined by its relationships to other actors in a network of such relationships. So here again, agency and structure are not comprehensible apart from each other.

There is no need at this point to argue for a particular version of sociogenerism. All that is needed is the general orientation toward viewing the individual and society as mutually constituting. Specific social structures produce specific types of individuals, and these individuals in turn reproduce the social structures in the medium of their own activities and practices, although not usually with complete faithfulness. So, neither in theory nor in describing examples can we assume that individuals are essentially nonsocial until they voluntarily enter into relationships with each other, or that social structures are the joint creation of contemporaneous individuals. To do so is to distort both the nature of the individual and the nature of multiple-agent action.

4   How to Improvise

> The premises from which we start are not arbitrary; they are no dog-
> mas but rather actual premises from which abstraction can be made
> only in imagination. They are the real individuals, their actions, and
> their material conditions of life, those which they find existing as well
> as those which they produce through their actions. These premises can
> be substantiated in a purely empirical way.
>
> —Karl Marx and Friedrich Engels,
> *The German Ideology*, Part I, A.1.

This chapter outlines a basic account of improvisation. Needless to say, this will not be a complete and exhaustive account of improvisation—that would be a book-length undertaking in its own right. This account of improvisation is based largely on actual examples gathered from a specific type of improvisatory activity—songwriting. With any luck, the results in this domain can then be generalized to improvisation in other domains of human activity. So the approach here is to ground theory as firmly and explicitly as possible in empirical data of a qualitative sort. This methodology is intended to contrast both with more standard philosophical methodologies based on thought experiments and hypothetical examples, and with more standard laboratory-based methodologies in cognitive science, psychology, and experimental philosophy.

The first section of this chapter explains why songwriting was chosen as the domain for investigating improvisatory activity. It also outlines how the songwriting data was gathered and analyzed. (Full details may be found in the Appendix.) The remaining sections articulate the account of improvisation based on these data. The observation that will serve as the springboard for an account of improvisation is that generating complex actions requires resources. Plans are one such resource. Not *the* resource, as typically assumed by proponents of the planning paradigm, but one resource among others (Suchman 2007; Agre and Chapman 1990; Chapman 1991; Agre 1997). So the question that will guide us here is: What *other* resources are available to the improvising agent? Prototypical plans set out a goal, actions needed to achieve this goal, and the order in which they must be concatenated. They are prepared in advance, thus relieving the agent of the burden of weighing options and making decisions at the time of action. This makes it possible to smoothly and quickly produce complex, coherent sequences of action over extended periods of time. Improvising agents do not have this resource available to them. Nevertheless, they, too, smoothly and quickly produce complex, coherent sequences of action over extended periods of time. How do they do it?

The second section, which takes up the bulk of the chapter, answers this question by identifying three improvisation *strategies,* as I will call them. Two of the strategies we will investigate—the appropriate-and-add strategy and the proliferate-and-select strategy—can be used either collaboratively or by individual agents acting on their own. The third strategy, turn-taking, is inherently collaborative. These strategies are not so much constraints on action as ways of enabling an ongoing, creative response to the world on the part of agents. So, unlike the case of planning, where the creativity of action is ideally relegated to the mental construction of plans that are then uncreatively executed, improvisation displays a kind of creativity distributed throughout the action itself.

The final section focuses on *practices* and *habits* as another kind of resource. As I understand them here, practices are procedures for generating and concatenating actions that are specific to particular cultures or subcultures. They are thus less general than strategies. Habits are specific to small groups and individuals, and are thus even more idiosyncratic than are practices. The main purpose of this section is to sketch the relationship between the constraints of sociality and the creative leeway enjoyed by each individual. This issue will be reopened with specific reference to material culture in Chapter 7.

WHY SONGWRITING?

Songwriting is an attractive domain for this investigation, for a number of reasons. First, it is both improvisatory and collaborative. It is comparatively rare for songwriters to sit down with the explicit intention of writing a song, and even rarer for them to have a settled idea of how they are going to proceed. Rather, songwriters typically begin with some small, serendipitously occurring fragment—a line of lyrics, a riff, or what have you—and then piece the rest of the song together, sometimes over a considerable period of time, and often in ways that might seem haphazard to an outside observer. In Bratman's terminology, songwriting is a purposive activity, but not a planful one. And this activity is frequently collaborative. Some of these collaborations are relatively ephemeral affairs. But often, collaborating songwriters work together over the course of many decades. On the other hand, some songwriters work mostly on their own. Thus, songwriting provides a good opportunity to compare multiple-agent improvisation with individual improvisation.

Second, songwriting is embedded in the wider domain of music making, which itself has several very attractive features. One is that music making appears to be a universal feature of human cultures. And focusing initially on such a universal activity will facilitate future cross-cultural study of improvisatory activity. Another attractive feature is that music making exhibits a rich and diverse material culture. Most obviously, there are musical instruments and their accessories—picks, slides, drumsticks, amplifiers, and so on. In addition to items like these with musical proper functions, there are also some very significant examples of the appropriation of items of material culture with nonmusical proper functions for musical purposes—spoons, washboards, jugs, saws, and so on. This is an important phenomenon with regard to the theory of function for material culture, as we shall see in Part II. And then there are numerous devices for recording or notating music. These range from good, old-fashioned texts such as tablature, to sophisticated digital recording equipment and storage media. Last but not least, songs themselves are arguably items of material culture. (Ask yourself why a song should be any less an item of material culture than a painting or a book, for instance.) If this is accepted, then studying songwriting provides an opportunity for studying the production of material culture side-by-side with its use. A final attractive feature is that music making involves improvisation in performance. This has been studied to some extent (Sudnow 2001; Sawyer 2001). But it is a poor choice as a model for improvisation in general. The constraints of performance in front of an audience result in an atypical and impoverished profile in comparison to non-performance forms of improvisatory activity. Nevertheless, improvisation in performance is clearly an important phenomenon. So, again looking ahead to future work, music making provides an opportunity to compare the performance and non-performance modes of improvisation within a single domain.

Third, songwriting is the subject of legions of published interviews with musicians and writers of popular songs. This huge but unsystematic body of material was of great importance at the beginning of this project as a source of inspiration for generating hypotheses and a provisional conceptual framework. I will continue to use it here as a secondary source of examples and supporting evidence. On the other hand, from a social scientific point of view, it is unsatisfactory because of the lack of consistency between interviews with regard to what questions were asked and how they were followed up. Moreover, it is pretty much impossible to get any information with regard to how the interviews were transcribed and edited. So, in order to test the initial hypotheses and refine the basic concepts in a more systematic way, I conducted a small, qualitatively designed study of my own. It consisted of semi-structured interviews with 10 songwriters, and was fairly evenly divided between people who usually write on their own and people who usually write collaboratively. The interviews were recorded on audiotape. I then transcribed the tapes myself, and analyzed them in accordance with standard ethnographic and qualitative procedures (Smith 1995; Charmaz

1995; LeCompte and Preissle 1993). I will be using the material from these interviews as the primary source of examples and evidence supporting the account of improvisation that occupies the rest of this chapter. Interested readers will find in the Appendix a more detailed description of how this study was conducted and how the interviews were analyzed.

Fourth and finally, the overtly creative nature of songwriting highlights the creative character of all human action (Joas 1996). This is the complement of sociogenerism. Although the individual is formed and constrained in an ongoing manner by her social environment, she nevertheless always retains a certain amount of autonomy in the face of this constraint. This freedom of social movement allows for a kind of continual creativity in action. Indeed, to a significant extent, the social constraints *enable* this creativity by providing tools and options. Cars and highways enable people to travel for their own purposes and by routes of their own devising, for example, while at the same time constraining where and how they drive. There are, to be sure, special and striking forms of creativity exercised by artists, scientists, and the like. But creativity in the sense to be explained here is not special or striking—it is ubiquitous and prosaic. It is like generativity in language, which enables any speaker to produce any number of different sentences and so to respond sensibly to what is said by others and to happenings in the world. Although we would be wise to suspect that the special and prosaic forms of creativity are on a continuum, we might still want to call the special and striking extreme innovative creativity to distinguish it from the more prosaic varieties. What holds the continuum together is that in both innovative and prosaic cases something is made that would otherwise not be there, and the making is relatively unconstrained, not determined by a preset template as it would be if the making were done by a machine in a factory.

To think about action as always having a creative dimension, then, is to think of it as a kind of relatively unconstrained making where what is made is the action itself. Some actions are productions, and then there is also a product that is made in addition to the action itself. Songwriting is obviously creative in the innovative sense, and it is a production. But what we will be focusing on in this chapter is the more prosaic kind of creativity inherent in the improvisatory *process* of songwriting, independent of the fact that this process is productive of new songs. More specifically, we will be looking at how improvisatory actions are creatively constructed over extended periods of time. The resulting account of improvisatory action based on the data from the songwriting domain is intended to be general in its application to improvisation in other areas of human action. So, everywhere we find improvisation—and we have argued that it is ubiquitous—we will have action with an inherently creative dimension.

But what about action that is not improvised, that is routine or planned? Let us start with planned action. The main difference is that in planning, the creative dimension is primarily a matter of *thinking* creatively in advance of acting; that is, it lies in the making of the plan itself. In improvisation, on the other hand, creativity is distributed throughout the activity rather than being relegated to an initial phase. Moreover, as we have already noted several times, plans are necessarily partial and often not executable as they stand. The filling in and revision that is then required during the execution of the plan is more often than not improvisatory. So plans also have a creative dimension in virtue of their dependence on improvisation in the execution phase. This last point will help us understand the creative dimension of routine actions as well. Take an action like unlocking your office door and flipping on the light. It seems entirely uncreative, since, unlike plans, routine actions appear to be executed over and over, *verbatim*. But this appearance is deceiving. Agents carrying out routine actions, like agents executing plans, are continually poised to interpolate or revise in light of the situation. So when you have mistakenly inserted the wrong key, you stop trying to turn it and look on your key ring for the right one. Or suppose you arrive at an unaccustomed early hour and bright sunlight is streaming through your one little window. You may pause with your finger on the light switch and then not flip it on. In other words, just as the individual retains some creative autonomy in the face of social constraints, so, too, the individual retains some autonomy in the face of the constraints of the routine and the preplanned.

The point about the creative character of human action, then, is not that every single action exhibits creativity, but that this creativity is a permanent possibility of all human action, and is often actualized. Were this not the case, human action would suffer from the same brittleness that still plagues artificial intelligence systems trying to operate in real time and real situations. So in part, what we are doing in this chapter is investigating the way this creativity surfaces in improvisation, as opposed to planning. In Chapter 7 we will return to this issue to investigate the role material culture—and particularly function in material culture—plays in underwriting the creative dimension of action. But for the purposes of this chapter, we may simply allow the innovative creativity of songwriting to orient us to the prosaic creativity of action in general.

STRATEGIES FOR COORDINATING ACTION

There is a sense in which improvising agents are faced with one and only one question—what to do next? On the one hand, it is a question of finding something—anything—to do next. This is not normally a problem, since in most situations there are numerous, easily identified options. But this leads directly to the other side of the question—which of the available options should be pursued? Improvisation is not formless or haphazard. What is missing in action theory as it stands is an account of how improvising agents can coordinate actions over time without a prior plan. Accordingly, this is not just a question of choosing among current options in isolation, but of choosing among them in such a way that they connect with previous choices to form a coordinated series of actions over time.

We may begin to understand how this is done by briefly considering Michael Bratman's (1983) account of the coordinating function of plans. On Bratman's view, plans have a dual coordinating function—both intrapersonal and interpersonal. According to Bratman, it is because plans ground expectations about future actions—your own or those of other agents—that they can support this dual coordinating function. What is it about plans that grounds these expectations? First, Bratman says, they are *conduct-controlling pro-attitudes*. They are, thus, both related to and distinguished from desires—related in that desires, too, are pro-attitudes; and distinguished in that desires only influence conduct rather than controlling it. A desire merely indicates a goal you are interested in pursuing, whereas a plan commits you to pursuing a goal through a specific course of action. But being a conduct-controlling pro-attitude is not sufficient to ground expectations—it is also necessary that plans be relatively *stable*. Bratman spells this out in terms of a disposition on the part of planning agents to resist reconsidering their plans unless they encounter 'a significant problem' (Bratman 1983, 274). Importantly, although Bratman does not mention it, reconsideration is also often prompted by significant opportunities that allow unexpected advances rather than require damage control. To sum up then, the *conduct-controlling* feature of plans grounds our expectations with regard to *what* we ourselves or other agents will do and *when;* the *stability* of plans grounds our expectations with regard to *how likely* we, or they, are to actually do it.

Plans also facilitate coordination by providing support for practical reasoning about further action (Bratman 1999b). This support flows from the interaction of two factors—the inherent demands for consistency and means-end coherence in planning, and the typically partial nature of plans. By explicitly specifying actions in advance, a plan can function as a set of constraints on reasoning about further actions that it does not explicitly specify. This is because the further actions must be consistent with the actions already specified in the plan, and even more stringently, must promote the overall means-end coherence of the plan. Moreover, the plan and the further actions that fill it in must both be consistent with background beliefs. Thus, plans clearly provide for intrapersonal coordination of actions. But they provide for interpersonal coordination as well, because plans can constrain the reasoning of agents other than the planner.

What Bratman does not explicitly acknowledge is that interpersonal and intrapersonal coordination can be accomplished by other means. Improvising agents have access to resources other than plans for coordinating their activities. Moreover, even in the case of filling in a plan, the plan is not the only source of constraints on relevant further action. So, to flesh out the account of coordination of action Bratman has begun, we will look at other ways agents can coordinate their actions both interpersonally and intrapersonally.

Plans ground expectations and support practical reasoning by establishing what we might call a *pre-existing action structure*. Thus, when the planning agent gets to the point of acting, she already knows what she is to do, at least in broad outline. But plans are only one kind of pre-existing action structure. There are lots of others, including laws, customs, habits, personal and institutional policies, and so on. We can distinguish broadly between *prescriptive* and *descriptive* pre-existing action structures. Laws, policies, and plans are prescriptive in the sense that they set out a template to which we are supposed to conform our actions, under the presupposition that we are not necessarily disposed so to act. Thus, you can have a law, policy, or plan in advance of anyone ever having acted in the prescribed way. These prescriptive action structures tend to be explicitly articulated, and reflectively applied. On the other hand, practices and habits are descriptive in the sense that they represent existing patterns of activity. Thus, a society or group cannot reasonably be said to have a practice unless at least some of its members already engage in the pattern of activity in question on some sort of regular basis. These descriptive action structures tend not to be explicitly articulated, and are typically applied non-reflectively. Contemporary action theorists have focused almost exclusively on prescriptive pre-existing action structures, and in particular on plans made and carried out by individuals. In contrast, we will focus here on descriptive action structures, and we will start with some that may well be species-wide in their employment. These are the pre-existing action structures I will call *strategies*. They are very basic and general procedures improvising agents use to organize their action. We will look at three of them: the *appropriate-and-extend* strategy, the *proliferate-and-select* strategy, and the inherently collaborative *turn-taking* strategy.

The Appropriate-and-Extend Strategy

Even if improvisation is not planned, it is still *situated* in at least two senses (Sawyer 2001). First of all, in everyday life, improvisation is always already situated at a particular place and time, in a particular material culture, and so on. Second, as the action proceeds, it defines the situation more and more precisely, thus creating a framework of constraints on what can or cannot sensibly be said or done next. The net effect is that by paying attention to where they are and what is going on around them, improvising agents enjoy roughly the same conditions and opportunities for coordination as do planning agents. As we saw above, one way in which plans facilitate coordination, on Bratman's view, is by constraining practical reasoning about further action—an important function in planning contexts, because plans are necessarily partial and must be filled in. Plans constrain the filling in by imposing consistency and means-end coherence requirements, thus providing a filter on what questions it is reasonable to ask and what options it is relevant to consider. Improvisation is *all* filling in, so to speak. But the developing situation, in tandem with the goals of the agents involved, generates consistency and means-end coherence constraints as surely as a plan does, although perhaps not with quite as much stringency. The other way plans facilitate coordination, according to Bratman, is by grounding expectations about future action in virtue of being conduct-controlling and stable. But the developing situation in improvisation also grounds expectations about future action. First of all, situations are as stable as plans, if not more so. You cannot normally reconsider being in a situation wholesale the way you can reconsider whether or not to scrap a plan, although you might on occasion radically revise your interpretation of a situation. Second, although a situation does not explicitly prescribe actions and so is not conduct-controlling in the way plans are, it is conduct-guiding just in virtue of the constraints on future action it generates.

Let us now take a closer look at some real-life examples of situational constraints in operation in the songwriting domain.[1] The songwriter in this case, Nathan Sheppard, usually writes on his own, and perhaps for that reason has particularly vivid memories of writing collaboratively on the few occasions when he has done that:

> 'Lying in the Grass,' with Will Greene. I was stuck on that. I had the riff for a long time, and then the song with no words. Will came over to my house one day, and this girl that I was living with at the time had painted this really huge picture of this girl lying in this tall grass on her side, and it had a bunch of planets in the background. And he goes, 'All right, I'll get you started, and then I'm leaving.' And he did the first two lines of the song, and then he walked out, and I finished it.

The structure of this activity is like stringing beads—take the string as it exists so far, add a suitable bead, repeat this operation until the string can be regarded as complete. Sheppard starts with a riff, adds a melody, but then gets stuck for lyrics. His sometime co-performer, Will Greene, appropriates the melody and adds the first two lines of the lyrics. Sheppard appropriates these lines and adds more until he regards the song as finished.

The second example is from Mike Mills, bass player for R.E.M. at the time of the interview, who almost always writes collaboratively and who here gets some help from singer and lyricist, Michael Stipe, during a practice session:

> [T]he song 'Me in Honey' off of *Out of Time*. I was sitting there, and the bass riff that is the song—it's the entire song—I was sitting there, I started playing that riff, just da-da-da-da-dum-da, da-da-da-da-dum-da, and I wasn't even thinking about anything. I was just sitting there doing it because I was killing time between songs. And Michael goes 'Keep going!' . . . And so I'm playing that, and he's inspired. So it's good to have him there, because sometimes he'll take things over that would never become songs otherwise. But because he puts lyrics and melody to

them, they become songs . . . And we said, 'Wow, that needs one more chord. Okay. A flat.' And that's it, that's the whole song. It's two chords. It's one of my favorite songs.

The important difference here is that the initiating contribution is produced *unintentionally.* These unintentional but accepted elements can enter in at any stage, and they are sometimes the result of outright mistakes or chance events, as reported in this example from Mamie Fike Simonds, keyboard player for the band Jackpot City at the time of the interview:

> [I]t was actually when we were recording. And I just made a mistake, and the mistake just kept happening. And then I just chose to use that note, when at first I was like 'Aargh! That's not the way that should sound!' But then by the end, that is the song I love because of that one note, because it just struck me as so different. Like who would have ever played that note there, you know? So I used it.

The role of such unintentional productions has not been noticed by action theorists, most probably because they are so focused on intentional action. But Annette Baier (1997) criticizes contemporary action theory for examining only intentional, initiating actions, and leaving out of account 'intentional continuings of what is already started' (16). And Andrew Harrison, in his unfortunately little-read *Making and Thinking* (1978), examines at length the idea that producing something at random and then assessing the result, rather than deciding beforehand what to produce and then producing it, is really how works of art, particularly paintings, are produced. So, being able to recognize already existing actions and products as useful or relevant even when they are not intended as a contribution to the project at hand is just as important a skill as being able to figure out in advance what would be useful or relevant for the project so as to produce it intentionally.

So far we have looked at examples of collaborative songwriting. But many songwriters work largely on their own, and they, too, employ this process. Here is an example from Russ Hallauer, guitarist for The Lures at the time of the interview, who describes the process as a continuous addition of new elements, each depending on the previous one:

> [T]here's a song called 'Best Thing' on the new album that I just wrote all the way through . . .[T]he riff progressed into a chorus, progressed into a bridge, back to the riff, and I had the whole arrangement done.

The point here is quite straightforward—what you appropriate and add to can just as easily be something you did yourself as something done by someone else. On the other hand, the collaborative examples indicate that this process may work better in a multi-agent situation, for at least three reasons. First, if you are stuck for something to do next, someone else may have something to offer that gets the ball rolling again, as described by Nathan Sheppard in the initial example above. Second, as the passage from Mike Mills shows, someone else may recognize something you have unintentionally produced as interesting or relevant when you do not. And finally and perhaps most obviously, many collaborative situations involve an expertise-based division of labor, so that someone else may be able to appropriate what you have done and add something you do not have the capacity to produce yourself. As Mike Mills puts it:

> That's the whole point of being in a band. I'm not dying to go off and do a solo record, because I can't write lyrics like Michael, and I certainly can't sing like Michael, and I can't play guitar like Peter. Therefore, my solo album would be a little more monochromatic.

Thus, although it is important to recognize that appropriating and adding can and does work perfectly well for the solitary improvising agent, it should also be recognized that its operation in multi-agent improvisation could be enhanced by factors peculiar to collaborative contexts.

Finally, we come to an important point about what it means to 'appropriate' something. What you are appropriating clearly constrains what you can or should add to it. But you do not want what your conversation partner or your songwriting collaborator does with your contribution to be either boringly predictable or disorientingly inconsistent. So the idea is to be creative, while not unduly violating the expectations and constraints of the situation.

But there are stronger and weaker construals of this idea. With the stronger construal, the expectations and constraints would be understood in terms of the intentions of the contributor, so that the rule would be: 'Take other contributions as the contributor intends them to be taken, that is, do not violate any expectations or constraints the contributor intends to create through their contribution.' This construal runs into trouble right away, of course, because we do not necessarily know what other people intend, based on what they say or do. This difficulty already surfaced in Chapter 1 when we discussed Randall Dipert's theory of performance. On his view, the performer *should* conform his actions to the intentions of the author of the work, but is only very rarely in a position to actually do this. Thus for Dipert, performance is creative *faute de mieux*—the performer must interpret the work to the extent that the intentions of the author are not known. Similarly, what other people say or do is not necessarily a very good or very complete guide to what their intentions are, but often we respond to what others say or do first, and get into a discussion about their intentions later, if at all. This is especially true of situations where action is very fast, as in a basketball game, or involves authoritative statements or orders, as in the military.

But in many cases, we may find that, far from insisting, the previous contributor does not *want* other contributors to conform their intentions to hers. Mamie Fike Simonds makes this clear in an example where she is reflecting on instances when her bandmates changed a bit of music she had brought in to work on:

> I like to think of it in terms of part of the process. Like maybe my idea could have been developed into something like that. And a lot of times, if I try to force them to hear what I hear, it never works. So the fact that we're all playing it together lends itself to whatever their ideas about the music are, versus mine. Trying to go 'No, no, no, no. I think you should do this'—then they're not really feeling it, and the thing for me in bands is for everybody to be comfortable with what they're playing . . . And sometimes my ability to hear the way it sounds and the ending result isn't that good anyway, so I kind of attribute it to 'Well, that's what it was supposed to sound like anyway.'

So, a second reason for not requiring that contributions be taken as the contributor intended them is that the contributor herself may not be at all attached to her intentions, often with good reason.

Finally, a third reason for rejecting the strong construal is that the intentions of the contributor are not necessarily—or even typically—precise or complete. Here is an example from Kelly Noonan, guitarist for Jackpot City at the time of the interview:

> I know I'm not like Brian Wilson that has every single note for everything and everybody. I couldn't do that. That's why I'm in a band. I can sit in my studio, and if I knew what to play and what would sound great all the time, I'd do it all. But I love having other people's input. They just make it into what it ends up being.

Sometimes this vagueness of intention is (as it were) intended, because fleshing the intention out or making it more precise would annul the advantages of collaboration, as this example from Mike Mills illustrates:

> I would almost rather give them just the essence of the song and say 'Okay, I trust you guys. Let's have some fun. Where should this go?' Rather than sitting there and putting down the bass, the guitar, the piano, you know, so that by the time I play it for those other guys there's not as much room for their input. I could do that, but I tend to enjoy their input. And then part of the way that I'm good for the band is I react to that . . . So I tend to hear someone else's ideas, and then say 'Well, that's good' or 'That's no good' or 'Why don't we do this with that?' I'm more of a shaper of things sometimes than a creator, in terms of adding things on to the initial song. I like to write the initial song, but in terms of adding things to it I tend to sometimes play off of other peoples' ideas more than come up with just essentially my own.

This vagueness of intention also shows up in the case of individual agents, who often do not have a settled idea about all aspects of what they are doing right from the beginning. Here is an example from Kevn Kinney, who typically writes on his own. Trying to show me (as opposed to tell me) how he writes a song, he picked up his guitar and started to play:

> If you're going to do a blues song, it's like . . . [plays a couple of chords and then starts singing] 'Find your own way home. Find your own way home. Find your own way home.' [speaking again] A lot of words coming from there. I'm not sure now what I'm going to do with it . . . What is home? What's the definition of home? Is he dead? Is home heaven? Is home getting home? Is home his past? What's the definition of all of these things? [plays and sings again] 'And it's a long way home.' [speaking again] Where is he, where does he need to go, is now the dilemma, to make it a song for me.

Thus, in the case of the individual, too, vagueness of intention is an important aspect of the creative process because it facilitates the exploration of many possibilities, a phenomenon we will examine more closely later on. But for now, the point to be noted is that in both the individual and the collaborative case, the intentions behind the previous contribution are often incomplete and imprecise, so even knowing what they were would not determine what contribution to make next, or even constrain it very tightly. Thus, an effort of creative interpretation is required.

But interpretation does change things. Sometimes it changes them quite radically, by taking them in a novel way instead of at face value. At the very least, it changes them by settling what they originally left open or by making explicit what they contained only implicitly. In other words, when you add your contribution, it effectively changes the previous contribution by settling on one of the many possible ways to go on from there. Here is an example from a published interview with R.E.M.'s Michael Stipe and Mike Mills:

INTERVIEWER: Do you listen to the music to suggest the words?

STIPE: Yeah, a lot. A lot of times the words can really change the music. We would have a song like 'Shiny, Happy People' that was originally like a stomp-rock kind of song.

MILLS: When I first wrote it, it was a quiet, little acoustic ditty. That's the weirdest thing about it.

INTERVIEWER: You wrote it on guitar?

MILLS: On acoustic guitar. It was fingerpicked, quiet, four little chords. The chords that comprise the chorus now. It sounds nothing like the song. And that's the way things go. When you start to get input from everyone, you start to use more instruments that you have at your disposal, and the songs evolve. They turn into final songs. Sometimes

> they still remain little acoustic numbers but sometimes they become 'Shiny, Happy People.' There's no way to tell. (Zollo 1997, 632)

So, on the one hand, the four little chords are still there. And they have constrained what else was added, perhaps by settling what key the song is in, for instance. But they no longer comprise a quiet, little acoustic ditty; they have been reworked as the upbeat chorus to a rollicking pop song. In short, the four little chords *have* been accepted, but they have also been changed. And they have been changed, in large part, through succeeding contributions to the song.

Moreover, sometimes change is a matter of explicit, intentional revision of earlier contributions, as in this rather complex example from Miria, a songwriter and performance artist who writes on her own, bringing in collaborators only at the stage where revisions or arrangements are in question:

> I wrote 'Perfect Day' in '92, but I've rewritten the melody for that three times, and the third melody I wrote with my producer . . . But the arrangement that he came up with kind of rearranged the order of the lyrics, too, to some extent. I would say the lyrics were not rewritten. They're the same lyrics; they're just in a different order because of the song structure.

Here we see, first of all, two different modes of revision: rewriting as contrasted with rearrangement of component parts. Second, we see revision both by the originator of the song, and by a collaborator at a later date. Finally, this example shows that sometimes it is the whole structure of an action or a production that is revised, not just a component part.[2]

Last but not least, outright rejection of contributions is routinely practiced in improvisation contexts, too. Here is another example from Miria:

> I would say that he [her producer] wrote about seventy five percent of the melody for the new version of 'The Perfect Day.' And it was completely his arrangement. He did that and I came back into the studio and he said, 'Here. What do you think of this?' And I said, 'Oh, that's great!' But he also had done that on a couple of other songs. It was like 'Oh, my god, that's so not me! What are you thinking?'

Miria went on to say that she felt comfortable rejecting her producer's contributions outright in these other instances, because she was paying for the recording project herself, and so understood herself to have final say. This is important, because it indicates how significant the pre-existing relationships of the collaborators can be with regard to what gets appropriated or added, and how this is done. This will differ especially between essentially egalitarian relationships as opposed to relationships where economic or social differences among the agents involved may mean that agents have a perceived right—or even a responsibility—to reject contributions from others that they consider inappropriate for some reason. Moreover, even in bands, where the relationships often are highly egalitarian, the songwriters interviewed reported rejection of contributions that were not considered very good by the rest of the band, or even just by the particular person who had originated the song in question, as described here by Kathy Kirbo, bass player for Jackpot City at the time of the interview:

> When you're writing with somebody, and you have this certain vision, you know, and they come up with something very different, sometimes it will turn out better with their idea, and sometimes you're like 'Oh, I wish you would do it the way I saw it, really.'

Here Kirbo not only reports feeling perfectly comfortable rejecting a contribution from a collaborator, but she reports being ready to do so on the basis of a prior idea she has about how a song she has originated should go.

So our original beads-on-a-string conception of improvisation was not right. This metaphor suggests that each succeeding contribution is simply added to a string of previous contributions that is supposed to be simply accepted as is, and not otherwise altered. But this conception is not adequate, because subsequent contributions always change previous ones, if only in virtue of interpreting them in a particular way. In addition, previous contributions are sometimes deliberately revised, or even rejected. Thus, contributions are not accepted so much as *appropriated*. That is, improvising agents make previous contributions their own by interpreting them, revising them or rejecting them. So, the process is not like stringing beads, but more like shaping a lump of malleable material such as clay; working each contribution in, not just adding it on.[3] Moreover, improvising agents in everyday situations are not following an explicit rule that instructs them how to proceed. So we will speak of the *appropriate-and-extend strategy* of improvisation. Finally, it is worth noting that there are limiting cases of this strategy where something is simply accepted and not extended. This might happen if a collaborator puts 'the finishing touch' on a song, for instance.

The Proliferate-and-Select Strategy

In the previous section, we talked mostly about the 'appropriate' component of the appropriate-and-extend strategy. In this section we will focus on the 'extend' component, which is itself typically the locus of operation of another important improvisation strategy I will call the *proliferate-and-select* strategy. So these strategies are typically related to each other in the following way:

Initial Action/Production → Appropriate → Extend → Appropriate → Extend
 ↓   ↑   ↓   ↑
Proliferate → Select   Proliferate → Select

Like the appropriate-and-extend strategy, the proliferate-and-select strategy can be used by solitary improvising agents as well as by collaborating agents, and its operation is typically enhanced by collaboration. The 'extend' component of the appropriate-and-extend strategy represents the introduction of some new action or production to carry forward previous contributions. The agents involved thus have the task of coming up with an appropriate next action or production. One side of this process has to do with the importance for improvisation of the situatedness of action. We already discussed this in the previous section, in terms of the expectations and constraints generated by the developing situation. The other side has to do with the creativity of the agent in introducing something new and quite specific into the situation. In other words, the situation provides a facilitating framework that narrows down the options for action with regard to what is relevant and what is not; but the agents involved still have to come up with specific candidate options and settle on one of them.

Like appropriate-and-extend, proliferate-and-select obviously consists of two distinguishable steps. Although in many of the examples that we will look at, proliferation and selection are inextricably entwined, in the interest of manageability we will focus first on proliferation and then go on to consider selection. As the term 'proliferation' indicates, the phenomenon to be investigated here involves generating multiple options for what to do next, and then selecting among them. This is not primarily a matter of imagining several different candidates, as you might do when constructing a plan, but rather of actually trying out several different ways of proceeding before settling on one. As with appropriate-and-extend, there are limiting cases of proliferation-and-select, of course. This happens when you generate just one option and go with it, without trying out any others. Limiting cases of proliferation are important, though, because they turn up regularly where there is pressure to do something quickly. When another vehicle veers into your lane, for example, you do not normally have time to think about different options for dealing with the situation, let alone the leeway to try several out, even in imagination, before settling on one. So you go with the first option you generate, for better or for worse. On the other hand, many driving situations do allow leeway for trying out more than one option. You can try out several different approaches to a parking space, for instance. So understanding the proliferate-and-select strategy in improvisatory activity will require looking at a range of cases, including the limiting one.[4]

To begin, then, let us look at a straightforward and very common type of proliferation—generating multiple candidates to fill a particular slot, as reported by Jason Slatton of The Lures:

> A quick one would be 'Surrounded by the Girl.' That was a thing where the verses definitely came very quickly, and the lyrics to go along with them. Where I hit a snag was with the bridge section, which is the section before the mellotron string section comes in. And I wrote 10 dif-

ferent bridges for that, because I couldn't find one that seemed to work and support the verses. And I finally settled on one that I really liked, but it took a long time to find that one section. A bridge is a really great thing, and a hard thing to write in a song, because it's pulled out of the song, but it's a break from it as well, you know.

We will call this type of proliferation *guided* proliferation, because it is typically quite highly constrained by the particular slot into which the candidate options must fit. In the case of the bridge of a song, there is a particular musical function the candidate options must fulfill. At the same time, the designated slot does not constrain the options so tightly that there is a determination of a uniquely right option, or necessarily even of a small number of especially suitable options. So, as Slatton says, the process of generating options can be quite time consuming and effortful. One final point: the process is not necessarily cumulative, such that each successive candidate is better than the one before and the one that is chosen is always the last in the series. The candidate options may represent radically different approaches to filling the designated slot, so the one that is ultimately chosen as the best may be anywhere in the series. To take a commonplace example from another domain: when getting dressed you might put on a number of different outfits before choosing one to wear, and the one you end up wearing might well be the first one you tried.

Not all proliferation is guided, though. Some is what we may call *free* proliferation. This is not to suggest that the options generated are devoid of structure, but only that they are not generated in response to a particular, pre-existing slot that needs filling. Thus, free proliferation is simply an ongoing, intermittent process in agents' lives and activity, where the options generated are connected to some goal or project of the agent only after the fact. In this sense, free proliferation is much more like biological evolution, which is not aiming at any specific result or trying to solve any particular problem, but is just generating possibilities at random to begin with, and selecting among them later on. Here is an example from Nathan Sheppard:

> I usually come up with a group of chord progressions on the guitar. What I do is I'll doodle with melodies and stuff. I'll get a chord progression, just something I like on the guitar. And I'll come up with a melody, record it, and save it. And when I get into words—have a concept as to what I want to do, verbally—I'll go pick out one of these tunes that I've recorded and write the words to it.

Later in the interview, Sheppard referred to this hoard of recorded tunes as a 'bank' from which he can withdraw a suitable melody when he needs one to fit lyrics generated separately. And, of course, this same process can be used collaboratively, as it is by R.E.M., for instance. The division of labor in this band was such that vocalist Michael Stipe wrote most of the lyrics and some of the melodies, and the band's instrumentalists wrote the instrumental components and some of the melodies for songs. As Mike Mills reports, they typically worked separately:

> There was really no sense for Michael to sit there and listen to us jerk the song around and try to mold it into a nice form, because we always wrote songs that were adaptable to what Michael needed. In other words, we wrote songs that if Michael needed a longer verse or a shorter verse or another chorus, we could always do that with a song.

And Michael Stipe reported in a published interview that, on his side, he generated and kept notes for lyrics and melodies:

INTERVIEWER: And do the lyrics come during this time of it?

STIPE: Yeah. There's no real set way that it happens. Sometimes I have an idea for a melody, or I've got this stuff written and I'm trying to figure out what to do with it.

INTERVIEWER: You write lyrics on your own and bring them to the band?

STIPE: Yeah, or I'm inspired by a song to write something. There's no real method. (Zollo 1997, 631)

So in this particular collaborative arrangement, two independently prolifer-ated 'banks' were available—one mostly devoted to lyrics and melodies, and the other mostly devoted to instrumental components of songs. These could then be drawn on to produce complete songs, usually by way of the instru-mentalists presenting a selection of their productions to vocalist Michael Stipe, who then focused on an even smaller number to pursue in light of on-the-spot inspiration or his own 'bank' of lyrics.

In the case of R.E.M. and Nathan Sheppard, the free proliferation of adapt-able musical snippets is a regular part of the songwriting process. But free proliferation can also be used as a more occasional resource when difficulties are encountered in the process of writing a song. For example, Jackpot City's Kelly Noonan showed me a notebook full of fragments of lyrics and notations of chord progressions she keeps in case they might come in handy later:

> I'll have my notebook I brought in there, my little composition book, and it will have tons of little pieces of paper stuck in there, because I'll be just driving somewhere and just writing down some stupid thing. But sometimes that little stupid thing, when you go back and look, when you need something—it's just what you need . . . So you learn to save all those little, weird things that you think about or realize, because you will need them when you've got nothing.

So for Noonan, the proliferation results in something that functions more like a cache of emergency supplies than like a bank from which regular withdrawals are made. It is a resource she can rely on when she runs out of ideas or gets stuck for what to do next, but that she does not necessarily draw on regularly for most songs she writes, as R.E.M. and Nathan Sheppard report doing.

Proliferation is central to the account of how improvisation works. But the production and collection variants of proliferation are doubly important in the context of the current project because they exemplify central ways in which material culture is involved in improvisatory action. The items produced or collected are, of course, usually items of material culture. But more importantly, items of material culture are utilized in both collection and production processes. Nathan Sheppard, in the example above, mentions using his guitar to come up with chord progressions and melodies that he then uses his computer to record. In addition, material culture is involved in post-production or post-collection storage of items. Songwriters store bits of music or lyrics in notebooks or on audiotapes or computer drives, for example. Thus, material culture provides an environmental infrastructure for improvisational activity. This infrastructure will repay further study.

Let us look first at what we might call the ground floor operation of proliferation in songwriting—coming up with initial bits of music to get the proliferate-and-select cycle going. For our purposes, we will not treat this as a matter of inspiration, but rather of what songwriters are *doing* when bits of music occur to them, and what they do next with those bits. This is not to deny that where songwriters get inspiration is an interesting issue. But in the first place, the sources of inspiration they tend to report are precisely what you would expect—listening to other people's music, wanting to write a song in a particular style or genre, wanting to write about a particular person or event, and so on. And this still leaves wide open the question of how any of these sources of inspiration is connected to actual bits of music. In the second place, how a songwriter gets from inspiration to actual music is no more and no less mysterious than how anybody gets from inspiration about anything to concrete ways of dealing with the world. For example, if you are inspired to rearrange your living room by an article in *Better Homes and Gardens,* how do you get from that inspiration to the actual rearrangement of your living room? You are not merely reproducing what you see in the magazine picture, any more than a songwriter is merely reproducing the music that inspires her. And finally, there is an obvious, if unsatisfying, answer to this question—human brains are set up to do certain sorts of things, among them making music and rearranging living quarters. But investigating what it is about human brains that makes this possible is a matter for neuropsychologists—or, in the case of songwriting, perhaps more specifically, biomusicologists. But what we can examine more closely and learn something from is what songwriters *do* and how they interact with their social, cultural, and natural environments in the process.

One thing songwriters typically report is that bits of music often seem to come out of nowhere while they are engaged in mundane activities such as making dinner or driving to work. Somewhat less frequently, but perhaps more interestingly for our purposes, these bits of music are touched off by environmental rhythms or sounds, as Mike Mills reports:

> I wouldn't know how to say where musical ideas come from. They just click in your head. Maybe you hear some rhythm of nature. Literally, the sound of a hubcap rolling down a street might set you off. (Zollo 1997, 633)

Whether or not there is an identifiable environmental stimulus, though, the end result is that the songwriter has an auditory image of a bit of melody, a riff, or something of the sort. But, they typically report, these auditory images are very hard to remember. Combined with whatever distraction might be caused by what they are doing at the time, this means that these bits of music quickly get lost, unless the songwriter does something to retain them. For example, Jason Slatton reports resorting to a variety of recording devices on different occasions:

> The worst instances have been when I don't have something to record with. What I'll have to do is write the music out, like a melody idea. I generally have a little tape recorder that I'll use and just sing something into it to try to remember it. I've even called my answering machine before and left it on voicemail, because I'll be somewhere, and I'll have an idea, and nothing to record it with. And that's not good, because you never remember it the same way. I think I've probably lost a lot of songs that could have been something good because I assume that I'm going to remember them, and I don't. So generally I will try the tape recorder. Or a notebook.

An alternative is to repeat the bit of music over and over in your head, and/ or to try to get to your instrument as fast as possible, as Russ Hallauer reports:

> Worst case is when it happens and you can't get to the guitar right away. I drive around a lot during the day with my job, and I'll be in the car sometimes and something will come and it will be eight hours before I can get home. And then you sit there and you try to hum it all day so you don't forget it . . . Because to me once you get it and you play it and you see where your fingers went, then it sticks a little harder.

Because so much cognitive energy is expended just trying to retain these musical fragments, it is no surprise that songwriters report that working on a fragment—appropriating and extending it—is not something they usually try to do in their heads in the auditory imagery medium. Instead, they 'transfer' the auditory image to an instrument to work on it. But this transfer is not necessarily easy, nor does it necessarily leave the musical fragment unchanged, as Mamie Fike Simonds reports:

> Sometimes when I go to the instrument and play what I thought I heard in my head, it changes. And so I'm thinking 'Maybe that wasn't what I was thinking at all.' And then maybe I use the instrument to carry that idea somewhere else. Or it might be that it is what I was thinking, and then I'll play around with it on the instrument and extend the idea, using the instrument.

Here we see the material culture infrastructure functioning not just as a physical support for improvisational activity, but as a cognitive support, and that in at least two ways. First, various kinds of material culture are used as external memory devices (analog recording, visual cues provided by an instrument, notation). Second, musical instruments are used as the medium in which further work is done on the initial fragment. And as we shall see in a moment, this is because the instrument actually aids the work, rather than merely preserving initial bits of music so that they can be worked on.

In light of the importance of musical instruments in the songwriting process, it is no surprise to learn that all of the songwriters interviewed reported that they also often come up with initial bits of music while actually playing. Most of them reported that writing on an instrument from the start is their usual and/or preferred *modus operandi*. And several of them explained that instruments help them write, as reported here by Debbie Norton, who at the time of the interview was singer and guitarist for the band Where's Anita? She plays both six- and twelve-string guitar, but prefers to write on twelve-string:

> You can actually hear a lot of the harmony in a twelve-string because there's so much sound. I think that's why I fell in love with it. It's just real rich sounding and it gives you ideas and tones, much more so than a six-string does. I almost always write with a twelve-string.

In addition to the sounds produced by the instrument, its structure can have an effect on the generation of musical fragments because of the constraints it embodies. In this regard, songwriters often favorably compare writing on piano as opposed to writing on the guitar, for instance, because the structure of the guitar fret board makes playing in certain keys or playing certain chords or chord progressions difficult, as Jason Slatton reports:

> Initially I was writing mainly on guitar . . . I read an interview with another songwriter who I really admire, who initially played guitar, and he talked about writing on piano, and how it was great because when you sit down with a guitar you're more inclined to play the same things over and over. And with a piano it's so much more free. And so I began writing on the piano. But that helped immensely. Melodic ideas, chordal

[ideas], because you can change the color of an entire chord with one key. On a piano you can. You can't really do that as easily on guitar. Guitar is a little more constrained, I think.

On the other hand, one songwriter's unduly constraining instrument can be another's inspiration. Jackpot City's Kelly Noonan avoids writing on bass, for instance:

> If I try to write on the bass, I get too attached to the one melody that I'm playing. With guitar, as I'm strumming a chord I can hear different things, you know. It suggests things, it helps me do it.

But her bandmate Kathy Kirbo often prefers the bass, especially as a change from other instruments:

> I think a new instrument kind of re-inspires you. Or changing over. That's one reason I started writing on bass. It just promotes a different style of writing and it kind of inspires you. So that's why I like dabbling around with different instruments.

Kirbo also reported an interesting example involving not a switch to a whole new instrument, but just changing the sound through amplification:

> I didn't have an amp in my house for probably a year or two, and then somebody brought by this little amp, and I wrote three songs in one night, just sitting on the sofa. And the band's like 'Yeah, you need to get an amp!' And it's just because I hadn't had it there before, and I was goofing around.

Finally, as Miria reports, creating a rhythm—or sometimes just hearing one that is environmentally produced—can promote the generation of musical fragments:

> There is one other way a song starts for me, which is just from rhythm. Like if I actually think 'I really want to write a song right now.' And I have nothing, you know, and not an idea. Then it starts from rhythm, I'll just like play out a rhythm . . . I haven't done this in years, but I used to every now and then hang out with a group of friends and just do hand drums and immediately I start putting words and melody to that rhythm. I think that's a really natural thing people do.

From all these examples, it is clear that working on an instrument is not a contingent matter for songwriters. Rather, an instrument is a material aid in proliferating initial bits of music, as well as in extending them. And the reason for this is that musical possibilities are inherent in the sound and the structure of the instrument itself.

But how do songwriters use their instruments to avail themselves of these inherent musical possibilities? The most consistent report is that they just sit down and play with no prior ideas or intentions to guide them, and, in effect, just let their hands wander over the instrument, as described here by Mike Mills:

> I'll sit down at a piano and I'll have no idea what key I'm going to play in until I've just hit it and started doing something. It could be a minor key. I tend to play a lot in flatted keys because on piano there's a nice rich tone that comes out of that. But you never know. Now sometimes you'll sit down to play another song that you already know; someone else's music or one of yours. And from that you will get ideas that branch out and lead you into another song. But for me, if you're really going to come up with something, a lot of times you just sit down and you just play. You just try to go from one chord to the next and see what happens, see if it's pleasing, or if it's interesting. If it sounds good, then you pursue it.

This passage brings out a number of interesting points. First of all, the songwriters interviewed were very clear about the lack of a guiding intention in this process. They regularly used terms such as 'doodling,' 'goofing around,' 'messing around,' or 'fiddling around' to characterize it. I will adopt 'doodle' as the term of art to refer to this phenomenon, not only because it was a term frequently used by the songwriters interviewed, but because it is etymologically related to 'tootle,' and is thus particularly appropriate for the music domain. Several of the songwriters reported doodling on their instrument while doing other things—watching television or talking on the phone (Kirbo), or listening to baseball games on the radio (Sheppard), for instance. In effect, then, they also sometimes use other items of material culture and/or aspects of the social environment as distraction devices, so that the doodling not only lacks a guiding intention, but also is not even the focus of conscious attention. In effect, songwriters sometimes intentionally arrange their environments so that unintentional productions are more likely to occur. This is further confirmation of the hitherto unremarked importance for action theory of unintentional productions.

Several of the songwriters who work collaboratively also reported multiple-agent forms of doodling, as Mike Mills reports:

> That was always a lot of fun, because it is truly of the moment creative. Whatever Peter or I would be doing, it was not necessarily something we'd been working on, because if it was something we'd been working on we would have taken the time to show it and say, 'Look, here's something I've been working on.' But basically it was total free form. Usually when we were just not inspired, we were out of ideas, we'd be sitting around and we'd literally just all three not even really be thinking about it, just be playing, but kind of consciously aware of the other

guy being there. And if you hear something, or if all of a sudden one of Bill's little drum things started going with the bass line I was making, then we'd follow that.

In a published interview, R.E.M.'s guitarist, Peter Buck, reported his sense of a connection between the use of distraction devices such as television while doodling and doodling in multiple-agent environments. The other respondent in this exchange is Bill Berry, the original drummer for R.E.M.:

INTERVIEWER: When you're writing, do you guide the music or do you follow it?

BERRY: Both.

BUCK: Both. When I'm sitting at home, I'll have the TV on and play to the TV, so I won't have to think of anything. I'll watch an old movie and just strum away to that. In the studio, it's the same thing, except there's no TV. I'll come up with a riff, and sometimes the band won't follow it but sometimes the band will go *boom!* And that's it. (Zollo 1997, 639)

R.E.M. sometimes used multiple-agent doodling quite consciously as a method for generating initial music fragments when no one in the band had brought in any individually generated fragments for them to work on collectively. Perhaps more commonly, it is just a serendipitous but regular happening in multiple-agent situations, as Kelly Noonan reports.

I don't know about most people, but when I sit down, I don't have anything that I'm getting ready to play. I'll just sit down and maybe start doing something, and then all of a sudden just by chance I might move my hand up here and go, 'Oh, that sounds cool.' And it happens in practice. Somebody's just doodling around, it's like, 'What is that?' 'Nothing.' And then it will start. It will just pick up on one of the little things she's doing and add to it or whatever . . . Just little doodlings can become songs if everyone cares about them, you know.

One thing it is important to note about both these reports is that it is not usually the producer of the interesting doodle who recognizes it as interesting and pursues it, but rather a bandmate, or the band, collectively. So, here again, it turns out that collaboration can enhance the operation of a strategy. In this case, not only does multiple-agent doodling mean a greater proliferation of potentially interesting musical bits, but the selection process is also enhanced, because individuals can rely on others to catch interesting bits they may themselves pass over. We will consider the selection step of the proliferate-and-select strategy in more depth in a moment, but first one final comment about doodling.

Several of the songwriters interviewed mentioned that sometimes playing over an existing piece of music, either their own or someone else's, can be a springboard for the generation of new bits of music through doodling. One way this sometimes happens is particularly interesting for our purposes. It involves something we may call *unfaithful* copying, in contradistinction to the faithful copying ideal of the planning paradigm. A good example of unfaithful copying is reported here by Kevn Kinney:

> Well, like 'Fly Me Courageous.' It started off [sings opening guitar riff]. That came out of me trying to play 'What'd I Say?' by Ray Charles. [Sings 'Fly Me Courageous' riff again, then sings . . .] 'What'd I say?' That's okay . . . I'm not that great of a guitar player. You know, when I play with Warren Haynes [of The Allman Brothers Band and Gov't Mule] he still puts my fingers on the frets, like 'No, this one here.'

Kinney is being very much too modest here in attributing the deviation from the original Ray Charles riff to his allegedly inexpert guitar playing. The truth of the matter is that copying is rarely exact, for any number of reasons. Sometimes the deviations are unintentional, and might be due to a different sensibility or background on the part of the copier, or to a different instrument being used, or to some combination of the two, for instance. Or the deviations might be intentional, and have reasons behind them. Unfaithful copying, then, occurs in both unintentional and intentional variants. Both these variants can be understood as appropriations of an existing production or action. But we can now see that in some cases where the copying is particularly unfaithful, it might be more correct to say that appropriation results in something new, rather than in an extension of what is being copied. Kinney's 'Fly Me Courageous' is not an extension of 'What'd I Say?' so much as a new song with a specific, historical relationship to Charles's original song.

Up to this point, we have been talking about the proliferation aspect of the proliferate-and-select strategy. Let us now go on to the selection aspect. Sometimes, selection takes place pretty much on the spot, as candidate options are being proliferated. With regard to free proliferation, we have just seen both individual and collaborative variants of this in the examples of individual and multiple-agent doodling. While doodling, agents keep a constant eye (or ear) out for anything that seems interesting and then pursue it—that is, they switch to the appropriate-and-extend strategy to develop it. In the collaborative case, there is the added advantage that someone other than the person doodling may be the one keeping an ear out. So, just as items of material culture can absorb some of the cognitive load of action, other people can absorb some of it, as well. In the case of songwriting, for instance, bandmates can take over some of the attention and recognition tasks that the individual would otherwise have to shoulder while doodling. In short, collaborative situations make possible a cognitive division of labor, not just a physical division of labor.

With regard to guided proliferation, selection also often follows immediately on the proliferation of candidate options. This is a common phenomenon in all domains of human action when an agent tries out on the spot a couple of different options for getting something done, and selects the most promising one. In the songwriting domain, for instance, this might involve trying several different possible chords in a chord progression, or in the cooking domain it might involve trying several different ways of getting the cake out of the pan. In some cases, this process is clearly a kind of trial-and-error problem solving. For example, to get the cake out of the pan, you might start by simply inverting it and tapping on the bottom; if that does not work you might run a knife around the edge and invert it again; and if that still does not work, you might resort to removing the cake in sections with a spatula. In cases such as this, there is a clearly defined problem and an equally clearly defined solution that must be reached—there is something that counts as failure, and something else that counts as success. But not all guided proliferation is like this. For instance, in trying out several chords in a chord progression, the task is not as clearly defined and there is no unique solution. There are chords that just will not work at all because they are in the wrong key, but which chord is ultimately selected is going to depend on the aesthetic sensibility of the songwriter, not on elimination after failure. Moreover, the choice of a surprising chord, one that might seem wrong at first blush, might in fact be the best choice artistically. In short, any number of chords might be perfectly fine, and the selection criteria are not rigidly constrained by clear criteria for failure or success.

The proliferate-and-select strategy can also be stretched out over long periods of time, however. This might be because the proliferation itself is intermittent, or because the selection process does not kick in immediately. This kind of extended timeframe may be more common with free proliferation, which involves no prior specification of a particular slot the proliferated items are to fill. So often these items are generated according to no particular schedule, and must be stored in case they might come in handy later on. As we discovered above, songwriters report that they often have difficulty remembering fragments of music they generate, and, therefore, resort to an array of recording devices and memory enhancing tactics in order to preserve the fragments long enough to work on them. And as we now realize, in many cases, this might involve fairly long-term storage. Songwriters in fact report that this is important not only for newly proliferated bits of music, but also for bits that have been worked on and extended, but are not in their final form as part of a completed song. In other words, both the proliferate-and-select strategy we are focusing on here and the appropriate-and-extend strategy we discussed in the last section sometimes depend on the capacity for relatively long-term storage.

The most obvious way of looking at storage is in terms of the clear advantages it provides. First, it makes possible a larger pool of items on which selection can operate. Second, it makes possible retention of items for appropriation and extension, especially when the ongoing process is intermittent, as it often is in songwriting. And given the vagaries of biological memory—which might with some justice be characterized as the world's first and most efficient *unfaithful* copying device—it would make sense to resort to material culture for storage, rather than relying on memory. Songwriters do indeed report this, both as individuals and as collaborating groups, but they also report some individual variation in what recording devices are preferred. Jason Slatton, for example, who is assiduous about recording musical bits he comes up with, prefers tape to notation:

> I could write down four bars, and then put the notes and everything. It'll generally come back. But sometimes it's just like a vocal inflection or one beat that you change a little bit, and it's generally better to go back to the most dumbed-down source, which is just tape.

The difficulty Slatton is pointing to here is that notation only records the bare bones of a bit of music, and this forces the songwriter to continue to rely a lot on memory. But several songwriters reported having very good memory for music, and being quite content with notation. For instance, Miria reports that taping herself singing makes her self-conscious, thus disrupting the songwriting process from another direction. So, she just writes down lyrics, and more rarely, uses an abbreviated form of notation for the music.

> For me the melody and the lyric come out at the same time. So what I'm doing is literally writing. I know the melody in my head and I write out the lyrics . . . I almost never write [the music] down. I just memorize it, and I'll sing it to my arranger who I'm working with. This is not a great way to work, necessarily! Sometimes it's harder to communicate it. But for me, as soon as I write the song I know the melody, and I don't have to write it down to avoid forgetting it. So occasionally I will do a little sort of primitive musical notation for my own benefit, just my own thoughts, nothing that someone else would really recognize as musical notation.

Similarly, Debbie Norton reports no compulsion to record what she writes:

> But I don't record them. The only thing I do is write down the words, and put the chords over the words. And then I remember it from there.

But Norton also reports some difficulties in working out the details of arrangements with her band, as a result of not recording what they come up with in practice sessions:

> For instance, I think the thing that happens the most is that we'll play a song one way one time, and we'll work a few things out, and I'll say, 'Okay, let's do this here, and this here.' And the next practice, Eddie may

or may not remember, or someone may or may not remember, or I may or may not remember. And I'll say, 'No, I said let's do it this way, didn't I?' and he's like, 'No, you didn't. You said let's do it this way.' And so I'll say, 'Well, let's try it both ways. Let's try it that way, and let's see which one we like better.'

In this case, not recording has the effect of forcing the band to repeat part of the arrangement writing process. This could actually be a good thing, if they come up with a better arrangement in the end—or, of course, a bad thing if the original arrangement they have collectively forgotten and/or disagreed about really was better. But in any case, as Norton hints, the slippage can cause friction in the collaborative relationship, because in the meantime there is a disagreement to be negotiated. For both of these reasons, some bands are assiduous about recording everything they are sure they want to keep track of from practice to practice, as reported about Jackpot City by Mamie Fike Simonds:

> Yeah, we'll always do that. Because we have a hard time—number one, are we going to agree about it? And then number two, are we going to remember it the next week in the same way? So if we come up with something we always do that. We're pretty religious about recording it so we won't forget it.

Thus, what we can see from these last few examples especially is that recording devices not only provide obvious cognitive advantages in the form of reliable retention of musical bits, but also provide support for collaborative relationships in at least two ways. First, as Miria suggests, they help with communication between collaborators. And as Debbie Norton and Mamie Fike Simonds report, they can also help minimize disagreements among collaborators with regard to previous results and decisions.

Both of these collaborative advantages rest on the 'transferability' of memory externalized and stored in items of material culture. This transferability also makes possible long-distance collaborations among songwriters. Sometime these are set up in advance, as in this case reported by Kathy Kirbo:

> Paul, when he went to Nashville, and then Ben Mize that I was in Greenhouse with—he's the drummer for the Counting Crows, it's a big band in L.A.—and when he moved away to L.A., we'd both do little four track things, and we'd send each other tapes, and try to write songs. So, yeah, that goes on. I've got a couple of friends I do that with.

Kirbo also reports an interesting and more serendipitous case:

> I have a friend that plays in a band called Thumb. And he recorded this song, and I liked it so much I recorded a guitar part over, with their song,

and sent it back to him. And he said at first it kind of freaked him out that I went to that much trouble to do that . . . But then he thought it was a great compliment that I liked it so much I made up a whole thing for it.

Thus, the transferability of tapes or notated scores makes possible collaborative relationships that would otherwise not be possible. So, here again, the involvement of material culture as a storage medium has both cognitive and social advantages associated with it.

The external memory embodied in various types of material culture thus supports both the appropriate-and-extend and the proliferate-and-select strategies, and does so in a number of different ways. But several songwriters reported that they intentionally do *not* use external memory devices in order to enhance the selection process in another way. Here is Russ Hallauer:

> I kind of use that [memory] as a judgment thing. If I can't hold it in my memory for three days until band practice, if it's not catchy enough to stay in your head, then maybe there's something wrong with it, and maybe you shouldn't be showing it to people!

Hallauer is expressing a 'survival of the fittest' view—he takes sheer memorability as an appropriate criterion of goodness with regard to musical fragments he generates, and counts on ending up with a smaller but better-quality body of fragments for further selection. This is, of course, very much in keeping with the whole profile of the proliferate-and-select strategy, which bears many resemblances to natural selection in biological organisms. We have already noted the sometimes non-intentional character of the proliferation step, for instance. Along these same lines, Mike Mills, who also reported using memory as a selection device in this way, voiced some skepticism as to whether it always does leave the fittest musical fragments standing:

> My feeling is if I don't remember it, then it probably wasn't worth remembering. That's not true. Because I have forgotten things that I'm really angry at myself for forgetting. But—I don't know why—I tend to resist the need to put it down immediately.

But Mills also mentioned several times in the course of the interview that neither he nor the band is often at a loss for musical ideas, so that proliferation typically results in a lot of material that is never used:

> We've written probably as many songs that didn't get finished as we have songs that did, if not more. Whether Michael was not inspired to finish them lyrically, or whether we just never felt that they were worth even presenting to Michael, sometimes it just never does happen . . . Which is a shame because there's a whole lot of really good stuff that's sitting

right behind us that never gets used. But it's always more exciting and more satisfying to try to come up with something new.

Putting these passages together, the overall view that emerges is that even if memory is not a terribly reliable selection device, proliferation is so reliable that there are always more musical fragments to take the place of any otherwise promising bits that are lost to memory lapses. This underlines the idea that action is inherently creative, by pointing to its inexhaustibility as a generator of options.

For collaborative songwriters, the selection process often takes place in two distinct stages, the first at the individual level and the second at the collaborative level. Although collaborators sometimes work together right from the beginning, generating initial fragments and extending them in a face-to-face situation, sometimes—and this appears to be more common— collaborators will come up with initial fragments on their own, and then bring them in to the face-to-face collaborative situation to be worked on by the group. These contributions have already undergone selection at the individual level. They are what are left after memory has taken its toll, for instance, or after the individual songwriter has deliberately picked them out of the pool of proliferated bits because she thinks they are particularly interesting. In addition, other selection criteria directly related to the collaborative situation may be applied. As Mamie Fike Simonds explains, both her sense of her collaborators' taste and musical genre influence her selection of musical bits to take in to her Jackpot City collaborators:

> I kind of know their taste, so if I'm going to write a song for Jackpot City, I'm probably not going to take it to practice unless I know there's going to be some interest from at least one member . . . I write different types of music. Jackpot City is a very pop oriented—you know, simple structure . . . Whereas if I write a classical piece or something like that— with no lyrics, just really trying to get into note structure—I wouldn't ever take a song like that to Jackpot City. I might write it down and maybe have my quartet play it, or something like that.

Thus, by the time a contribution is brought into a collaborative situation, it is typically already the result of several different types of selection applied by the individual songwriter. Then, selection is exercised again at the collaborative level. The group may or may not choose to work on a given contribution, since it is in fact commonplace for collaborating improvisers to reject contributions from other group members rather than accepting and extending them. Russ Hallauer is again insistent that such rejection by collaborators is a reliable indication that the fragment lacked 'fitness' to begin with:

> And as a songwriter, if you bring it up a couple times and it doesn't take, that's your judgment of a song, really. If you can't get your band members

interested in it, how are you going to get anyone else interested in it? So I think you kind of trust your band members to judge you that way . . . It's just that if you keep bringing it up and they don't like it enough to work with it, then maybe there's something wrong with it. Maybe that's why you just leave it alone and you move on to the next one.

Several of the other songwriters interviewed expressed less equanimity about this phenomenon, admitting that they were sometimes disappointed when their collaborators showed no interest in one of their contributions, or annoyed when the contribution was appropriated, but developed in a direction they had not anticipated or did not particularly like. But, they all pointed out that the reason they bring their contributions in to collaborators—and more specifically, the reason they have commitments to particular collaborative relationships—is to have the benefit of better judgments and significant improvements they would not have been able to make on their own. So having some contributions rejected is an acceptable trade-off. Here is a typical example of this point of view, expressed by Jason Slatton:

A lot of times, you split the difference between what somebody wants. Because I do have to respect the fact that these guys want to play with me. And even though I'm bringing in what I feel is an idea, I have to respect the fact that they want to help me with that idea. And I could get another bassist or drummer, or whatever, but it wouldn't sound the same.

Thus, the selection process is complex. It may take place over extended periods of time; may involve not only multiple criteria, but different types of processes (biological memory, material culture in the form of recording devices, sociality in the form of collaborative relationships); and may have distinct individual and collaborative stages.

To conclude our discussion of the proliferate-and-select strategy, let us briefly consider its significance with regard to our overall picture of human action. Philosophical action theory has traditionally focused on the characteristically *directed* nature of human action. More specifically, it has focused on the role of mental structures, such as intentions and plans, in controlling subsequent action. But our consideration of the proliferate-and-select strategy and its use in improvisational activity shows that this traditional focus is one-sided. Human action is not just characteristically directed—it is characteristically *prolific*. Along with creative appropriation, this prolificness is an aspect of the creativity of everyday action. This characteristic prolificness and the important role it plays in human life has not been noticed in action theory, except insofar as the prolificness is purely mental and dedicated to plan construction. But, giving an account of improvisation forces us to recognize and investigate the prolificness of action, because in improvisation much of the directedness of the action emerges from the actual proliferation of actions and productions in the world and their subsequent pruning rather than being imposed in advance through armchair deliberation. Recognizing prolificness as a leading characteristic of human action, in turn, directs our attention to important aspects of human action that underwrite it. For instance, we doodle. We fiddle with stuff constantly, half the time not with any particular purpose in mind. In the process, we unintentionally produce things or actions that can be appropriated if they are interesting for some reason, and at the very least we learn a lot—how to manipulate different kinds of materials, for instance. In addition, we constantly stockpile stuff for which we have no immediate use. This is not just a matter of producing or collecting things; it also has an analogue in non-productive action when we learn repertoires of actions for which we have no immediate use. This is a salient phenomenon in sports and the arts, for instance, where we practice plays and techniques that we may or may not ever have an opportunity to use. Now these stockpiles, repertoires, and results of doodling are all available and important for planning, of course. But they are also available for improvisation, and are even more essential for this aspect of human action, which necessarily depends so much more heavily on the current resources of both agents and the environment.

Turn-Taking Strategies

The two strategies we have considered so far can be used either by individuals acting alone or by groups acting collaboratively. In this section we will consider, somewhat more briefly, a strategy that is inherently collaborative—turn-taking. Turn-taking is a very basic way of organizing multiple-agent action. It is also a surprisingly complex phenomenon. To begin with, we may distinguish a macrolevel structure and a microlevel structure. At the macrolevel, we have turn-taking phenomena that concern fairly large and easily recognizable 'chunks' of action, where rules governing the turn-taking are often explicitly formulated, either by the agents involved or in institutional forms such as *Robert's Rules of Order*. At the microlevel, on the other hand, there are 'rules' and practices that govern action at a much finer grain, and that are typically not formulated explicitly by the agents involved. Indeed, they are typically discovered only by researchers doing careful analyses of action.

The microlevel structures of turn-taking practices in one thoroughly improvisational collaborative activity—conversation—have been extensively studied by a branch of sociology known as ethnomethodology, and more specifically by an ethnomethodological subfield known as conversation analysis (CA). The central tenet of ethnomethodology is that everyday activity is highly organized, and that this orderliness is accomplished locally by agents orienting to normative practices in producing and accounting for their own actions and the actions of others. Ethnomethodology is the study of these folk practices (ethno-methods) in operation. Its leading edge has been conversation analysis, which was started in the 1960s in conjunction with the newly available technology of audiotapes, which made possible an unlimited source of data in the form of taped, naturally occurring conversations. Conventions for transcribing such tapes in minute detail were quickly developed. What emerged from the analysis of these conversations in particular was a rich understanding of turn-taking in conversation, which is very orderly and quite complex in its structure. At the macrolevel, of course, everyone is aware that the parties to a conversation are supposed to take turns speaking. In some institutional contexts, the rules for who gets to speak when and for how long are even explicitly set out. But what CA discovered is that the parties to an ordinary conversation implicitly recognize a number of different kinds of possible transition points at which another speaker can enter the conversation and take a turn. In addition, there is a set of implicit practices governing which speaker gets the next available turn. And there are practices governing the construction of turns—how long a turn is, what speakers do to indicate the approaching end of a turn, and so on. The parties to the conversation do not normally recognize these microstructure 'rules' in any explicit or conscious way. Conversation analysts have used these initial findings, based largely on a corpus of informal telephone conversations in American English, as a benchmark for the analysis of conversation data from other cultures and from various more formal institutional settings in both North American and other cultures (e.g., conversations between doctors and patients, or retail store clerks and customers). They have discovered both interesting commonalities among these different conversation situations, and also interesting differences between them.[5]

The importance to an account of improvisation of ethnomethodology in general, and conversation analysis in particular lies largely in its focus on the agent-induced orderliness of action at the microlevel, and the methodological tools it has developed for studying this. Its detailed descriptions of turn-taking practices in conversation are especially impressive in this respect because they focus on precisely what we said an account of improvisation needs to do—show how action that is not preplanned is nevertheless organized on the spot by agents into coherent, extended sequences of action that provide for intrapersonal and interpersonal coordination over time. This ethnomethodological analysis of microlevel turn-taking practices in conversation would be especially useful for an account of improvisation if it were connected to more wide-ranging descriptions of turn-taking at both the macrolevel and the microlevel in other domains of action—turn-taking in sports or music, for instance, or in material culture contexts where division of labor is an important factor. Unfortunately, conversation analysis has not really broadened its scope to include action in general, but has remained focused on communicative interaction in natural language. There has not even been much use of videotape (as opposed to audiotape) to develop an analysis of gesture, direction of gaze, and so on in conversational interaction. Most strikingly in this regard, conventions for transcribing videotaped action have not been developed to complement the conventions for transcribing audiotaped conversation.[6] So the resources for studying the microlevel turn-taking structure of action in general are not yet in place. Consequently, the interview study of songwriting with which we have been working was not designed to study turn-taking at the microlevel. But it does provide some data about aspects of turn-taking at the macrolevel.

To begin our discussion, let us consider an example in which the way turns are taken is regulated by explicit rules that are the subject of conscious attention by the agents involved. Turn-taking in professional baseball, for instance, is quite complex and carefully regulated and monitored.[7] On the one hand, there are turns taken by whole teams as they rotate from fielding to batting and back. There are rules that specify under what conditions this rotation takes place, how many cycles of the rotation must occur before the game is concluded, and so on. On the other hand, there are turns taken by individual players—perhaps most obviously, turns taken at bat. Here again, there are rules that specify when one player's turn at bat is over, which player goes next, and so on. These rules, too, are very complicated. There are a number of different ways a turn at bat can terminate, for example. The player may be struck out, or walked, or may hit the ball in a number of different ways with different results for the termination of the turn (e.g., a home run terminates a turn; a foul ball ordinarily does not). Although these rules for taking turns at bat are very precise, the transitions must sometimes be negotiated, because it is not always clear which of the precisely prescribed conditions actually obtain. For instance, it may not be clear whether or not a batted ball crossed the foul line, or a checked swing crossed the plate. Decisions on such matters often determine whether the batter's turn is over or not. But these decisions may involve discussions among the umpires, appeals from managers, official transfer of decision-making power from one umpire to another, and so on. In other words, there are rules that settle the matter—rules that the players, umpires, managers and fans all know and to which they can refer. But figuring out what actually happened and which rules apply may be a lengthy process, and transitions between turns can be caught in limbo in the meantime.

This example exhibits the important features of turn-taking. It is orderly—in this case because of explicit rules. But it is not mechanical or deterministic—the transitions between turns have to be actively identified and/or decided. We can also see from this example that in ordinary action, unlike in conversation, turns may be simultaneous in addition to being sequential. When it is your turn at bat, it is simultaneously the opposing pitcher's turn to pitch, for instance. Finally, the rules governing turn-taking provide for local, ongoing organization of activity that is fundamentally improvisatory in character. In other words, they provide a framework of constraints that make intrapersonal and interpersonal coordination of a particular sort possible in improvisatory activity. It might be objected here that games such as baseball are not fundamentally improvisatory. Not only do individuals and teams have a plan *to* play a game, they have a plan *for* playing the game provided by the rules of baseball, including the turn-taking rules. Thus, the rules constitute a very schematic plan for a game of baseball that is filled in by particular teams on particular occasions. But even if this is the right way to look at the matter, the plan represented by the rules of the game is so very sketchy that the actual game consists mostly of improvisatory filling in. This is especially the case with competitive games such as baseball, where there is something of a premium on remaining open and flexibly responsive to unpredictable moves made by opposing players. So, even if baseball players are executing a plan for a game, they can only do it by improvising constantly. With regard to turn-taking in particular, neither the number of turns to be taken nor the length of the turns can be reliably predicted, and must therefore be constructed improvisationally while the game is going on. The turn-taking rules make it possible for this aspect of playing baseball to be carried out in an orderly manner. For instance, you cannot plan for the length of a turn, but there are procedures for judging reliably when it is over.

The unusual thing about turn-taking in games such as baseball, of course, is precisely its regulation by explicit rules, well-known not only to the agents involved but to their audience, as well. In other domains, the role of explicit rules is often taken by practices, some of which are readily articulated by the agents involved, and some of which are not. Let us consider turn-taking practices in the music domain to get a better sense of this kind of turn-taking organization. One obvious example is the widespread practice of instrumentalists taking solos during the performance of a song. In jazz ensembles, all the players may take turns soloing, for instance, and ideally this should be done seamlessly. In some cases, the order of the solos may be decided in advance, but if not, the players themselves must indicate when a solo is ending and decide who is to take the next one while continuing to play. Graham Collier (1995, 9) calls this 'structural improvising,' and suggests that the turn-taking practices it involves are for the most part local habits that may vary somewhat from ensemble to ensemble:

> Such groups, by their very nature, get to know each other very quickly, so this process, and the unwritten vocabulary of nods and winks and gestures and shorthand actions which any group of people known to each other use to communicate, can soon be absorbed. The entries and exits of the musicians and their control over the overall color and shape of the performance, what I have termed structural improvising, occur as naturally as breathing. (Collier 1995, 15–16)

Similarly, the length of a solo is not necessarily determined in advance, but is constrained by practices well known to jazz musicians. For example, solos typically consist of an indefinite number of repetitions of the main melody, or chorus. So, the other musicians are prepared for a possible transition to a new soloist whenever the end of one of these repetitions is approaching, although they cannot know for sure whether a transition will occur there or not. And the nods, winks, and gestures Collier mentions are the micro-level structures for which the players will be on the lookout as a possible transition point comes along. Because these practices and local group habits are not hard and fast rules, individual agents have a lot more leeway with regard to turn-taking. A jazz soloist has a lot more say about how long his solo is than a baseball player does about how long her turn at bat is, for example. And a second important difference is that the practices governing turn-taking in performance are not explicitly set out anywhere, for the most part. Consequently, it is not clear that these practices are always reflectively known to the agents who participate in them, let alone their audience, or that they would even be easily formulated by these agents.

Another kind of practice-based turn-taking that occurs in the music domain is predicated on division of labor. For example, in collaborative songwriting, there is often a division of labor between writing lyrics and writing music. So having written some music, say, one collaborator will hand it over to another collaborator who is regarded as responsible for the lyrics to work on in their turn. Russ Hallauer describes two different versions of this, one from his old band, Sunbrain, and one from the band he was in at the time of the interview, The Lures:

> Some Sunbrain songs I would actually have a guitar riff, but then also have what I thought would be the melody. I would play it to the singer and say, 'Here's the melody; you fill in the words.' With The Lures I don't even do that. I strictly just write a guitar part, and then say, 'Okay, Jason, here's the guitar part, and then you make it shine.'

This kind of turn-taking is, of course, endemic to material culture contexts, where both the use and production of material culture items typically involve division of labor. Turn-taking practices predicated on division of labor also reflect the physical and technical requirements of the tasks involved.

The macrostructure and microstructure of turn-taking are, thus, important resources for improvising agents in collaborative contexts. But as we have seen, these structures are implemented in practices that are often culturally local; or even in habits that are specific to small groups of people engaged in a common activity. So in the next and final section, we will look briefly at the role of practices and habits in improvisation.

PRACTICES, HABITS, AND THE LIKE

The examples we have been looking at are not just a matter of action in accordance with strategies, but simultaneously involve other kinds of pre-existing action structures, such as cultural practices, personal or group habits, institutional or personal policies, and so on. Investigating all the different kinds of pre-existing action structure and their roles in human action would be another book (at least). But it is important to look at least briefly at the relationship between practices, habits, and strategies.

Let us start by considering the relationship between practices and strategies. Strategies are very general and basic action structures. Because they are so general, agents must implement them in terms of more specific action structures. For example, as ethnomethodologists have discovered, turn-taking as a strategy is so general as to be common to all cultures and to all or most domains within any given culture. But cultures, or domains of activity within a culture, must have more specific practices for implementing such general strategies. Cross-cultural studies of turn-taking in conversation have revealed some very different practices with regard to how turns are constructed, how much overlap between turns is allowed, and so on (Sawyer 2001; Furo 2001; Moerman 1988). Similarly, even within North American culture, conversations in different activity domains depend on distinct turn-taking practices. Talking to your doctor is not the same sort of thing as chatting with a friend, for instance. So, it is not surprising that songwriters implement not only turn-taking but also the appropriate-and-extend and proliferate-and-select strategies in terms of culture-specific musical practices. Here is an exchange between myself and Debbie Norton about the genesis of her song 'Hale Bopp Times,' which illustrates this. (Hale Bopp, you will remember, is a comet.)

NORTON: I thought, 'Well, it needs to sound a bit planetary.' So I tried to capture that sound, to a degree. And chords will fall into a category of words. An E, for instance, to me, in my world, is a very serious chord. Which I happen to use a lot!

ME: Is this E major we're talking about?

NORTON: E major, yeah. Well, E minor is pretty close, too. But, yeah, E major to me is that kind of chord. So I found the chords that for me sounded like a planetary, kind of more ethereal song. And then once I found some chords, I started writing with those chords.

Here, Norton has a particular kind of sound in mind, and proliferates and selects chords in light of that. But in so doing she is also operating in terms of cultural practices governing musical structure—major and minor modes, for instance, and keys. It should be noted that an agent does not necessarily have to be able to explicitly formulate such practices in order to use them effectively. Russ Hallauer, who has no formal training in music, makes this clear:

There were years when I first started playing in bands where I would just kind of know where to put my hands. I wouldn't exactly know, if someone asked me, what key I was in. I would be like, 'I have no idea. Here's where my hands are.'

Nor is it always the case that these practices are adhered to slavishly, as Mamie Fike Simonds reports about a typical exchange with Kelly Noonan in practice sessions:

> She's like, 'Okay, well, what chord is it?' And I'm going, 'Well, it's just this chord right here I made up. It's not really a chord.' And then she'll say, 'Well, where's the chorus?' 'Well, it's not really a chorus, it's just this part right here that you could call a chorus if you want' . . . So she'll tell me that my songs are disjointed, or whatever, and then she'll take it and make it into 'This is your chorus, this is . . .' So that helps me.

It should be noted that of all the songwriters I talked to, Fike Simonds is probably the one with the *most* formal training. So deviations from standard Western musical practices in her songwriting are more likely to reflect creative bending of the 'rules,' not lack of knowledge. Nevertheless, she indicates at the end of this passage a willingness to have her contributions taken back in the direction of the standard practices, although she does not say why. Miria, who also often writes songs that do not have standard structures, reports a similar experience with her producer. But she does explain why, in her case, it sometimes makes sense to let her work be revised back in the direction of conformity with more standard song structures:

> Usually he's very much keeping commercial possibilities in mind, and trying to get my songs to fit in a more traditional song structure. And obviously if I were working with a different producer the outcome would be somewhat different. For instance, Alanis Morissette and Glen Ballard—Ballard doesn't have her do that. And a lot of her songs are not in any way the traditional song structure, and they're working within that. Arguably some songs are going to be easier for people to remember, easier for them to sing along with, in some more traditional song form that they're going to recognize, and go, 'Okay, here comes the verse again. Here comes the bridge.' So sometimes I felt like it made it a better song, or that I liked it. And sometimes I didn't want to change it because I felt like enough of my friends already knew it the way it was written; that to me that was the song, and changing it did change the integrity of the song. So I try to take his suggestions whenever I think he's right, and do it.

Here, it is clear that a major reason for not deviating too much or too often from the standard practices has to do with communication with a potential audience, and hence with commercial success, as well. On the other hand, Miria also makes it clear that adhering to the standard practices is neither a necessary nor a sufficient condition for communication and commercial success. The most important point to be derived from these examples, though, is that whether conforming to or deviating from the common musical practices of their culture, these songwriters are always implicitly or explicitly aware of what these practices are, and, thus, are, always acting in light of them. So, cultural practices provide a useful and necessary resource for implementing the strategy-embedded operations of turn-taking, appropriation, extension, proliferation, and selection.

Such practices are one of the primary ways in which sociality surfaces in individual action. And in light of our discussion of suigenerism *versus* sociogenerism in Chapter 3, a couple of observations are in order. First, the songwriters in the interview study regularly referred their actions in writing songs and playing music back to these practices as normative constraints on what they should or should not do—and/or what they are aware other people think they should or should not do. It is clear that these practices pre-existed the musicianship of these individuals as a cultural accumulation inherited by learning to make music. So, as individual musicians, these songwriters are sociogeneric products of a particular musical culture and its local practices, just as Gilbert's Jack and Sue turned out to be sociogeneric products of the local practices governing the taking of walks. Just as importantly, though, these individuals do not just conform to these musical practices, but creatively deviate from them or bend them to unusual uses, either as a matter of unfaithful copying or as a matter of a more reflective departure from what is expected. So, the practices are not a cloning device, but a set of resources that are used flexibly and creatively in the structuring of action. As the ethnomethodologists prefer to put it, individuals 'orient to' such normative practices, rather than conforming to them.

But cultural practices are still very general, with respect to specific actions of individuals. Modes and keys, for instance, are a resource that offers a whole range of options, and this range has to be narrowed down to a specific mode or key for any particular song. So, whether conforming or deviating, songwriters appropriate the cultural practices in more specific forms geared to their own habits and preferences. As we saw above, for example, Debbie Norton has a predilection for the E major chord and uses it often. Her characterization of E major as a serious chord is an idiosyncratic perception. I was surprised by this characterization and asked her to confirm that she meant E major (as opposed to E minor), because I do not share her perception of E major at all, to be honest. To me, E major is a rather colorless, boring chord that I would probably not use for anything if I didn't have to, let alone for a serious song. E minor, now, that is a different matter. Most of my favorite serious songs are in E minor. So if required to write a serious song, I imagine I would start with E minor. Or possibly D minor. But certainly not E major. Such idiosyncratic preferences and the individual habits to which they give rise are the main way individual agents appropriate and deploy cultural practices in individual action. So just as more specific cultural practices implement generic strategies, so even more specific habits implement relatively generic cultural practices.

It will be helpful to look at some more complex examples illustrating the interplay between habits and practices in the implementation of strategies. This is from an exchange between Kevn Kinney and me about doodling. He was playing his guitar while talking. My descriptions of what he was playing are interposed in square brackets:

ME: When you sit down to play the guitar, what is it that you play? Do you play other people's songs, or your old songs, or you just kind of improvise and hope something comes out of it?

KINNEY: Well, you know, when you've been playing as long as I have— I'll be in a certain mood, I'll know what key I want to sing in, I'll know . . . yeah?

ME: So you just start playing some chord that's appropriate for—

KINNEY: Can I get my guitar for a second?

ME: Yeah, sure. Uh-oh. [*sotto voce*, realizing this is trouble for transcription]

KINNEY: [Strums once] This is open. [i.e., the guitar is in an open tuning, most likely open D, in which the strings are tuned to the notes of a D major chord]. I play every morning and every night before I go to bed. [plays several chords] Just do it for hours. Like for an hour, I'll just . . . [plays several more chords in the same vein] I was doing that for a while, and then . . . [plays a different series of chords] An Indian thing . . . [plays a bit that sounds like a sitar] because I love sitar music, you know . . . [plays more of the sitar sounding bit]. If you're going to do a blues song, it's like . . . [plays several chords of a blues].

Here, the proliferate-and-select strategy seems to be implemented fairly directly in terms of a personal habit of doodling for several hours, morning and evening. But Kinney explicitly relates the *content* of his doodling to the musical practices of both Western and non-Western cultures, including practices involved in the use of material culture, such as alternative guitar tunings. A similar example from Miria illustrates the implementation of the appropriate-and-extend strategy in terms of what Michael Bratman (1999b) calls a 'personal policy':

But usually it [a song] will start with a fragment and the question is how much time I have right at that moment to take it the whole way to a complete song. If I have a lot of time to myself, then I usually can take it the whole way. And I have a rule that anytime I am inspired to write a song, no matter what else I'm doing I drop it and I write the song. Doesn't matter where I am. I've written songs in the middle of business meetings at work, because I bring a notebook with me and I write in my head and pay no attention to the meeting. I'll pull over by the side of the road—doesn't matter. So that's the rule. Because everybody does that differently, too, you know—certainly songwriters who can write on a schedule, and get up and write a tune, or whatever. I don't really work like that.

Having a personal policy of dropping other activities in order to work on a musical fragment that has serendipitously appeared is an effective way of implementing the appropriate-and-extend strategy, while simultaneously dealing with the risk of forgetting such fragments mentioned by so many of the songwriters interviewed. Miria here also displays her awareness that there are other, equally effective personal policies for implementing this strategy employed by other songwriters. But here again, the habit implements the strategy *via* cultural practices, if in a subversive way. Miria is in the habit of bringing a notebook to business meetings—a habit that in the usual case would implement the practices involved in business meetings by conforming to them, but which in Miria's case implements songwriting practices while appearing to implement the business meeting practices.

The strategies that improvising agents use to organize their ongoing activity are, thus, dependent for their actual implementation on cultural practices, which, in turn, depend for their implementation on individual habits. And we could continue this analysis, since habits are, in turn, implemented by even lower-level structures, such as embodied skills. Having a habit of using the E major chord a lot is one thing; being able to play it on any particular instrument is another, for instance. We do not have time to discuss embodied skills here, but the general idea should now be clear. Improvised action sequences are coordinated through the simultaneous use of multiple resources at multiple levels. And this use may honor pre-existing action structures as much in the breach as in the performance; that is, the use may be creatively deviant rather than conforming.

In Chapter 2, our complaint was that by treating spontaneous actions as planned, action theory deprives itself of any way of explaining the concatenation of actions in improvisatory sequences. Now we have grounds for two further complaints. By treating habits, practices, and other pre-existing action structures all indiscriminately as plans, action theory misses or underestimates two further important features of human action. First of all, it misses the layered implementation structure of action that we have been describing in this section. Because habits, practices, policies, and so on are all equally plans, on this view, there is little incentive for exploring how these different pre-existing action structures relate to each other, or function synergistically in the generation of action sequences. Second, it misses the element of interpretive or creative deviation that we emphasized, particularly in our discussion of the appropriate-and-extend strategy, but which has turned up in our discussion of practices, as well. The planning view is thinking in terms of prototypical plans, and the prototypical use of such plans is to conform your subsequent actions to them. But if we think of practices, habits, policies, and so on as resources for structuring action, it is more apparent that their use is not just as a pattern to which to conform, but as a springboard, a deceptive screen, an opportunity to revolt, or the like (Certeau 1984). Thus, in our improvisatory picture, action is creative in an ongoing way as it turns a changing array of available resources to good use. This contrasts sharply with the planning picture, which relegates creativity to the mental construction of plans, thus depriving the action itself of any real, theoretical interest.

This completes the action theory part of our analysis. Obviously, there is much more to be done in terms of working out the details, but the importance of switching gears and proceeding to a consideration of function in material culture is twofold. First, it will enable us to see the issues involved in an analysis of material culture from the side of the things that are made and used, as opposed to the agents who make and use them. Second, we will be able to confirm and extend our understanding of the overarching themes that have emerged here in Part I—the problem of centralized control, the distinction between a suigeneric and a sociogeneric approach to the relationship between individual and society, and the role of creativity in everyday life and action. All of these themes will reemerge in Part II in forms specific to function theory rather than action theory.

Part II
Function

5   Proper Function and System Function

However well one has grasped the *utility* of some physiological organ (or of a legal institution, a social custom, a political practice, a form in the arts or in religious cult), one has still not comprehended anything regarding its genesis: as uncomfortable and unpleasant as this may sound to earlier ears—for from time immemorial one had thought that in comprehending the demonstrable purpose, the usefulness of a thing, a form, an arrangement, one also comprehended the reason for its coming into being—the eye as made to see, the hand as made to grasp. Thus one also imagined punishment as invented for punishing. But all purposes, all utilities, are only *signs* that a will to power has become lord over something less powerful and has stamped its own functional meaning onto it; and in this manner the entire history of a 'thing,' an organ, a practice can be a continuous sign-chain of ever new interpretations and arrangements, whose causes need not be connected even among themselves—on the contrary, in some cases only accidentally follow and replace one another.

—Friedrich Nietzsche, *On the Genealogy of Morality,*
Second Treatise, §12

In Part I, our project was to lay some foundations for a philosophy of material culture, starting from the side of the agents who make and use it. Since making and using are actions, we were able to ground our discussion in philosophical action theory. This was a signal advantage, not only because it provided a springboard, but also because a philosophy of material culture that did not connect with ongoing philosophical concerns would be an odd duck, indeed. But we also discovered a number of problems in action theory that had to be addressed. Specifically, traditional action theory has focused on the centralized control model of action, and has consequently lost sight of the sociogeneric nature of the relationship between individual and society, the importance of improvisation, and the prosaic creativity improvisation embodies.

Here in Part II, the project is to lay some foundations for a philosophy of material culture starting from the side of the things made and used. This poses more of a problem with regard to defining an approach that will connect well with ongoing philosophical concerns. The study of material culture in other disciplines is extremely varied with regard to what aspects of material culture are emphasized (Tilley et al. 2006; Hicks and Beaudry 2010). Choices range from studies of particular kinds of material culture, such as clothing, vernacular architecture, or photographs, to studies that focus on broader aspects, such as consumption, embodiment, style, or technological change. In comparison, the philosophical study of material culture has been quite narrowly focused. As we pointed out in the Introduction, it has been largely confined to art, sophisticated modern technologies, and to the metaphysics of artifacts.

One option that has important advantages for us, though, is function in material culture. First, function is one of the salient aspects of items of material culture. It would be hard to understand why we would even have material culture unless it were functional in the sense of doing something for us. Second, and more importantly for our purposes, function is an aspect that has been of interest to writers on material culture across the disciplines, including philosophy (Conkey 2006; Crilly 2010). So, although we will be focusing on philosophical theories of function here, we will at the same time be building bridges to the more wide-ranging work in material culture studies for use in future research. Third, function connects nicely with other aspects of material culture that we might have chosen instead—the cognitive aspect of material culture (Clark 2008; Sterelny 2010; Malafouris and Renfrew 2010), for example, or its social aspect (Appadurai 1986; Schiffer and Miller 1999; Boivin 2008). Some of the ways in which function plays into the cognitive and social aspects of material culture will become apparent as we proceed, although we will not be able to spend much time investigating these connections.

Finally, focusing on function will allow us to relate our discussion here in Part II to the themes broached in Part I—centralized control, sociogenerism, and creativity. Chapter 5 will provide the necessary background in philosophical function theory and raise the issues that need to be resolved in order to have an adequate philosophical theory of function for material culture. In Chapter 6, we will address one of these issues—the role of intention in establishing function in material culture. The common opinion that it is the intentions of the creators of items of material culture that establish their function is a form of the centralized control problem we discovered in action theory, and it is no more salutary for function theory. Resolving this issue will again highlight the importance of the non-intentional and of sociogenerism that we noticed in the chapters on improvisation and collaboration. In Chapter 7, we will address issues surrounding the reproduction of items of material culture. This is not merely the reproduction of material structures, but of functions, of the human purposes corresponding to those functions, and of particular types of human agents who entertain those purposes. Thus, the theme of sociogenerism carries over into Chapter 7. But here it is paired with the theme of creativity, which arises out of a consideration of how cultural change takes place in and through the reproduction of material culture.

The business of Chapter 5 is to ground a theory of function for material culture in existing philosophical function theory. This theory is well developed in philosophy of biology, but much less attention has been paid to function in material culture (Preston 2009a). The obvious strategy is to investigate whether existing theories of biological function can provide the resources for an adequate theory of function in material culture, just as in Part I we investigated whether existing philosophical action theory could provide resources for an adequate account of the production and use of material culture. As we shall see, a pluralistic account of function that combines the complementary insights of Ruth Millikan's (1984, 1993) theory of proper function and Robert Cummins's (1975) theory of system function[1] does provide an adequate, basic understanding of function in material culture. But some important adjustments and extensions are required, and these will not be entirely completed until Chapter 7.

In the first section, a phenomenological description of function in material culture will orient us to the phenomena that an adequate theory of function in material culture will need to encompass. In the second section, we review and compare the theories of function advanced by Millikan and Cummins and the two different concepts of function they support. This leaves us with the question of how these concepts of function are related to each other. This question is taken up in the third section. One view argued for by a number of authors is that one of these concepts subsumes the other. The other main possibility, also supported in the literature, is that neither concept is reducible to the other, but that, on the contrary, both are needed to cover all the phenomena of function. As we will see, this second view is the more plausible one. It leaves us with a pluralist theory of function. But this pluralist theory was originally devised with biological function in mind. The last section of this chapter begins the work of adjusting the biologically oriented concepts involved to fit the case of function in material culture. These adjustments will continue through Chapters 6 and 7.

PRELUDE: THE PHENOMENOLOGY OF FUNCTION

In order to properly ground our theory of function, it will be helpful to start with a discussion of the phenomena such a theory should explain. This section explores the readily observable aspects of function in material culture, and results in a list of the main phenomena for which our theory should account. This list does not pretend to be exhaustive or to settle any issues with regard to the relative importance of the phenomena listed.

A central feature of the structure-function relation in material culture is the *multiple realizability of function*. Any function can ordinarily be realized in a variety of materials and/or forms. Take spoons, for instance. Historically, besides just about any metal you care to mention, they have also been made from wood, shell, horn, bone, pottery, porcelain, and more recently plastic and silicon. Some materials are not suitable, of course. You do not hear of spoons made of water or cotton batting. The shape, too, is variable, although here again, some shapes are just not suitable. The bowl of a tablespoon may be oval, round, pointed, or even fluted—but not spherical, a foot wide, or razor sharp on the edges, for instance. Function does constrain structure, then, but does not determine it. This underdetermination makes multiple realizability possible. Because of the multiple realizability of function, material cultures often contain multiple types of things, all designed to serve basically the same function. Brooms, mops, vacuum cleaners, and Swiffers are all good for cleaning uncarpeted floors, for instance. And, of course, the same function is often served by different types of things in different material cultures. The function of conveying food from plate to mouth is carried out in Japan with chopsticks and in the United States with a fork, for example.

A second central feature of the structure-function relationship is the *multiple utilizability of structure.* Any item of material culture can ordinarily be used for a variety of different functions, and in particular for functions it was not designed to serve. For example, ordinary tablespoons can be used as musical instruments, to open cocoa tins, transplant seedlings, measure cooking ingredients, hold down papers, help prevent a glass from breaking when boiling water or hot tea is poured into it, and so on. In this case, too, we have an interplay of constraint and underdetermination. Structure does constrain the possible uses of an item—spoons are only marginally useful as weapons, for instance, and are no good at all as umbrellas or towels. But because structure underdetermines function, we can use items of material culture for an indefinite number of purposes. Just as multiple realizability of function has the consequence that the same function may be served by different types of things, so, too, multiple utilizability has the consequence that items of material culture often are designed to have multiple functions. For example, there are large spoons made specifically for cooking and serving, and small spoons made specifically for eating, but in between are tablespoons that can serve either function quite well. Some of the most important examples of such multiple functions involve the layering of social functions over technical ones. A souvenir spoon can be used for eating (technical function), but is more specifically designed to be collected and displayed as a memento of some event or place visited (social function).[2] In general, then, the relationship between function and structure in material culture is in principle—and more often than not, in practice—a many-many relation. This relationship can be described more precisely in terms of the twin features of multiple realizability of function and multiple utilizability of structure.

A third important feature is that the functional structures of material culture are not merely produced but *reproduced*; that is, they have standardized forms and uses that are relatively stable over years, generations, or even millennia. As in biology, of course, the process of reproduction in material culture ordinarily allows for some variation. But material culture processes sometimes actually promote variation and innovation. So it would be best to consider this phenomenon as a combined process of *reproduction and variation.* It is worth noting here that innovation in material culture is not a matter of creation *ex nihilo,* but of extending or varying what is already there. For example, computers are the latest entry in a long history of calculating machines and devices, and could have arisen only on the basis of such a history. Similarly, when a material culture does encounter an instance of radical innovation, it is typically an import from another material culture. We will investigate this phenomenon in more detail in Chapter 7, where it will be central to our discussion of creativity in material culture.

A rarely remarked set of phenomena integral to reproduction and variation are processes such as maintenance, repair, rebuilding, and recycling (Preston 2000). We may call this the *maintenance-recycling continuum,* because it concerns more or less radical modifications of structure and function. Most items of material culture must be maintained in order to continue to perform their functions effectively. Sometimes, the need for maintenance is a direct result of the exercise of the function—spoons become encrusted with food during use and must be washed, for instance. In other cases, the need for maintenance results from natural deterioration of the material of which the item is made—a silver spoon will need to be polished from time to time, even if it is not used, for example. Most items of material culture are also subject to damage that calls for repair. Here again, damage is sometimes the result of normal functioning, as when socks get holes in the toes or heels; and sometimes the result of misuse or accidents, as when a spoon is bent while being used to pry up floor tiles. Items of material culture more complex than socks or spoons sometimes undergo a radical type of repair, usually called rebuilding or remodeling, in which an item is completely disassembled and put back together, usually with some new parts. Maintenance, repair, and rebuilding all are intended to return the item to its original function. But at the far end of the continuum is recycling, a cluster of processes that start with existing items of material culture and use them in the production of new items, usually with different functions. One type of recycling makes slight modifications to the structure in order to suit it for a different function. In effect, this is multiple utilizability, but with some modification of structure so that the item is no longer usable for its original proper function. For example, the bottoms can be cut off soft drink bottles to make cloches for young lettuce plants, or the handles of old silver spoons can be bent to make key chains or jewelry. A closely related phenomenon is the reuse for a new function of items that are no longer repairable, as when old tires are used as swings or planters. Further along the continuum are cases where the structure is so radically modified that the original item is no longer clearly identifiable, as when old clothes are cut into strips and braided into chair mats, or old tires are cut up to make sandals. And, finally, there is what we usually think of as recycling—breaking the structure down so thoroughly that it is returned to the raw material state and can be used to produce new items, usually of a different type, as when plastic containers are recycled to make carpeting.

A fourth and very important phenomenon associated with the functional structures of material culture is *malfunction*. The possibility of malfunction is something a theory of function needs to account for, just as theories of representation need to account for misrepresentation. A malfunction is not so much something going wrong with the function itself, but with the structure that is supposed to subserve the function. Thus a soup spoon malfunctions if its handle is bent so badly it cannot be used to transfer soup from bowl to mouth, or if a manufacturing defect results in a hole that allows the soup to leak out, or if an inappropriate choice of material means that the heat of the soup melts the spoon. So, malfunction may be due to a variety of causes, among them misuse, manufacturing defects, poor design, or simply wearing out as a result of normal use.

Finally, there is a peculiar little phenomenon I will call *phantom function*. This occurs when a type of item is regularly reproduced to serve a specific function, but no exemplar of it has ever been structurally capable of performing that function. A mundane case is bug zappers, alleged to rid your yard of mosquitos by attracting and then electrocuting them. There is considerable evidence that not only do bug zappers not kill very many mosquitos, but that they may actually increase the population of mosquitos in your yard by attracting them from your neighbor's. Still, bug zappers continue to be manufactured and bought, because people believe they get rid of mosquitos.[3] A less mundane case is *fengshui* mirrors, which are supposed to deflect evil spirits and bad *qi* from a household when placed over the front doorway.[4] On the assumption that there are no evil spirits or bad *qi* to deflect, no *fengshui* mirror ever has—or ever could—carry out this function. Nevertheless, as with bug zappers, these mirrors continue to be made and used by people who believe there are demons and that these mirrors can repel them—as well as by people who do not believe this, but participate in the practice of *fengshui* for other reasons (e.g., tradition, trendiness, aesthetics, and so on). Thus, an adequate account of function in material culture must accommodate the possibility of types of structure that do not have the capacity to perform the function with which they are popularly associated and for which they are produced. We will explore this phenomenon at length in Chapter 6, where it will be central to our discussion of the role of intention in establishing functions.

We have now identified five central phenomena associated with the functional structures of material culture: multiple realizability of function, multiple utilizability of structure, the process of reproduction and variation with its associated maintenance-recycling continuum, malfunction, and phantom function. Again, this does not pretend to be an exhaustive list of the phenomena that a theory of function for material culture would have to cover in order to be complete. But it does orient us to the central phenomena any such theory must take into account in order to be minimally adequate.

BIOLOGICAL FUNCTION: TWO THEORIES

The concept of function was of interest in the first instance to philosophers of science trying to understand the ascription of function to biological organs, such as the heart. Subsequently, philosophers of mind acquired an interest in function, motivated by the hypothesis that to ascribe meaning to a mental representation is, at least in part, to say what its function is in the mental economy of the organism. But consensus on a theory of function has proved elusive, in large part because two main conceptions of function have been articulated in the literature and there is a lack of agreement about their relationship to each other. In this section, we will examine these two notions of function and how they developed. In the next two sections, we will use them to start constructing a basic account of function in material culture.

The initial problem for function theory was that a thing might engage in all sorts of performances, many of which have nothing to do with its function, intuitively gauged. For example, the heart both circulates blood and makes a characteristic noise. In a pivotal analysis, Larry Wright (1973) addresses this by connecting functions to performances, which account for why the thing is *there* in the first place. For Wright, there are two things you have to do to produce a function ascription in the service of a functional explanation. First, you have to look at what the thing in question has the *capacity/disposition* to do. Second, you have to look at the *history* of the thing in question so as to determine which of its capacities/dispositions account for its being there.

The problem with Wright's analysis is that these two criteria have proved difficult to blend into a harmonious single account of functional explanation. An early and significant challenge to Wright's account came from Robert Cummins, who pointed out that the current performance of a biological organ does not necessarily have anything to do with the evolutionary reasons why it is there. Here he discusses the contractile vacuoles, which in fresh water protozoans perform the crucial task of expelling excess water:

> For it might seem that natural selection provides the missing causal link between what something does in a certain type of organism and its presence in that type of organism. By performing their respective functions, the contractile vacuole and the neurofibrils help species incorporating them [protozoans and ciliates, respectively] to survive, and thereby contribute to their own continued presence in organisms of those species, and this might seem to explain the presence of those structures in the organisms incorporating them.
>
> Plausible as this sounds, it involves a subtle yet fundamental misunderstanding of evolutionary theory. A clue to the mistake is found in the fact that the contractile vacuole occurs in marine protozoans that have no excess-water problem but the reverse problem. Thus, the function and effect on survival of this structure is not the same in all protozoans.

Yet the explanation of its presence in marine and fresh-water species is almost certainly the same. This fact reminds us that the processes actually responsible for the occurrence of contractile vacuoles in protozoans are totally insensitive to what that structure does. (Cummins 1975, 750)

Other biological examples can be adduced, such as the panda's thumb (actually a modified wrist bone) made famous by Stephen Jay Gould, or the wings of flightless birds, which may be used (e.g., by penguins) for swimming. This phenomenon is even more common in material culture, where things designed for one function are frequently used for something else. Consider the old tire that is now a swing, the jelly jar that is now a drinking glass, and the orange crate that is now a coffee table. In such cases, there is indeed a story about why these items are *located* where they are, which appeals to their current capacities/dispositions—it is because the orange crate has a nice flat top that it makes a good coffee table, for instance. But there is a completely different story to be told about why these things are there in the sense of being *in existence,* and it need make no such appeal, since the thing may no longer even have the capacity/disposition that is responsible for its coming into existence. The tire that is now a swing is almost certain to be treadless, and the penguin's wings are not capable of lifting it off the ground. Such cases show that *current* capacity/disposition and selection history are, in principle, divergent. The difficulty, in short, is that Wright's formulation 'X is there because it does Y' does not necessarily hold. X may be there because it *used* to do Y, although now it cannot do Y at all, as in the case of the tire swing. Or it may be there because its ancestors *did* Y, although it has never been able to do Y itself, as in the case of the penguin's wings.

The underlying problem, according to Cummins, is that Wright and other previous writers on this topic misunderstood how functional explanation in science works. It is not, as they assumed, a causal–historical account of how something got there. Rather, it is an account of the current capacities of a whole system in terms of the capacities of its components, just as the capacity of a Detroit assembly line to produce a car can be explained in terms of the tasks accomplished by the workers at each station:

Functional analysis in biology is essentially similar. The biologically significant capacities of an entire organism are explained by analyzing the organism into a number of 'systems'—the circulatory system, the digestive system, the nervous system, etc.—each of which has its characteristic capacities. These capacities are in turn analyzed into capacities of component organs and structures. Ideally, this strategy is pressed until pure physiology takes over. (Cummins 1975, 760–61)

The capacities of the components of the system are, according to Cummins, precisely what we want to call the functions of those components—the functional roles they play within the system as a whole. So in this case, functional explanation does have a necessary connection to the current capacities/dispositions of things. Cummins, thus, retains the second criterion from Wright's analysis of function, but replaces the first criterion—the one that claims that functional explanation is based on selection history—with an alternative notion of functional explanation, which appeals only to current system context. In what follows, I will refer to this notion of function as *system function*.[5]

But even if the justice of Cummins's criticism of Wright is granted, the plausibility of his alternative analysis as a definitive and complete account of biological function is weak, since he fails to respond adequately to the consideration motivating Wright's claim that functional explanation must appeal to selection history. What drove Wright to this conclusion was the necessity of separating out from all the transient and accidental performances in which things may engage those which are tied in with their 'real' function. Intuitively, for Wright, that the heart makes noise is accidental, a mere by-product of its real function, which is pumping blood. Adverting to the selection history of hearts confirms this intuition. Cummins's account, on the other hand, makes it impossible to draw the function-accident distinction where Wright wants to draw it. This is because the notion of a system is extremely open-ended, comprising almost any orderly arrangement of interacting things. Thus, for the majority of performances something manifests, it is possible to describe a system in which it is a functioning component.

So, for example, if you consider the cardiac diagnostic system, the sounds the heart makes do indeed appear as a functional component, interrelated with others, such as the results of various tests and measurements. Cummins tries to downplay this inconvenient inclusiveness of his view by pointing out that, in some cases, it will not be possible to specify any sort of interesting containing system for a given performance, so that there will, indeed, be cases where system-functional explanation is just not possible or appropriate. For example, Wright mentions the case of a belt buckle saving its wearer's life by deflecting a stray bullet. Here, it is hard to imagine what system could be described such that this singular event would come out as a function of the buckle, rather than as just a lucky accident. So a Cummins-style analysis and a Wright-style analysis would draw the function-accident distinction in the same place in cases like this. But in general, Cummins's account still draws this line a great deal more liberally than Wright and many others are willing to countenance.

It is, therefore, no surprise to find Ruth Millikan seconding Wright's contention that functional explanation is causal, and that, consequently, selection history is essential to it. On this foundational assumption, she constructs an account of what she calls proper function:

> Biological categories are carved out not by looking at the actual structure, actual dispositions, or actual functions of the organ or system that falls within the category, but by looking at (or speculating about) its

history . . . In like manner, every body organ or system falls in the biological or physiological categories it does due to its historical connections with prior examples of kinds that have served certain functions or, typically, sets of functions. So whether or not it is itself capable of serving any of these functions, every organ or system is associated with a set of functions that are biologically 'proper' to it, functions that have helped account for the survival and proliferation of its ancestors. I call these functions 'proper functions' of the organ or system. (Millikan 1993, 55–56)

Hearts, for example, have proliferated not because they make noise, but because they circulate blood. Thus, even a heart that comes into the world so badly deformed that it is never capable of circulating a single drop still has circulating blood as its proper function. It is still relevantly similar to ancestors that did circulate blood, and whose circulation of blood in the past accounts for the production of the deformed heart (although not for its deformity) in the present. Similarly, vegetable peelers have proliferated because they remove peels from fruits and vegetables. So, even if a manufacturing defect makes it impossible for one of them to peel anything at all, peeling is still its proper function. An analysis in accordance with Millikan's notion of proper function draws the function-accident line where Wright thinks it should be drawn, and it does so in virtue of the same reliance on selection history. It is not any old performance in which a thing engages that constitutes its proper function, but only those specific performances that enabled its ancestors to survive and reproduce. On the other hand, Millikan agrees with Cummins's contention that selection history and current capacity/disposition do not necessarily march in lockstep, as Wright's analysis assumes, but may, in fact, march in quite different directions. So, instead of connecting selection history directly with what a thing now does—its current capacity/disposition—she connects selection history with what the ancestors of a thing did in the past (or what previous exemplars did, in the case of items of material culture). So, where Wright says 'X is there because it does Y,' Millikan says 'X is there because some of its ancestors did Y.' This fixes the problem noted by Cummins, since what the precursors of a thing did just is part of the selection history that accounts for its existence, and there is no appeal to the problematic current capacity/disposition.

What we have just described is, strictly speaking, what Millikan calls 'direct proper function.' She also wants to account for cases where, intuitively, we have a proper function, but there is no selection history to ground it. She calls such functions 'derived proper functions,' and gives a separate account of how they get that status. A central case of derived proper function is that of prototype items of material culture—a new kind of can opener that works on entirely different principles from any existing kinds, for instance. We will examine this case at length in Chapter 6. Moreover, the distinction between direct and derived proper functions is not germane to the rest of what we need to do in this chapter. So, in the interest of expositional simplicity, we will defer our discussion of derived proper function until Chapter 6. For the remainder of this chapter, then, the reader should assume that 'proper function' means 'direct proper function.'

A distinguishing feature of Millikan's notion of proper function is that a correlative notion of malfunction falls out directly.[6] If you can say what a thing is supposed to do, then you can also say when it is failing to do it, that is, malfunctioning. The problem for Cummins is that relying on an appeal to current capacity/disposition for the determination of function makes it difficult to distinguish between malfunction and just not having a function. Consider someone born blind. Her eyes simply never have the capacity to see, and so on a Cummins-style analysis, where the sensory system is the containing system, they do not contribute to the functioning of the whole sensory system at all, and so do not have a function. Millikan's point is that it would be useful for us to have a notion of function that would enable us to say that they do have a function, but are unable to perform it. And it is only when we let go of current capacity/disposition as the determining criterion of function that we are able to do this.

Thus, in addition to drawing the function-accident distinction very liberally, the notion of system function is also non-normative in the special sense in which proper functions are normative. Things either have a capacity/disposition or they do not; but on this view, there is no particular sense to be made of the claim that there are capacities/dispositions that they *ought* (in a nonjudgmental sense) to have, but are temporarily or permanently unable to exercise. Thus, a crucial difference is that proper function is normative in a special sense that is lacking in system function. In particular, the normativity that defines proper function is not reducible to statistical regularity. It might happen that even the vast majority of a certain type of thing is unable to fulfill their proper function without this compromising in the least their possession of that proper function. Millikan employs the telling example of sperm, the vast majority of which do not or cannot fertilize an ovum, although that is still what each of them is (in a nonjudgmental sense) supposed to do. An example from material culture is nuclear weapons, the vast majority of which are—thankfully—never used. Millikan employs the capitalized term 'Normal' to signify this special sense of normativity. I shall follow this convention and refer to proper function as Normative and system function as non-Normative. It is important to bear in mind, though, that system function may be normative in other senses, such as the statistical sense, and that Millikan (1999) does recognize these other senses of normativity.

So Wright's original notion of function has split in two. Cummins took one element of Wright's analysis, the idea that function has to do with current capacity/disposition; jettisoned selection and reproduction history as irrelevant to it; and came up with the non-Normative notion of system function. Millikan took the other element of Wright's analysis, the idea that function has to do with history of selection and reproduction; jettisoned current capacity/disposition as irrelevant; and came up with the Normative notion of proper function. Each of these notions of function has associated with it a proprietary mode of explanation. System function is associated with explanations taking the form of compositional analyses of the capacities of containing systems in terms of their component parts. Proper function is associated with explanations taking the form of causal–historical accounts of why a thing is there in the first place. Thus, it seems we now have two quite distinct but equally well-motivated accounts of biological function.

WHAT PRICE UNIFICATION?

How are proper function and system function related to each other? Two distinct options are evident in the literature. First, there is what we may call the *subsumption* option. This is the view that one of these notions of function subsumes the other as a special case or subcategory. The most common version of this option is to subsume proper function under system function (Griffiths 1993; Walsh and Ariew 1996; Buller 1998; Davies 2001). Kitcher (1993) takes the opposite tack and subsumes system function under proper function, by attempting to bring both under the overarching rubric of design—a concept more closely allied to proper function because of its implications about what something is supposed to do. Second, there is the *pluralist* option. This is the view that there are two accounts of function, because there really are distinct functional phenomena to be accounted for (Millikan 1989, 1999, 2002; Godfrey-Smith 1993; Allen and Bekoff 1995; Preston 1998b).[7] We will see that a pluralist account of function is needed for material culture. Similar considerations may well obtain in the case of biological function, but we will not try to sort that out here.

   It is important to note at the outset that however distinct proper-function and system-function phenomena may be, they are also related to each other in two ways. First, they have an epistemic relationship. Proper-function analyses and system-function analyses typically coincide, in the sense that the performance of a proper function can be given a system-function analysis. For example, the brakes on your car can be given a proper-function analysis, by explaining what brakes in previous cars did that contributed to the reproduction of cars with brakes. But your brakes can also be given a system-function analysis, by specifying the car as the containing system and asking about the role the brakes play in it, regardless of whether any previous cars had brakes or not. This coincidence of proper- and system-function analyses is due to the fact that the kinds of things in both biology and material culture with histories of selection and reproduction are for the most part systems and/or components of systems. So we can advert to their history and talk about their proper functions, or we can advert to their current capacities and talk about their system functions, depending on what our explanatory or descriptive project happens to be.

The epistemic importance of this coincidence resides in the clues that prior knowledge of proper function can provide for system-function analysis and *vice versa*. For example, if you have been told what the proper function of something is—what it is supposed to do—then you know what the overall capacity is that must be explained by the capacities of its components. This is the basic epistemic strategy of reverse engineering. On the other hand, if you can figure out what something currently does using a system-function analysis, then you have a clue as to what its proper function might be, if it has one. But it is essential to understand that in neither case does the epistemic advantage amount to demonstration of one type of function on the basis of knowledge of the other. Because of the multiple realizability of function, knowing what something is supposed to do will not tell you exactly how it does it; and, because of the multiple utilizability of structure, knowing what something now does will not tell you for sure what it is supposed to do. So, the epistemic advantage lies only in providing a principled direction for investigation.

In addition to their epistemic relationship, proper function and system function have a historically conditioned ontological relationship to each other, because the performance that eventually constitutes a proper function through being selected and reproduced over some historical time period starts out as a pure system function. Consider the well-known history of Post-it notes, for example.[8] The adhesive was invented by a 3M engineer who was trying to make a really sticky adhesive and came up with a not-so-sticky one instead. He spent the next five or six years trying to find something to do with it. Then another engineer realized he could use it to solve a personal problem—the tendency of the slips of paper he used as bookmarks during choir practice to fall out of his hymnal. He coated the bottom of each slip with the not-so-sticky adhesive, *et voilà*—system-functional bookmarks that could be repositioned easily while not falling out. Several years and a lot of product development work later, what we now know as Post-it notes were in regular production for the general proper function of 'self-stick removable notes' (as it says on the package). No doubt there are defective Post-it notes—too thin a film of adhesive, for example—and there certainly are worn-out Post-it notes that no longer stick, as a result of being repositioned frequently. But otherwise, every Post-it note has the capacity to perform its proper function, and that capacity is roughly identical to the system function carried out by the prototype hymnal bookmarks. From this point of view, proper functions look like stabilized system functions.

On the other side of this ontological relationship, system functions are often proper-functional performances co-opted for some other purpose than the one for which the proper-functional item was reproduced. Consider this example given by Robert Cummins:

> In my horse pasture, I have a device that opens, at a pre-set time, a gate dividing the pasture in two. Here is how it works. There is a wind-up

alarm clock. When the alarm on the wind-up alarm clock goes off, a string wound on the key-stem unwinds, releasing a ratchet on a pulley. A weight on one end of a rope over the pulley falls, jerking open the gate latch attached to the other end of the rope. (Cummins 2002, 158)

If part of the proper function of an alarm clock is to go off at a preset time, then arguably, this one is still performing it. But this performance is now an integral component of a gate-opening system rather than of the human-agent-awakening system for which the alarm clock was made. Thus, just as proper functions can be seen as stabilized system functions, so, too, can many system functions be seen as 'liberated' proper functions. Other system functions, of course, take advantage of structurally based capacities and performances that do not contribute to the proper function of the item. For example, the unwinding of the first bit of string by the turning of the key-stem is not a co-opted proper-functional performance. The proper function of the key-stem is to wind up the clock by being turned in the opposite direction. But in order to be wound up it has to wind down, so it *can* unwind a bit of string, and in Cummins's gate-opening device that is its system function.

The main consideration that makes the pluralist option attractive, though, is that proper functions and system functions do not always coincide. There are cases where only a system-function analysis is possible, and other cases where only a proper-function analysis is possible (Millikan 1989; Preston 1998b). Material culture items with proper functions but no corresponding system functions are those that are unable to perform their proper function. One category here is malfunctioning items, including those that are defective from the start (e.g., Post-It notes with too thin a film of adhesive) or damaged thereafter (e.g., an originally perfectly good Post-it note pad that has been left out in the rain), and perhaps worn out items (e.g., our frequently repositioned and, thus, no longer sticky Post-it note). Another category includes items the proper use of which renders them henceforth unusable for that purpose, for example, matches that have been struck, the quantity of dish detergent washed down the drain, and so on. A system function is a current capacity or disposition to fulfill a certain role in a containing system, and items in these categories have no such capacity. But, there is something they are supposed to do in virtue of their history of selection and reproduction, so they retain their proper functions, even though they are not able to perform them.

Items with system functions but no corresponding proper functions are legion in material culture because people constantly co-opt proper-functional items for system-functional uses. Some of these uses are what I have called *ongoing system functions*—system functions that are repeated but never consolidated into proper functions, because they never contribute to the reasons for reproducing the item (Preston 1998b). Ongoing system functions may be further classified into standardized and idiosyncratic forms. *Standardized* ongoing system functions occur as a matter of widespread cultural practice. For example, people regularly stand on chairs for a variety of reasons. Similarly, they use dish detergent to find leaks in tires, antique flatirons as doorstops, spoons as musical instruments, and so on. Despite being the subject of recognized and widespread practices, these items are not reproduced for these uses and so never acquire them as proper functions. If you want a pair of spoons to play, you go to Walmart or a thrift store, not a music store. *Idiosyncratic* ongoing system functions are not connected with culturally recognized practices in this way, but, rather, represent creative uses of items of material culture by individuals or small groups such as families. Cummins's gate-opening device is a good example. Idiosyncratic ongoing system functions do sometimes become standardized by diffusion. Now that Cummins has published a description of his device, perhaps other people with a need for a gate-opening device will copy it. Indeed, many popular magazines, do-it-yourself books, and web pages report and/or recommend such ongoing system-functional uses for the benefit of their readers. Consider the unfortunate diffusion of information about how to make explosive devices using such things as alarm clocks, pipes, nails, synthetic fertilizer, and the like.

Another material culture category of items with system functions but no corresponding proper functions are natural objects co-opted for cultural purposes. Shade trees are a good example. The species involved are not usually subject to artificial selection and reproduction; and people often acquire them by either leaving some of the trees that are already there when they build a house, or transplanting saplings from the wild. Similarly, plants (e.g., dandelions, pokeweed, lambs quarters, blueberries, elderberries, etc.) and mushrooms are often gathered from the wild, even in agricultural cultures. In addition, people co-opt sticks and stones and leaves and bark for a variety of purposes. Small stones may be used in a slingshot, larger ones as edging for a garden bed or to hammer in a stake, and still larger ones in a wall, for example. Such uses do not contribute to the reproduction of the items involved, either because reproduction is not relevant (e.g., stones) or because it is accomplished independently of human use. Indeed, some human uses curtail attempts to reproduce—every dandelion flower you gather to feed to your rabbits is a dandelion flower that does not produce seeds, for instance. And other uses do not contribute much, if at all, to the reproduction of the organisms in question. Blueberries owe a lot to birds, for instance, but very little to us these days, given that we have a tendency to deposit their seeds in out-of-the-way places such as septic tanks and sewer systems. We can add to this category the numerous system functions of parts of the human body—the use of hands, feet, etc., as weapons, of the skin as a substrate for permanent (tattoos) or transient (paint) decorations, locks of hair as keepsakes, and so on.

The existence of items that have system functions with no corresponding proper functions, or proper functions with no corresponding system functions, demonstrates a clear difference in the extensions picked out by these two concepts of function. The intersection of these two extensions is not empty, but neither extension is a proper subset of the other. This also reinforces the point made at the end of the last section. What we seem to have in the notions of system function and proper function is two distinct forms of explanation, grounded in quite different concepts and criteria, and resulting in function ascriptions to different sets of cases. It is these clear differences in the form of explanation and the consequent differences in the extensions picked out that impress pluralists at the outset.

Proponents of subsuming proper function under system function typically do not deny these differences in concept, extension, or explanatory mode.[9] But they typically emphasize the ontological and epistemic relationships between proper function and system function to argue for an understanding of proper function as a special case of system function. There are various ways of doing this, but they are all versions of a single idea—that you do proper function analysis by doing a particular kind of system-function analysis, so proper functions are just a subcategory of system functions. Specifically, there are no restrictions on what overall capacity of a system is analyzed. So, if you choose the individual organism as the containing system, and its capacity to survive and reproduce (fitness) as the overall capacity to be explained, your analysis will yield system-functional performances of traits as the explanation. And since superior fitness is what causes selection and differential reproduction, you eventually end up with the history of selection and/or reproduction you need in order to identify proper-functional performances of traits. In other words, if you choose your initial overall capacity carefully, you can then help yourself to all the proprietary concepts of proper-function analysis (selection, reproduction, fitness, history, lineage, etc.) for free.

But this raises an important question—can you add conceptual resources to the theory that underwrites your *explanans* via your choice of *explanandum* without really changing the character of the initial theory? Or is there a theoretical sleight of hand here that changes the terms of the analysis radically, while contriving to appear not to do so? We can get some clarity on this issue by looking at exactly how the system-function analysis here proceeds, and exactly where and how the additional conceptual resources are deployed. We start by specifying the individual organism as the containing system, and the capacity of the organism to survive and reproduce (fitness) as the capacity to be explained. Now there are a lot of system-functional performances that may contribute to the fitness of an individual but that *cannot* become proper functions because they are not subject to reproduction, or that *do* not become proper functions because they are not selected. For example, acquired characteristics often contribute to the survival of an individual, but these are not genetically reproduced in offspring, and they are not necessarily socially reproduced, either. A particular deer might learn how to get into your vegetable garden by lifting the gate latch with its nose, and in a drought year this might mean that deer survives when others do not.

But this is not the sort of behavior deer learn from other deer (we may hope, and thank the goddess for small favors!), so this deer's offspring would not exhibit the behavior, even as a matter of social reproduction. Similarly, a feature that contributes to the fitness of an individual may be outmatched by other individuals' version of that feature and so be selected against, the benefit it confers notwithstanding. This is because selection has to do with the relative fitness of individuals, not absolute fitness (adaptedness). For example, the fawns of American white-tailed deer have light-colored spots that they lose during their first year, and that are surmised to enhance camouflage by mimicking dappled sunlight. A fawn born without spots would still benefit from the camouflage provided by the uniform brown coloration it shares with adults, but the ubiquity of spotted fawns indicates a selective advantage for spotted over plain brown juvenile camouflage, even though both color schemes presumably contribute to fitness.

In short, the system-function analysis of any single individual in terms of its capacity to survive and reproduce does not immediately yield proper functions. Rather, the crop of fitness-enhancing functions it yields must be pruned to yield those that are selected and/or reproduced in the next generation. And this process must be iterated across some indeterminate number of generations until the traits and their associated functions have stabilized sufficiently. It is this historical stability that allows us to ascribe a proper function to tokens of a trait type. In other words, once the history of selection and reproduction has been reconstructed, a proper function can be ascribed in light of this history alone, rather than in light of the capacity any particular token has. So, are we still within the realm of system-function analysis in reconstructing such histories and using them to ascribe proper functions?

On the one hand, it seems that we are. Some system functions contribute to fitness; others do not. Surely there can be nothing wrong with identifying the ones that do as a subcategory. Moreover, some fitness-enhancing system functions are selected and/or reproduced, whereas others are not, allowing us to narrow the subcategory even further. And if you carry out this subcategorization operation over many individuals and succeeding generations, an evolutionary history of selection and reproduction can be reconstructed for some traits on the basis of patterns that emerge at the population level. On the other hand, two things here should give us pause. First, reconstructing this evolutionary history is not just doing system-function analyses and classifying the results under various headings, but connecting system-function analyses of individuals together in a historically conditioned series. And in order to do that, you have to make use of concepts such as reproduction, inheritance, and selection in ways that go beyond classification of system functions. In other words, these concepts are no longer just a way of specifying the overall capacities of individual organisms that you wish to explain; they are a theoretical apparatus for connecting the cases you wish to explain together in a very particular sort of way over historically or evolutionarily defined periods of time. And this type of historical connection between cases of system function is not provided for by the concepts native to system-function analysis. Indeed, this operation is entirely antithetical to one of Robert Cummins's basic theoretical insights—that many function phenomena are completely independent of the evolutionary history of the organism and must be analyzed without reference to it. So, reconstructing such evolutionary histories in the service of function ascription is something system-function analysis was originally set up *not* to do.

The second thing that should give us pause here concerns how this reconstructed history of selection and reproduction is used. Even if you were just doing straightforward system-function analysis all the way along in order to reconstruct the history, once you start using it to ascribe proper functions independently, you are arguably operating outside the ambit of system-function analysis altogether. And the problem is that in order to capture the distinctive Normative character of proper function that is exactly what you have to do. Specifically, in order to capture the phenomenon of malfunction, you must be able to ascribe functions to tokens that are defective, damaged, or worn out and that no longer have—or never had—the capacity in question. Such malfunctioning tokens are not susceptible to a system-function analysis, because they are not making any current contribution to the overall capacities of the embedding system. So the only way to ascribe functions to them is by appeal to their evolutionary history. The result is a class of cases that is *not* a subcategory of system functions. The Normativity of proper function—the possibility of talking about what something is supposed to do, even when it lacks the relevant capacity—is usually claimed as a signal advantage of history-based function ascription over system-based ascription. But accounting for this phenomenon requires not just the use of a panoply of concepts not native to system-function analysis, but also an exclusive appeal to those concepts in the face of the failure of system-function analysis to apply at all. It appears that the project of subsuming proper function under system function fails, then, because it cannot capture the distinctive Normativity of proper function, especially as exhibited in the phenomenon of malfunction.

So, it looks like the only way to salvage the project of subsuming proper function under system function is to give up on Normativity. Paul Sheldon Davies is one proponent of the subsumption option who does take this tack, arguing that there is no reasonable sense in which there is something a biological trait is supposed to do (Davies 2001, especially chapters 3 and 7). But is this a realistic option in the case of material culture? Davies himself does not take a stand on this question, although he does remark that the functions of items of material culture depend on human intentions, which do not enter into an account of function for the biological traits that are his sole concern (Davies 2001, 7–8). So it would be open to Davies to argue that the special features of material culture give rise to a Normativity that is just not present in biology and to accept a pluralist account of function in material culture while maintaining his subsumptionist account of function in biology.

We can take advantage of this opening provided by Davies to mount a phenomenological argument in support of a pluralist theory of function in material culture. Let us start with the idea that there is something an item is 'supposed to' do, and is regarded as malfunctioning if it cannot do. This idea surfaces when a manufacturer or distributor of the item can be held ethically or legally responsible for its failing to do what it is supposed to do, for instance. Beer is supposed to be a potable liquid with certain character-istics, such as fizziness and a specific taste. So, if you cannot drink it because it tastes awful or makes you ill, you have a legitimate complaint and can demand your money back. On the other hand, if you use the beer as slug bait (a common practice among some organic gardeners), and your local slugs are not attracted to it or it does not drown them, you cannot reasonably demand your money back. Similarly, warranties for appliances often state the proper uses of the item and warn that other uses that result in the item no longer being able to function as it is supposed to function void the warranty. Phenomena of this sort indicate that malfunction in the Normative sense is culturally distinguished from simply not working for a given purpose, and that there is a cultural recognition of the difference between official uses and alternative ones. This amounts to a distinction between proper function and system function embodied in the legal and ethical practices of some societies.

A similar and even more ubiquitous phenomenon involves social criticism or sanctions for using an item of material culture for something other than what it is 'supposed to' be for. In some cases, any use other than the proper one is frowned upon. For example, if you insist on drinking your morning coffee from a consecrated chalice borrowed from your church, or you buy a United States flag only to burn it at the protest the next day, you may face religious or legal sanctions, and you will surely face criticism. In other cases, use other than what is deemed official is criticizable only in certain contexts. If you use your salad fork for the main course at a black-tie dinner, that is a *faux pas*. But if you use it to eat a slice of pie or even stir your coffee at an informal family dinner, criticism is unlikely. The other side of this coin is that in some contexts, using an item of material culture for something other than its official use is singled out for praise for creativity or ingenuity. Cummins's alarm clock-based gate-opening device is the sort of thing that would gener-ate this kind of a response, for instance. Phenomena such as these are further confirmation that a distinction between official uses and alternative uses is widely recognized. They also show that the ramifications of this distinction go well beyond any concern with malfunction, since both official and alter-native uses are evaluated differently from context to context.

To sum up, we now have arguments from two directions for pursuing a pluralist account of function in material culture. From a negative direc-tion, we have seen that attempts to unify theories of biological function by subsuming proper function under system function are problematic at best, and that the most consistent (Davies's account) succeeds by dint of simply giving up on Normativity, rather than accounting for it in system-function terms. From a positive direction, we have just seen that a distinction between Normativity and Non-normativity and the concomitant distinction between proper function and system function are built into various ethical, legal, and social practices common in Western culture, at least. So we will proceed on the assumption that whatever may turn out to be required for an explication of biological function, function in material culture requires a pluralist account.

PROPER FUNCTION AND SYSTEM FUNCTION IN MATERIAL CULTURE

If we want to use the concepts of proper function and system function to theorize about material culture, we must make sure that they apply straightforwardly and not vaguely or metaphorically. And here the translation from biological function to function in material culture begins to look rather dicey, because both system function and proper function are defined primarily with biological function—and, therefore, biological concepts and phenomena—in mind. In the case of system function, the issue is whether items of material culture are appropriately analogous to biological organisms with respect to system analysis. In the case of proper function, the issue is whether items of material culture are appropriately analogous to biological organisms with respect evolutionary analysis and its attendant concepts, such as selection and fitness.

Let us begin with system function. The first question here is whether the conception of a system is the same with regard to both biology and material culture. Interestingly, the example Cummins uses to explain this concept is drawn from material culture:

> Assembly-line production provides a transparent example of what I mean. Production is broken down into a number of distinct tasks. Each point on the line is responsible for a certain task, and it is the function of the workers/machines at that point to complete that task. If the line has the capacity to produce the product, it has it in virtue of the fact that the workers/machines have the capacities to perform their designated tasks, and in virtue of the fact that when these tasks are performed in a certain organized way—according to a certain program—the finished product results. (Cummins 1975, 760)

If we think of this as an automobile assembly line in Detroit, for instance, it is easy to see that the cars it produces are also systems. Each car consists of subsystems (e.g., the electrical system, the fuel system), which have the capacity to perform subtasks that contribute to the capacity of the whole car to function as a road-worthy transportation device. Cummins claims that this model is exemplified in biological organisms in exactly the same way.

In a sheep, for instance, the capacities of organs and other sub-systems (e.g., the digestive system, the nervous system) contribute to the capacity of the whole organism to carry out its life activities (e.g., foraging, reproducing).

The second question we have to answer here—whether biological organisms are analogous to items of material culture with respect to system-function analysis—is a little bit more complicated. You can select examples that make the analogy seem entirely straightforward, as we just did by comparing a car and a sheep. But a closer look reveals a possible disanalogy. In biology, we tend to talk about the functions of traits, but not about whole organisms as having functions; whereas with regard to material culture, we are just as apt to talk about the functions of whole items as of their parts. A car has the function of transporting people and goods, just as its spark plugs and alternator have functions. But this apparent difference begins to evaporate when we consider that ethologists and ecologists, if not biologists, do talk about the functions of whole organisms. For example, in a particular ecological community, it might be the function of sheep to eat certain plants and be eaten by certain predators. The general point is that systems are instantiated simultaneously in a hierarchy of levels, so function analysis can be extended up to a macrolevel or down to a microlevel. A preliminary attempt to map this hierarchy comparatively for biology and culture yields something like this:

	Biology	Culture
Macrolevel	Ecological communities	Material cultures
	Conspecific groups/ populations	Suites/toolkits[10]
	Individual organisms	Individual items
	Organs	Parts
Microlevel	Physiological properties	Structural/chemical properties

But another possible disanalogy threatens this schema. Even very simple organisms—viruses, say—have component systems with different capacities and, thus, different functions. But there are items of material culture that do not seem to have discernible parts with different capacities. Paper, window glass, flour, string, wire, and soap are all good examples. The problem here seems to be that the 'parts' of such items are homogenous. Paper is made up of many separate fibers, but except in the case of special papers, such as that used by the Department of the Treasury for printing money, all of them are alike and seem to be doing roughly the same job. It is their collective structural relationship to each other that explains the capacities of the paper. However, different kinds of paper do have different overall capacities, which can be analyzed in terms of this microstructure. The fiber structure of writing paper provides a rigid sheet with a hard surface so that writing instruments will glide over it and you can hold it up to read it. The fiber structure of a paper towel provides a flexible sheet with a soft surface so that it will absorb liquids and can be scrunched up or wrung out. Now you can write on a paper towel or—with somewhat more trouble—mop up a spill with a piece of writing paper; and a function analysis will explain those capacities of paper towels and writing paper, as well. But it will also explain why the capacity of the paper towel to absorb liquid is greater than that of the writing paper, and this bears on the function of these different papers in the suites of items of material culture to which they belong. In short, the problem here is just that some items of material culture lack any analogue of organs, and so are missing one level of the hierarchy for the purposes of system-function analysis. It is important to recognize this, but it is not a problem, in principle. System function, then, is on firm footing with regard to its application to material culture. The sense of function analysis outlined by Cummins is the same in both domains, and the possible disanalogies between organisms and items of material culture with regard to the ascription of function are not problematic.

The situation with regard to proper function is more difficult, due to its more intensive grounding in biological concepts. In the case of system function, the clearest examples are drawn from material culture in the first place. But as Ruth Millikan (2002, 117) remarks, the best examples of proper function are biological traits that are reproduced genetically under Darwinian natural selection. The operative concepts here are selection and reproduction. But it is clear from the outset that these terms cannot be univocal across biology and material culture. Selection in material culture involves the intentions of intelligent agents, and, thus, is different from the mechanical processes that characterize natural selection. And reproduction in material culture is not genetic. So the question becomes whether selection and reproduction in material culture are sufficiently analogous to selection and reproduction in biology that the concept of proper function can be translated sensibly into the cultural realm.

Let us start with selection. For an evolutionary biologist, a trait has been selected only if it has coexisted with variant traits, and if it has been so much better at contributing to the fitness of its possessors that it has persisted and proliferated, while the variants have slowly but surely disappeared. Natural selection is, thus, selection *over* alternatives. So, if cultural selection is to be analogous to natural selection, it must at the very least involve competing variants. In material culture, such processes occur in at least two areas. First, design often involves the building and testing of a number of prototypes, one of which is then selected for production. Second, the economic processes of marketing and distribution often involve the appearance of a number of competing variants of a type of item, one of which proliferates while the others disappear. For example, quill pens fell into disuse with the advent of fountain pens in the late nineteenth century; and Microsoft Word has arguably out-competed other word processing systems currently available. So, at first blush, it looks like selection among alternative variants is a feature of material culture just as it is of biology. But a closer look raises some concerns.

Karen Neander (1991b) suggests that one problem with attempts to construe cultural selection in accordance with natural selection is that there may be only one way—or only one way apparent to the agents involved—to realize a given function, so no alternatives may be produced either in reality or in virtuality. Consider two hypothetical, prehistoric cultures with flaked stone knives. In one culture, knives have never been made of anything but stone, because in this region no other suitable material is available. Alternatives are inconceivable to the inhabitants. In the other culture, knives used to be made from bamboo, but when pressure flaking of flint was invented, the bamboo knives gradually disappeared. Given the strict biological definition of selection, we are forced to say that the flint knives in the first culture do not have a proper function, whereas those in the second culture do. We may call this the problem of *absent variation*. There is also a problem we may call *persisting variation* where variations are produced but there is no selection of one over the others. This is more obvious when we consider selection as an economic process, where the operative concept is market share, not sink or swim. For example, fountain pens may have lost market share in the wake of the introduction of ballpoint pens, but they are still available and preferred by some consumers.

Consideration of the marketplace as the locus of variation and selection leads to another worry, as well. When a variation does disappear, the reasons for its disappearance do not necessarily have anything to do with how well it fulfilled its erstwhile function. Perhaps it actually worked better than all the competing variations, but the company was poorly managed and went under, or it ran afoul of Microsoft, or the advertising or distribution were not adequate, or the colors were unfashionable, or whatever. This phenomenon is like genetic drift in biology, where the frequency of genes in a population can change for reasons extraneous to natural selection, like natural disasters that randomly wipe out members of a population with no regard to their fitness. Let us call this phenomenon *cultural drift*. The problem here is that the winnowing out of variations has been carried out by a non-selective process. So here again, we would have to say the variation left standing at the end has no proper function.

Absent variation, persisting variation and cultural drift raise doubts about the possibility of settling what should count as a proper function in material culture by appeal to any analogue of natural selection. But this should not be very surprising, since similar doubts have also eroded the appeal to natural selection as a criterion for proper function in biology (Preston 2009b). Because absent variation, persisting variation, and drift can occur in the biological realm as well as the cultural one, accounts of biological proper function that do not appeal to natural selection as the decisive criterion (Schwartz 1999, 2002) or that appeal only to fitness and heredity instead of natural selection (Buller 1998) have been proposed. These accounts are motivated by the perception that there are a fair number of cases of what seem intuitively to be proper functions in which natural selection cannot be part of the account of how these proper functions came to be established. But there are worse problems in the offing.

Robert Cummins (2002) has re-entered the function theory fray with a much more fundamental critique. On his view, natural selection does not account for the establishment of proper functions, even in the cases in which it does occur. The target of Cummins's argument is a widely held view he calls *neo-teleology*. On this view, natural selection accounts for the existence of proper-functional traits, because it builds complex traits incrementally. Second, it accounts for the spread of such traits through populations, and thus for their existence in individual organisms. With regard to the building of traits, Cummins (2002, 168–69) agrees that natural selection is largely responsible for this, but points out that it works by means of a piecemeal, long-term process that is entirely insensitive to the proper function of the trait that is the ultimate result. With regard to the spread of traits, Cummins (2002, 164–65) again agrees that this is often accomplished by natural selection, which in this case *is* sensitive to function—but only to the relative success with which a function is performed by the current variants. For example, natural selection does not select between winged pileated woodpeckers and wingless pileated woodpeckers, but between pileated woodpeckers with better and worse wing designs. And the crucial point here is that both better and worse wings already *have* the proper function of enabling flight. In short, in the case of both the building and the spread of traits, what natural selection selects for does not correspond in the right way to the proper functions of these traits.

Does an analogous argument go through for material culture? Let us first consider spread. It does seem that cultural selection, like natural selection, spreads items of material culture by selecting among better and worse variants with the same proper function. Quill pens and fountain pens both have the proper function of writing, but fountain pens are more efficient because they have a larger ink reservoir. So they proliferated, while quill pens fell into disuse. Nor does the ink reservoir—which, as a component part, is more nearly analogous to the wings of the pileated woodpeckers in our biological example—represent a new proper function. The hollow shaft of a quill pen is also an ink reservoir, but an inefficiently small one in comparison to that of the fountain pen. And while there may be some rare cases in which a completely novel structure capable of a novel performance is introduced, this is a vanishingly rare exception rather than the rule, in both material culture and biology. So cultural selection, like natural selection, does not spread items with a particular proper function by selecting them over variants with different proper functions, but rather selects among variants that all have that particular proper function but perform it more or less well.

Next, and more importantly, we must consider the sheer existence of proper-functional items of material culture—why are they there at all? Cummins calls this a Paley question, with reference to the watchmaker analogy made famous by William Paley. Paley's point was that if you find a complex item of material culture, such as a watch, on a deserted beach, you naturally assume it must have had an intelligent designer. Likewise, if you find an eye or a stomach, you should assume an intelligent designer of these complex biological items. But, what evolutionary theory shows is that you do not have to answer Paley questions about biological traits or organisms by appeal to intelligent design, because the observed results can be achieved by long-term, incremental processes that are insensitive to the eventual complex structural 'design' or function. So, now it is widely assumed that Paley questions about material culture just have a different kind of answer than Paley questions about biology. Specifically, cultural selection is thought to be necessarily sensitive to function and design, whereas natural selection is not. But if Cummins's argument is to go through for material culture, we are now going to have to insist that Paley questions in both domains do in fact have the same kind of answer—but an answer opposite to the one favored by Paley. In other words, we must insist that the existence of a watch on a deserted beach is in fact to be accounted for by a long history of incremental variations that was not aimed from the beginning at the creation of watches.

We have already observed that radical novelty is vanishingly rare in material culture. Rather, human inventiveness consists in making incremental changes in existing types of items rather than producing radical novelty out of nowhere. In light of this observation, let us consider the history of mechanical watches of the sort Paley had in mind, the early forms of which appeared in the sixteenth century. First of all, such watches depend on the development of two basic technologies, glassmaking and metallurgy, both of which have histories stretching back many millennia. Second, they depend on the development of machining techniques for producing very small parts capable of precise operation. Finally, watches depend on the prior history of mechanical clocks, which first appeared in the fourteenth century in the form of large, weight-driven tower clocks in public buildings. It is certain that early glassmakers and metallurgists were not aiming at watches. Neither were early machinists. And, arguably, neither were the early clockmakers, who were working on a vertical mechanism driven by large weights that was not even conceivably portable. It was only with the invention of a spring-driven mechanism and early portable clocks (e.g., for use onboard ships) that the sort of personal, portable clock we now know as a watch could be realistically designed, let alone made. The point is this. Positing an intelligent agent with an understanding of the proper function of a watch and its parts only just begins to explain the existence of the watch on the deserted beach, because the existence of such an agent itself requires an explanation. An agent capable of designing or making a watch is not even remotely conceivable without the long history of the underlying technologies sketched above, since no human being, however intelligent, could possibly have invented such a thing utterly from scratch. In other words, a watch may imply a watchmaker, but a watchmaker implies a cultural history during which the requisite technological resources and techniques are incrementally built up through the work of many intelligent agents who did *not* have an understanding of the proper function of watches or their parts. Thus, the existence of watches is not explained by appeal to watchmakers, but only by appeal to the history of technologies and techniques on which watchmakers are utterly dependent and without which their production of watches is inconceivable. So an analogue of Cummins's argument against neo-teleology goes through for the building of items of material culture, just as it did for the spread of such items.

Let us consolidate our results so far. Since standard theories of biological proper function appeal to natural selection, it seems we need an analogue in cultural selection. But, instead, we find that the appeal to natural selection encounters a number of serious problems—absent variation, persistent variation, and drift—in both biology and material culture. Worse yet, if Cummins's critique of neo-teleology can be sustained and extended to material culture, selection cannot do what theorists of proper function need it to do, anyway. The most reasonable response is to abandon selection as a central concept in a theory of proper function. But what other options are there?

We may look for inspiration to a non-selectionist account of biological proper function proposed by David Buller. Here is his definition:

> A current token of a trait T in an organism O has the [proper] function of producing an effect of type E just in case past tokens of T contributed to the fitness of O's ancestors by producing E, and thereby causally contributed to the reproduction of Ts in O's lineage. (Buller 1998, 507)

Like the selectionist accounts, this non-selectionist account appeals to the history of reproduction of a trait. But it grounds that history in *contributions* to fitness, not in the stricter condition of selection over other variations because of superior fitness. So now, instead of looking for a material culture analogue of natural selection, we must look for analogues of reproduction and fitness.

Let us start with fitness. This is a fraught concept in biology and philosophy of biology. First of all, it has been used in a number of different senses (Endler 1986, 33–50). In addition, it has been alleged to be tautologous, or at least lacking in explanatory power, because those organisms that survive and reproduce are by definition the fitter ones (Sober 1984, chapter 2). In general, fitness is a propensity to survive and reproduce, but the grounds of this propensity are usually spelled out so as to dispel the air of tautology. Buller (1998, 509) appeals to a widely accepted and allegedly non-tautologous conception of fitness with four components: viability, fertility, fecundity, and ability to find mates. Are there analogues for these four components in material culture? We can eliminate the ability to find mates immediately, since reproduction in material culture is not sexual; but this does not seem to be a problem, since in biology, much reproduction is asexual anyway (e.g., among plants). What about viability? This is important to the fitness of biological organisms because they have to survive to maturity in order to achieve fertility and fecundity. But for items of material culture, there is no such point in their 'life cycle.' You can start mixing up a new batch of brownies before the first one is out of the oven, for instance. Similarly, you could conceivably bake a new batch of brownies even if all previously existing brownies had already been eaten. In short, reproduction in material culture is not absolutely dependent on the survival of individual items in the way that reproduction in biology typically is, because it is ensured by us, not by the items of material culture themselves. Finally, fertility and fecundity—the capacity to produce offspring, and lots of them—might seem to have an analogue in that there are higher and lower rates of reproduction among items of material culture. For example, there always seem to be a lot more chocolate cakes around than red velvet cakes. But here again, fertility and fecundity in biology are characteristics of individual organisms, whereas in material culture being reproduced at a higher or a lower rate is, instead, a characteristic of types of things. In connection with this, it is worth remarking that no reasonable sense attaches to the idea that the red velvet cake you are now baking is the offspring of the previous one you baked. The underlying difference that prevents analogies from taking hold here is the difference between reproducing and being reproduced.

It is perhaps because of the kinds of disanalogies described above that Paul Griffiths (1993, 419–20) says fitness in material culture is a vaguer notion than in biology, referring merely to a propensity to be reproduced. But this lands us squarely in the realm of tautology, since a propensity to be reproduced on the part of items of material culture will now be supposed to account for their having been reproduced. Griffiths (1993) is sensitive to this, since he immediately connects the propensity of an item to be reproduced to its intended use, asserting that 'its ability to fulfill its intended use gives it a propensity to be reproduced' (420). This is promising. Items of material culture are made to be used, and whether or not they continue to be reproduced does seem to depend in some way on whether they have, in fact, been useful.

We can now formulate a provisional definition of proper function for material culture that does not depend on a concept of selection:

> A current token of an item of material culture has the proper function of producing an effect of a given type just in case producing this effect contributed to the *usefulness* of past tokens of this type of item, and therefore to the *reproduction* of such items.

As with Buller's non-selectionist definition of biological proper function, this provisional definition of proper function in material culture appeals to a history of reproduction, but grounds this history in contributions to usefulness (the analogue of biological fitness) rather than in selection for superior usefulness over other variants. But this is only the first step in defining proper function in material culture, since even if usefulness is an acceptable analogue of fitness in biology, all the details remain to be worked out and some of them promise to be problematic.

One set of problems is associated with the concept of usefulness. Griffiths introduced this concept in terms of the *intended* use of items of material culture. We were spared questions about the role of intention in cultural selection, because an appeal to selection turned out to be neither necessary nor desirable. But now we will have to address it with regard to usefulness. And it will not all be clear sailing, because as we shall see, questions about the role of intention reintroduce the problem of centralized control in a new guise. For example, what if the real usefulness of a type of item is not the use intended for it by its makers and/or realized by its users? As writers from Marx to Foucault have pointed out, the uses of material culture are not necessarily transparent to the human agents involved, and this indicates some slippage between intended use and actual use. How will this affect our provisional definition of proper function in material culture? Similarly, the phenomenon of phantom function, where an item is reproduced even though it has no real ability to fulfill its intended use (e.g., deflecting evil spirits in the case of *fengshui* mirrors), is problematic. Should we say such items do not have proper functions? Or if they do, how can we account for these proper functions in the absence of any actually useful performance, as our provisional definition requires? We will deal with these issues in Chapter 6.

Another set of problems is associated with the concept of reproduction. As we noted above, reproduction in material culture seems to be quite different from reproduction in biology, largely because items of material culture do not reproduce themselves but are reproduced by us. This did not affect our provisional definition of proper function in material culture, because there was still a history of reproduction to which we could appeal. But in the wake of our discussion of intention in Chapter 6, some issues about reproduction in material culture will surface. One concerns the strictness of the distinction between reproducing and being reproduced, which at first blush seems to divide nature from culture so sharply.[11] A closer look reveals a more complicated picture and a more blurred division. In particular, we will discover that what is reproduced in material culture—or perhaps more precisely, along with material culture—are the intentions and purposes of the human individuals born into that material culture, and so in a very real sense those individuals themselves as they result from the developmental processes they undergo in the context of their material culture. This brings us back to the issues of sociogenerism and creativity broached in Part I, and returning here in a new guise. We will deal with these issues in Chapter 7.

6   The Use and Abuse of Intention

> For a *large* class of cases—though not for all—in which we employ the
> word 'meaning' it can be defined thus: the meaning of a word is its use
> in the language.
>
> —Ludwig Wittgenstein,
> *Philosophical Investigations*, §43

In the previous chapter, we started with theories of function oriented primarily to biology and went some distance toward a theory of function in
material culture. This had the effect of de-emphasizing the role of intention
in the establishment of function. Direct proper function is established by
a history of reproduction, and system function by a role in a containing
system. So, while human intentions undoubtedly play a significant role in
the implementation of cultural histories and systems, the appeal is not, in the
first instance, to these intentions. This approach, thus, runs contrary to the
more common view that the functions of cultural objects are established by
the intentions of human agents. Following Vermaas and Houkes (2003), we
may call this the *intentionalist theory* of function in material culture. And we
can see that it is the centralized control model manifesting itself in function
theory, for just as in action theory plans control action, here the intentions
of designers control function in material culture. So, we must now take a
closer look at the role of human intentions in the establishment of proper
functions, in particular.

The first section describes the main features and general problems of the
intentionalist approach. The second section shows that the plausible move
of appealing to the intentions of designers to establish proper functions for
novel prototypes in fact causes more function-theoretic problems than it
solves. In addition, the (mostly unconscious) motivations behind this move
are shown to be suspect. The third section shows that the equally plausible move of appealing to the intentions of users to establish the proper-
functional status of phantom functions is no more successful, because
these intentions do not track the actual history of reproduction and use
of phantom-functional items very well at all. This critique of the centralized control model as it appears in function theory also results in a further

refinement of the definition of proper function in material culture. Even usefulness is too strong a notion. Instead, an appeal to historical patterns of actual use and reproduction for that use is recommended. The resulting account of proper function is non-intentionalist, in the sense that it appeals in the first instance to what people do, rather than to their intentions.

INTENTIONALIST APPROACHES TO FUNCTION IN MATERIAL CULTURE

One version of the intentionalist theory traces the functions of items of material culture unequivocally to their creators. For instance, in their introduction to a collection of papers on biological function, Ariew and Perlman write:

> Humans often create objects with a purpose in mind, endowing the objects with particular functions. It is taken to be relatively unproblematic to have artifacts receive their functions from the intentions of their inventors. For example, can-openers are invented with the function of opening cans. (2002, 1)

This view gives rise to some obvious questions. First of all, who is to count as the creator of an item of material culture for the purposes of establishing its function? On the one hand, there is a crucial difference between the maker and the designer/inventor, because the maker in principle need not know the function of the item she is making. This could be cleared up expeditiously by specifying the intentions of the designer as the operative ones, even if she has no hand in the actual making of the item. But this leaves us with another problem—which designer? The very first inventor of a type of item? Or the more immediate designer of a contemporary version?

But these problems pale in comparison with a pair of problems concerned with the relationships among agents in these contexts. First, as we discovered in our foray into action theory, the design and making of items of material culture is typically a group activity. Moreover, this activity is complex, messy, and poorly understood. The invention of Post-it notes is an excellent illustration of just how problematic this makes any appeal to human intentions in function theory. The engineer who invented the Post-it note adhesive *intended* to invent a strong adhesive but ended up with a weak one, for which he could find no good use. It was another engineer at a later date who adopted this adhesive for a purpose not envisioned by the first engineer. And then it took a whole team of production engineers to turn his prototype into the office product we know and love today. So where in all this is *the* intention to create Post-it notes and endow them with the proper function they now have? The most obvious way for intentionalist theories of function to incorporate this sociality is to appeal to some notion of collective intention, as John Searle does:

> Given an apparatus that includes both collective intentionality and the intentional imposition of agentive functions on physical objects, it is no big step to combine the two. If it is easy to see how a single person might decide to use some object as a chair or a lever, then I believe it is not difficult to see how two or more people together could decide to use some object as a bench on which they can all sit or to use something as a lever to be operated by several people, rather than just one. Collective intentionality can generate agentive functions as easily as individual intentionality. (1995, 38–39)

This may not be as easy as Searle thinks, though. As we discovered earlier, existing theories of collective intentionality are not designed to deal with improvisatory group activities, let alone with improvisatory activity stretched over a considerable time period, as illustrated by the history of the invention of Post-it notes. Searle gives no inkling of these typical but much more complex cases, because he focuses his examples solely on simple situations where a group of agents comes to an explicit consensus on a specific occasion about the function of an individual thing. So, appealing to collective intentionality is not an easy fix.

A second problem concerns the relationships between designers and users of items of material culture. This relationship is important, first, because even if users do not endow items of material culture with their functions in the first instance, they may play a necessary role in sustaining those functions, as Peter McLaughlin suggests:

> The function of an artifact is derivative from the purpose of some agent in making or appropriating the object; it is conferred on the object by the desires and beliefs of an agent. No agent, no purpose, no function . . . Although, given the social nature of intelligent agents, the function of any one particular agent's product may be independent of the continued existence of that particular agent, nonetheless it is dependent on the existence of some agents that share the relevant beliefs and desires. (2001, 60–61)

Thus, the stability of proper functions depends on the transmission of intentions from designers to users, and from one user to another. McLaughlin does not suggest a mechanism for this. But Wybo Houkes and Pieter Vermaas (Vermaas and Houkes 2003; Houkes and Vermaas 2004) build a communicative relationship into their account for this purpose. On their view, functions are ascribed in accordance with a use plan intentionally communicated by the designers to the users, and by users to other users (Houkes and Vermaas 2004, 65). Thus, intentions are transmitted in virtue of being embodied in use plans that are the explicit content of intentional acts of communication among agents. As in the case of collective intentions, this plan-based account is less straightforward than it seems, if only because it depends on the sort of planning-oriented action theory problematized by our discussion in previous chapters.

The other side of the designer-user relationship highlights the divergence that occurs when users deploy items of material culture for purposes not intended by their designers. Much of this kind of use is system-functional use of proper-functional items. This common phenomenon raises a number of questions for intentionalist theories. First, it is not entirely consonant with acknowledging only the designer (creator/inventor/maker) as endowing items of material culture with functions, because it seems that users can change the functions of items of material culture, or add functions in addition to those anticipated by the designer. For example, museum reproductions of coins, bronze axes, and so on are not intended to fulfill the functions intended for such items by their original designers, but rather to function as collectibles or souvenirs. Arguably, there has been a change in proper function in such cases. Similarly, aspirin tablets were originally designed to relieve fever and pain, but are now prescribed for the prevention of cardiac problems, as well. Here the added function qualifies as a proper function, since aspirin manufacturers market specially formulated tablets for this purpose. So, proponents of the intentionalist view owe us an account of how and under what conditions the intentions of users can override or supplement the intentions of designers.

The intentionalist theory of function in material culture, initially so appealing and apparently straightforward, thus turns out to be a mare's nest of loose ends and little-recognized problems (Perlman 2004; Lewens 2004). This is an indication that it is not so much a worked-out theory as an intuition that has become a commonplace without any real theoretical development. Assessing a theory that is in such an unsettled state is difficult, at best. But we may gain some clarity about its prospects by focusing on the specific phenomena of function in material culture that have been thought to necessitate an appeal to human intention. If the intentionalist approach cannot handle these cases in a satisfactory manner, its overall viability is questionable. We will look at two cases—*novel prototypes* that lack any history of reproduction, and *phantom functions* of items that are constitutionally incapable of fulfilling the functions they are thought to have.

NOVEL PROTOTYPES

A prototype is the first full-scale model of a type or design of thing to be produced. Most prototypes are neither interesting nor problematic from the point of view of function theory, because they involve no significant innovation. Consider the prototype of next year's automobile model, for instance. Perhaps there are some cosmetic changes, such as spiffier upholstery. And perhaps there is some new equipment, such as side-impact airbags. But these new components do not themselves represent novel functions or structures;

nor, of course, is the function or overall structure of the whole car novel. However, there are prototypes that do represent either a novel function, or a completely novel way of implementing an existing function. The prototype of the first can opener had a novel function, for instance; and if someone now were to patent a device that opened cans by some entirely new means, that would be a novel implementation of an existing function.

Ascribing *system* functions to such novel prototypes is not a problem. Take the prototype of the first can opener. If it did indeed open cans, it succeeded in fulfilling a role in a containing cultural system involving food preservation and storage devices, including cans. Prototype can openers that work have the system function of opening cans, then, and prototype can openers that do not work simply have no system function. But there is a strong intuition that such novel prototypes have *proper* functions, not just system functions. More specifically, the intuition is that there is something novel prototypes are supposed to do, such that if they do not do it they are malfunctioning. This Normative feature is the hallmark of direct proper functions. But novel prototypes do not have the history of selection and reproduction that is required for Millikanian direct proper functions. The response has been to appeal instead to the intentions of the designer—there is something the designer intended the prototype to do, and this is its proper function.

In Chapter 5, we determined that selection is not a desirable element of an account of proper function for material culture. But now it seems that in order for novel prototypes to have proper functions, we must appeal to a form of selection—intentional selection by a designer—because there is no history of usefulness leading to reproduction to which to appeal. Our discussion here will lead to the conclusion that the notion of intentional selection by a designer is extremely problematic; that we are better off sticking to our guns and leaving selection of any kind out of our account of proper function in material culture; and that we should accept the consequence that novel prototypes do not have proper functions. To start, let us look at some accounts of how intentional selection is supposed to work.

Vermaas and Houkes (2003) point out that design—particularly engineering design—is not a matter of simply intending in a cognitive void, but of applying knowledge about materials, techniques, and so on in the formation of an intention such that the artifact resulting from the carrying-out of that intention has a reasonable chance of working as anticipated. At the very least, the designers must be able to provide an explanation that justifies their expectation that the artifact will work (Vermaas and Houkes 2003, 287). In a more recent paper, they have articulated this view more precisely in terms of use plans shared between designers and users (Houkes and Vermaas 2004). This theory copes easily with the attribution of proper function to novel prototypes. The designer of the prototype has a use plan in accordance with which the prototype is constructed, and which is communicated to potential users. The capacities of the prototype that are highlighted in that plan are its proper function (or 'standard function,' as Houkes and Vermaas term it).

Ruth Millikan provides for proper functions for novel prototypes within her overall account, but in virtue of a much more elaborate theoretical apparatus than is offered by Houkes and Vermaas. The part of her account we discussed in Chapter 5 is, as we noted, an account of what she calls *direct* proper function—proper functions a thing has in virtue of its history of selection and reproduction. This is a non-intentionalist component of her account. But Millikan also has an intentionalist component—she distinguishes a type of proper function she calls *derived* proper function (Millikan 1984, 1999). When a thing has a direct proper function that it accomplishes by producing some other thing, the product is said to *derive* a proper function from the producer. Thus, the product does not itself have to have a history of selection and reproduction for this precise function (Millikan 1984, 41–43). So, if a spark plug has the direct proper function of initiating combustion by producing a spark, the spark it produces on any particular occasion has the derived proper function of initiating combustion. This theoretical apparatus has a special application to human makers. On Millikan's view, the intentional states of intelligent organisms have direct proper functions. Intentions, for example, have the direct proper function of getting themselves fulfilled. And some intentions get themselves fulfilled by causing the production of a thing that does the actual fulfilling. So the thing derives a proper function from the content of the intention. For example, if my intention is to open cans and I invent a device to do that, then the device has the derived proper function of opening cans. So, Millikan solves the novel prototype problem by providing for appeal to human intentions within the compass of an overall theory that accounts for direct proper functions without any such appeal.

Unfortunately, these tidy intentionalist solutions to the novel prototype problem result in stresses and strains elsewhere. The intentions of designers are taken to be sufficient for the establishment of proper functions, on this view. But what about the intentions of users? They do not necessarily coincide with the intentions of designers, and so can result in something being used for a different purpose than the designer intended—for example, the use of pipe cleaners for craft projects. Do the intentions of such users establish derived proper functions, as well? And if so, are all system functions in material culture actually derived proper functions? Houkes and Vermaas are committed to preserving the distinction between proper function and system function (which they call 'accidental function'). On their view, all artifact functions are equally capacities highlighted in a use plan. But they then distinguish between proper functions and system functions by introducing a distinction between standard and non-standard use plans. For example, the standard use plan for beer highlights its capacity to serve as a beverage for humans, and this is its proper function. A non-standard use plan for beer might highlight its capacity to attract and drown slugs when poured into saucers and left overnight in the garden. Thus slug bait is an accidental (system) function of beer.

Houkes and Vermaas claim that there are three sources of use plans—innovative users, designers, and tradition. On their view, the last two sources are privileged:

> The concept of standard use can be explained straightforwardly by maintaining that a use plan that stems from the last two sources, i.e., communicated traditions and designing, holds a privileged position in the set of available plans. Standard use of an artifact is then the execution of a plan approximately identical to the designed or traditional use plan . . . By contrast, non-standard use is the execution of a plan of a different type than the designed or traditionally evolved one, e.g., a plan devised by the user herself or one that is made up by a fellow user. (Houkes and Vermaas 2004, 60)

Non-standard use plans can become standard over the course of time by becoming entrenched and traditional. But in the interim, the intentions of the users only establish system functions, not proper functions. So for Houkes and Vermaas, the intentions of designers are efficacious in a way the intentions of users are not. A use plan devised by a designer is *ipso facto* a standard use plan, and thus immediately establishes a proper function. But a use plan devised by a user, no matter how innovative, can at best *become* a standard use plan, and then only provided it meets the conditions of success and communication from user to user over some significant period of time. Thus, the decisive factor in the case of user-devised use plans is a basically non-intentional history of success and transmission, not the users' intentions.

Thus, what initially appears to be an egalitarian view of the genesis of function in material culture—its origin in human intentions—is transmuted into a hierarchical view, without either explanation or justification. All artifact functions, for Houkes and Vermaas, are capacities highlighted by use plans. Thus far, their account is egalitarian. But Houkes and Vermaas preserve the distinction between proper functions and system functions by introducing a hierarchical distinction between standard use plans and non-standard use plans. If this move is not to be *ad hoc*, the privilege of designers' use plans must rest on something other than the desire to preserve the distinction between proper functions and system functions. This privilege does not stem from any feature of the plans themselves, for a standard use plan and a non-standard one may be identical. A standard use plan for putting in screws, for example, would specify a series of actions to be undertaken with a screwdriver. A non-standard use plan for putting in screws might specify the same series of actions to be undertaken with a table knife. Indeed, a user unfamiliar with screwdrivers might find one and devise a plan serendipitously identical to its designer's plan. But the user's plan would still be non-standard and would not establish a proper function for the screwdriver. In short, it is the *source* of the plan that is decisive, not any internal feature of the plan itself. Whence this special authority of designers and lack of authority of users? We are not told.

Millikan's quasi-intentionalist theory also privileges designers over users with regard to the establishment of derived proper functions. She stipulates that artifacts only get derived proper functions from the intentions of their makers, not their users (Millikan 1999, 205). In other words, intentions that get themselves fulfilled by causing the *production* of some other thing that fulfills them endow the produced thing with a derived proper function. But intentions that get themselves fulfilled by causing the *utilization* of some already existing thing that fulfills them do not endow the utilized thing with a derived proper function. So, for example, if my desire for a weapon to fend off intruders results in my buying a length of seasoned ash and carving a baseball bat-shaped bludgeon out of it, the produced item does have the derived proper function of fending off intruders. But if, instead, I buy a standard model Louisville Slugger from a sporting goods store with this same purpose in mind, it does not have the derived proper function of fending off intruders. It has, on the one hand, the direct proper function of hitting baseballs, and on the other hand, the *system* function of fending off intruders if I use it for that purpose and it works. So, on Millikan's account, too, the intentions of designers are efficacious in a way the intentions of users are not. Designers' intentions are sufficient to endow their products with derived proper functions, which are full-fledged proper functions with all the Normative characteristics of direct proper functions. Users' intentions, on the other hand, are not sufficient to establish derived proper functions, although presumably Millikan would agree with Houkes and Vermaas that a user-originated system function might become a direct proper function over the course of time, and with a suitable history of selection and reproduction. But like Houkes and Vermaas, Millikan vouchsafes no explanation or justification for this privileging of designers' intentions over users' intentions.

To summarize, the novel prototype problem arises from the intuition that novel prototypes have proper functions. But the usual proper-function analysis in terms of a history of selection and reproduction is blocked. The accounts we have been considering solve this problem in what seems like the only possible way—by maintaining that designers' intentions are sufficient to endow novel prototypes with proper functions. But this move creates a new problem. It would be natural to think that if designers' intentions are sufficient for establishing proper functions, so, too, are innovative users' intentions. But both the accounts that we have examined deny this. This is because they seek to preserve the phenomenologically well-grounded distinction between proper functions and system functions. For if users' intentions *were* sufficient for proper functions on the same footing as designers' intentions, virtually *all* functions in material culture would be proper functions (Preston 1998b). In other words, it seems that in order to ascribe proper functions to novel prototypes *and* simultaneously maintain the distinction between proper function and system function, designers' intentions must be privileged over users' intentions. But neither of the accounts we have been considering provides any independent grounding for this claim of privilege. Thus, it is either an unreflective assumption or an *ad hoc* stipulation. Moreover, if it should turn out that this claim of privilege ought to be rejected on independent grounds, we would be back in the position of having to choose between ascribing proper functions to novel prototypes on the one hand, or maintaining a distinction between proper functions and system functions on the other (Preston 2003).

So what independent grounds might there be for privileging designers' intentions? You might expect an intentionalist approach to look first for some qualitative difference between designers' intentions and users' intentions. One possibility, for instance, is that designers' intentions are cognitively distinct from innovative users' intentions. But it is hard to see what cognitive difference there could be, since designers and innovative users alike are commonly thought to engage in means-end deliberation resulting in a plan, which is then executed. From a formal point of view, then, it looks like there is no cognitive difference between the intentions of users and designers. But what about the content of their deliberations and plans? Houkes and Vermaas (2004) suggest there is one difference—the intentions of designers involve not only a use plan but a 'description of a type of artifact' (58). This is a bit vague, but what they most likely have in mind is a construction plan for an artifact. Thus, the intentions of designers would contain two plans—a use plan and a construction plan—whereas the intentions of users would consist only of a use plan. Unfortunately, this is not going to yield a principled difference either, because innovative users do often modify the items they use. For example, I cut up non-recyclable plastic cups and containers to make plant labels. This is not a matter of design—the bought ones are pretty much better, and mine are extremely variable in size, shape and efficacy. Rather it is a matter of not having to buy labels on the one hand, and getting some use out of frustratingly non-recyclable plastic stuff on the other. No doubt, there is a continuum here. Some innovative use involves nothing more than relocation or repositioning of an unmodified artifact for a new use, whereas other cases involve considerable modification—reconstruction, if you like. But the point is that innovative use plans are often accompanied by what is for all practical intents and purposes a construction plan, just as designers' use plans are. So, there does not seem to be any principled difference along these lines in the content of the intentions guiding standard and non-standard use.

If cognitive features do not distinguish designers' intentions from users' intentions, perhaps there is some measure of creativity that might distinguish them. For instance, it might be suggested that designing is privileged creatively, in that it brings something new into the world—at least in the case of novel prototypes—whereas use simply operates with what is already there.

But on this score, it seems even clearer that no principled difference exists. Designers, we said, may be creative in two ways. They may design something to serve a novel function, or they may design something to serve an existing function in an entirely novel way. With regard to the latter, it seems clear that designers are in no way more creative than are innovative users. Consider the recent innovative and devastatingly effective use of fully fueled airliners to implement the existing function of incendiary bombs, for instance. Such novel implementations of existing functions probably account for most instances of novel prototypes, as well as most instances of innovative use. Moreover, innovative uses can also involve novel functions. Consider the first food cans, for instance. No provision was made by the designers for opening these cans, and as Henry Petroski (1992) reports in a chapter aptly entitled 'Closure Before Opening,' the original military users of these cans resorted to 'knives, bayonets, and even rifle fire' (185–86). Here, a novel function is being carried out by innovative use of existing items of material culture. In short, the same kinds of creativity exhibited in the design of novel prototypes are also exhibited in innovative use. So here again, there do not seem to be any grounds for privileging designers' intentions over users' intentions.

But a deeper problem stems from the requirement, inherent in this view, that there be a bright line distinction between design and innovative use. In order to privilege designers' intentions, we have to be able to distinguish design contexts from innovative use contexts in a reliable manner. And the problem is that designing typically proceeds *via* innovative use. The history of Post-it notes again supplies a clear example. For several years, the engineer who originated the not-so-sticky adhesive fruitlessly tried to convince product developers at 3M to consider it as a spray or coating for bulletin boards. Another engineer heard one of these presentations, and it was he who came up with the innovative use of the adhesive as a backing for notepad slips. Here we see the importance of the fact that design processes are typically collaborative. This means that something designed by one agent for one purpose can be used innovatively by another agent for another purpose in the context of designing something else.

This is only a special case of the fact that designers typically make innovative use of pre-existing components. For example, the designers of the first electric guitars had almost all the main components they needed—including, of course, guitars:

> For amateur inventors all the technology required to increase the guitar's volume was readily at hand. They were not dealing with revolutionary new concepts but with equipment they had been playing with for years: microphones, record players, radios, and vacuum tubes. The technological pieces were all around them, waiting to be put into place. Even musicians were taking microphones apart and attaching them to guitars. Others were taking the magnets and coils from telephone receivers to make pickups. Amplifiers were being fashioned out of parts of

radio sets and record players. Les Paul was not the only experimenter who took the pickup of an electrified phonograph and jammed it into the strings of a guitar to amplify the sound of the strings. [George] Beauchamp got hold of a Brunswick phonograph, took the pickup out, extended the wires, and mounted it on a 2-by-4-inch block of wood with a single string. (Millard 2004, 47)

Here we see the importance of the fact that design processes are not just typically collaborative, but universally social, in the sense that they are dependent on pre-existing social and cultural resources. Design and invention are not a matter of creation *ex nihilo* resulting in radical novelty, but rather of incremental improvements or extensions of existing material culture resulting in relative novelty.

Let us sum up the discussion so far. First, we observed that the privilege of designers' intentions is not grounded in any qualitative differences between their intentions and those of innovative users. Then we observed that all design involves use, since designers depend on the material and practical resources of the surrounding culture. So, in principle, a design process could consist of nothing but standard and innovative uses of pre-existing technologies and devices. The design of the first solid-body electric guitars may well be an example. This makes a bright line distinction between design and innovative use impossible to draw in a principled way, and so casts doubt on the assumption that there is a theoretically significant distinction to be had here at all. And without a theoretically significant distinction to start with, any attempt to distinguish design from innovative use for the purpose of claiming some sort of privilege for designers' intentions begins to look like a rather quixotic enterprise.

At this point, then, in addition to the question of why designers' intentions should be regarded as privileged, we also have the prior question of why there is such a strong tendency to assume a bright line distinction between design and innovative use in the first place. A closer look at the invention of the solid-body electric guitar will put us on the right track to answer both of these questions.[1] It is pretty clear that no one person or integral group of people designed and built the first solid-body electric guitar. The motivation for developing such an instrument was practically universal among both players and manufacturers, because guitarists were struggling to make their instruments heard in the dancehall bands of the time. Electric amplification was the obvious way to go. But attempts to simply electrify hollow-body acoustic guitars did not meet with much success, due to interference effects between the electric and the acoustic amplification. So solid-body guitars depending solely on electric amplification were also a fairly obvious way to go. The result was a lot of people separately working along the same lines. Some of them were performing musicians, such as Les Paul. Some, like Paul Bigsby and Leo Fender, were individual craftspersons and/or entrepreneurs. And some, like the Gibson guitar company, were established instrument manufacturers with teams of designers and engineers at their disposal. But if you ask the person in the street who invented the solid-body electric guitar, you will almost certainly get one of three names: Les Paul, Leo Fender, or Adolph Rickenbacker. Not coincidentally, all three of these individuals eventually lent their names to a line of electric guitars. But, in all three cases other, less-well-known individuals also had a hand in the design of the guitars. Les Paul's case is instructive. He built, and sometimes played in public, a primitive solid-body electric guitar he called 'the Log,' because the central element of it was simply a length of four-by-four. Early on, he took this prototype to the Gibson company in an effort to interest them in developing a more-refined instrument based on his ideas, but Gibson was not receptive. Then Leo Fender put out the Fender Telecaster, the first solid-body electric guitar to be mass-produced rather than custom made. Observing the Telecaster's growing popularity, Gibson had their engineers design a solid-body electric guitar from the ground up, and then sought out Les Paul as a design consultant who would also lend his (even then famous) name to their product. It is terminally unclear how much Paul actually contributed to the design of the Gibson Les Paul—Gibson and Les Paul have somewhat different accounts of this—but it may, in fact, have been very little. Thus, although Paul designed and built several prototype solid-body electric guitars on his own, and although he is officially the designer of the first Gibson Les Paul electric guitars, it is almost certainly the Gibson team of engineers who were responsible for most of its design. And no one but a music historian would now be able to name any of the individuals who worked on this project for Gibson other than Les Paul.[2]

André Millard (2004, 42) suggests that the reason for this is that only some of the people involved fit the nineteenth-century image of the 'heroic inventor'—the individual who succeeds in accomplishing great technological feats through sheer persistence and ingenuity. Les Paul fits this image, for example, whereas the Gibson employees do not. Extending Millard's line of thought here, we may note that a more recent avatar of the heroic inventor is the highly educated, highly paid design engineer, wearing a white coat and inhabiting a laboratory replete with gleaming instruments. We have a stereotype of the designer based not so much on their actual design activity as on other aspects of their social role and associated social status. Les Paul gets to be one of the major figures in the invention of the solid-body electric guitar less because of having designed and built 'the Log' than because of his preeminence as a performer, for example. Thus, privileged social roles involving fame, wealth, education, access to sophisticated technology, and so on influence who is identified as a designer in the first place. Arguably, then, it is the prior privilege attaching to these roles that also grounds assumptions about the privileged position of designers *vis-à-vis* the establishment of proper functions in material culture.

This analysis poses a serious difficulty for the intentionalist view. Social roles and their associated privileges do little or nothing to make manifest actual facts about human activity. Indeed, they are often the operative factor in masking such facts from the view of both the person in the street and the investigator in the academy. To mention just one egregious example, the nature of women's work as well as its economic importance and social value have until only recently been routinely masked by the privilege accorded to men's work. So, the privilege accorded a particular social role in a particular culture is in general not a firm foundation for theory construction in science or philosophy.

Furthermore, there is reason to believe that the social role of designer and the privilege attaching to it is specific to recent Western culture, raising the additional worry of parochialism. One line of evidence for this has already been broached in the form of Millard's suggestion that current ways of understanding the design and production of material culture owe more to lingering nineteenth-century preoccupations with heroic individualism and genius than to actual observation or historical research (2004). Another line of evidence pointing in the same direction comes from Plato and Aristotle, who make a distinction between user and maker, but delineate no separate role for the designer. Here is Plato on flute making, for instance:

> It's wholly necessary, therefore, that a user of each thing has most experience of it and that he tell a maker which of his products performs well or badly in actual use. A flute-player, for example, tells a flute-maker about the flutes that respond well in actual playing and prescribes what kind of flutes he is to make, while the maker follows his instructions. (*Republic* 601d–e)

Aristotle is even more explicit, associating knowledge of form and function with the user, and knowledge of materials and construction techniques with the maker (*Physics* 194a35–194b10).

Thus, for Plato and Aristotle, the designer's role is, in effect, just an aspect of the user's role, and not a separate activity or capacity at all. Consequently, for them there is not even a marked difference between the designer and the *ordinary* user, let alone the innovative user. Every user is potentially a designer, in virtue of the kind of knowledge involved in use. Thus, just as the ancient Greeks did not recognize any significant distinction between art and craft the way we do—it was all *techne* to them—so they did not recognize any significant distinction between design and use. This suggests that the assumptions of the intentionalist view as to the existence of a bright line distinction between the designer role and the user role and as to the privilege of the former do not reflect natural cleavages or features of the phenomena, but rather some parochial, entrenched ways of thinking about certain social roles and who is or is not a candidate for filling them.

We can carry this line of argument a step further. There is a fundamental assumption built into the intentionalist theories that we have been considering—the assumption that novel prototypes *must* be construed as having proper functions. This is a strong intuition in many quarters, but what grounds it? One motivation might be the fact that non-novel prototypes uncontroversially have proper functions. The prototype of next year's Ford Mustang, for instance, has the proper functions associated with previous models, and with cars in general. But then it has been copied, with minor changes, from last year's model, so it gets its proper functions in the ordinary way, in virtue of its history of reproduction from ancestors that performed those functions successfully. So, it is not clear why the proper functionality of such non-novel prototypes has any bearing on the functionality of novel prototypes, which are novel precisely because they *lack* a history of reproduction from relevantly similar and successful ancestors. And this is a feature they share with innovatively used items of material culture, which may well have a history of reproduction, but not for the use to which they are now being put. So, why not just classify novel prototypes with innovative uses and analyze them the same way, since these phenomena have more relevant features in common than non-novel and novel prototypes do?

In defense, the intentionalist might argue that what makes designers' intentions special is just that designers intend the items they design to have proper functions, whereas innovative users do not so intend with regard to the items they use. In other words, in addition to aspects concerned with the features and construction of the item, the complex intentions of designers' may include a 'founding' intention with regard to proper function. But there are two problems with this claim. First, there is no guarantee that the intentions of individuals independently identified as designers or users will have or lack such a founding intention, as required. The complex intentions of both designers and innovative users have in common the intention that the item fulfill a certain purpose. Consider two people pouring a brown liquid into saucers and placing them in the garden to trap slugs. In one case, the brown liquid is beer; in the other case it is designer slug bait—a mixture of secret ingredients prepared in accordance with a carefully guarded formula. In both cases, the brown liquid is supposed to trap slugs and is so intended by the pourer. So, the founding intention must be something over and above the envisioned purpose. Perhaps the designer intending to establish a proper function must in addition intend to promulgate this purpose in some way—intend to communicate the use plan, as Houkes and Vermaas suggest, for instance, or intend to reproduce the item. But then it seems that the intentions of independently identified designers and users really do not have or lack founding intentions, as required. People often design and make items for their own idiosyncratic and sometimes transient purposes, with no thought of either communicating the design or reproducing the item for use by others. Professional inventors are proverbially prone to filling their living spaces with such one-off devices, for instance. On the other hand, innovative users often *do* communicate the new use and/or encourage the reproduction of the item for this new use. Gardening techniques like the use of beer for slug bait provide a good example. The pages of popular gardening magazines—not to mention innumerable websites—are rife with reports of such innovative uses and recommendations to others to adopt them. Arguably, then, founding intentions are neither universal among designers nor lacking among innovative users.

Second, and more importantly, such founding intentions are problematic in and of themselves. On the intentionalist view, they are infallible in the sense that what is intended cannot fail to be achieved. In other words, all a designer has to do to endow a novel prototype with a proper function is to intend that it have that function, and straightaway it has it. The problem is that we normally think of intentions as intrinsically subject to failure or frustration. Their successful execution depends on how the world is, not just on our mental state. I may intend to make a device that opens cans, but that does not ensure that it will. But on the intentionalist view, my intending it to have the proper function of opening cans does ensure that it has that proper function. There are, indeed, some intentions that cannot fail to achieve what is intended—intending to form a specific intention, for example, or intending to try to do something. In both cases, the intention must be a present-directed intention, though, for a future-directed intention of the same type can fail. For example, suppose that in the middle of the afternoon I form an intention to try to make a soufflé for dinner (having never made one before and having heard they are tricky), but I am too exhausted on arriving home from work to even try, and I go straight to bed without eating. I not only fail to make a soufflé for dinner in this case, I fail to try to make one. On the other hand, if I form a present-directed intention to try to make a soufflé forthwith, I may fail to make the soufflé, but I can hardly fail to try.

Present-directed intentions to form an intention or to try cannot fail to achieve what they intend because they merely shadow the very intention now being formed or the very activity now being attempted. Thus, they are infallible, but in a trivial sense. They have no substantive, independent content that could be frustrated by the world. Intending that an item you have designed have a particular proper function, however, does have substantive, independent content. It is substantive, because a proper function is what a thing is supposed to do; what it can be faulted for not doing; what you, as its designer, can be sued for not having ensured that it can actually do; what other users are supposed to conform their actions to on pain of voiding the warranty, and so on. And it is independent, since the thing may not be capable of performing the proper function you intend it to perform. In short, on the intentionalist view, even if the thing does not look the way you intend it to look, or work the way you intend it to work, it still has the proper function you intend it to have, no doubt about it. So if a designer intends a proper function for something she has designed, she is not just engaging in internal self-management, as in the case of present-directed intending to intend or intending to try. Rather she is creating a public Norm by fiat.

This is quite an extraordinary claim on the part of intentionalist theories. A close analogy to this kind of prerogative vested in ordinary individuals might be the naming prerogative you have with regard to your children, pets, or boats.[3] The names you give them are the names they have, the names others are to call them by, the names that go on legal documents, and so on. But even in this case, the world can frustrate your intentions. There may be legal or religious restrictions on allowable names, for instance. Or the person officially recording your choice of name may make a mistake. Or it may turn out that you are not legally or socially in a position to give a name to the child, pet, or boat in question. But apparently, nothing at all can frustrate your intention that a thing that you have designed have a certain proper function. Knock two sticks together, call yourself a designer, and you get to say what the proper function of the two-stick device is, without let or hindrance. Another close analogy might be to sports umpires, whose calls cannot be appealed.[4] The play is taken to be whatever the umpire says it is, and the game continues on that basis. But here again, the disanalogies weigh more heavily. An umpire is treated as infallible for the purposes of regulating the playing of the game. But everyone is aware that umpires are not, in fact, infallible—they can and do make mistakes, which are then discussed at great length in the sports news. What is extraordinary about the claim that designers' intentions are privileged, then, is that these intentions cannot in principle be frustrated at all. In other words, the right analogy would be to umpires who were, in fact, infallible.

So founding intentions have two strikes against them. First of all, they do not seem to be either universally present in the complex intentions of certifiable designers or universally lacking in the complex intentions of innovative users, so even if they exist they may not serve the intentionalist's purpose. Second, even if we assume they exist and exhibit the required pattern, in order to guarantee that novel prototypes have proper functions the founding intentions of designers must be infallible. This renders designers' intentions uncomfortably unique in comparison to intentions in general. In short, the appeal to designers' intentions is, in fact, rife with difficulties at least as knotty as the novel prototype problem this appeal is supposed to solve.

Fortunately, there is a simpler and more workable alternative. We can disregard our intuitions and stop insisting that novel prototypes have proper functions. Indeed, this is what we should do, since, as we discovered above, the antecedents of this insistence are suspect. Instead, we can analyze novel prototypes the same way as novel uses of existing items. If the novel prototype or innovatively used item performs successfully, it has a system function. A novel prototype or innovatively used item that does not perform successfully has no function, either proper or system. In the course of time, the copies of a novel prototype that is reproduced and proliferates on account of its successful performance acquire a proper function, just as a novel use of an existing item may become a proper function over the course of time. This alternative is non-intentionalist, in the sense that it appeals to systematic material culture contexts, on the one hand, and processes of reproduction, on the other hand, rather than to the unmediated intentions of individuals. It has the signal advantage of preserving the phenomenologically well-attested parallels between design and innovative use. In particular, it does not run afoul of the fact that much of what is classified as design actually consists of innovative uses of various sorts. But most importantly, from our point of view, it preserves the phenomenologically and theoretically well-grounded distinction between proper function and system function which is threatened by intentionalist theories should they fail—as we have argued they do fail—to articulate a real and significant difference between users' intentions and designers' intentions.

PHANTOM FUNCTIONS

But even if it fails for the novel prototype problem, the intentionalist approach is not dead. The phantom function problem seems to require an appeal to the intentions of individuals. Phantom functions are cases where an item of material culture is constitutionally incapable of performing a function it is widely taken to have. *Fengshui* mirrors are taken to deflect bad *qi,* bug zappers are taken to reduce local mosquito populations, rabbits' feet are taken to bring good luck, vitamin C is taken to prevent colds, and so on. These uses have all the earmarks of proper functions. In particular, the utilized items are often reproduced and marketed for these precise purposes. But their reproduction cannot be contingent on actual successful performance of the alleged function if they are not in fact capable of this performance. So, the reproduction of such items must be contingent on something other than actual success. The phantom function problem, thus, parallels the novel prototype problem in that there is an insistence on an analysis in terms of proper function in both cases. But the frustration of this insistence is different. In the case of novel prototypes, there is no history of reproduction at all to underwrite the analysis, whereas in the case of phantom functions the history of reproduction is pathological.

In an earlier paper, I proposed solving this problem without any appeal to the intentions of designers or users:

> Do we want to say that artifacts reproduced largely on the basis of such illusory success have the relevant proper functions or not? Alternatively, should we say that they do have a proper function, but just not the one they are popularly perceived as having? I think this second tack is the right one to take. Bug zappers *are* successful at killing lots of flying insects. It is that real success which underwrites their reproduction, because it allows the illusion that they are killing a lot of mosquitos, and thus ridding the vicinity of them, to take root . . . In other words, the artifact case is the same as the biological case in that reproduction is contingent on a successful performance, and it is that performance which establishes the thing's proper function . . . But people can be, and often are, mistaken about what an artifact does successfully, and this leads to a mistaken attribution of proper function. (Preston 1998b, 245–46)

But this proposal will not work. On this view, phantom functions are not real functions at all—they are simply mistaken attributions of function to things that in reality have a different function altogether. This does have the virtue of preserving successful performance as the basis of the reproduction that in turn underwrites proper function. But one problem is that it does not work at all for cases such as the rabbit's foot amulet, which does not do anything much, other than possibly weighing down the pocket or the keychain of its possessor. A second problem is that this proposal conflates the phantom function with an obvious ordinary function in some cases. *Fengshui* mirrors do what ordinary mirrors do, and with this proposal that would be their only real function. This does nothing to explain why people make them, acquire them, or use them for purposes quite different from those reserved for ordinary mirrors. Moreover, the connection between reflecting things (the ordinary proper function) and deflecting bad *qi* and evil spirits (the phantom function) is at best metaphorical, whereas the connection between killing a lot of flying insects and killing a lot of mosquitos is clearly causal, even if equally mistaken. In the case of the bug zapper, then, it is easy to see how a mistaken attribution of function might occur. It is very hard to see how there could be any such simple mistake in the *fengshui* mirror case. In short, the fatal problem for this proposal is that on the face of it, phantom functions *are* proper functions and not just fantastical parasites on items with some other proper function.[5]

The failure of this non-intentionalist solution makes an intentionalist approach seem more attractive. Perhaps the best way to account for phantom functions is not in terms of what their bearers actually do, but what they are believed or perceived to do. Paul Griffiths has proposed a solution along these lines to a problem he says is specific to material culture:

> Consider the tapered tail of an old racing car. This feature is intended to streamline the car, to reduce its drag coefficient. But it does not do this, and nor have any of the other designs it has 'evolved' from. They are all based on a false theory about drag. It is hard to see how there could be a selective explanation of a trait of this kind. There have, it seems, been no episodes when it has performed well, and hence been selected. This type of situation cannot arise with biological functions. Natural selection can only operate on a trait in virtue of something it actually does. (Griffiths 1993, 420–21)

This is, of course, the phantom function problem. In order to solve it within his selectionist view, Griffiths resorts to a thoroughly intentionalist consideration—what goes on in the designer's head during the design process:

> The solution to this difficulty is . . . to create a more abstract notion of 'selective process' by allowing selection amongst hypothetical alternatives. This selection amongst hypothetical alternatives occurs in a hypothetical environment constituted by the beliefs of the designer. When the

designer has false beliefs about the real world, this results in artifacts functioning well in his hypothetical environment when they do not function in the real environment. The tail of the facing [*sic*] car did perform its function, but only in the mind of its designer. (Griffiths 1993, 421)

In the case of non-phantom functions, this imagined selection process would be grounded in a set of relevant and correct beliefs about the world, so the imagined success or failure would correspond to actual success or failure. But in the case of phantom functions, some or all of the beliefs about the world are false, and imagined success then corresponds to actual failure. In many cases, no doubt, the actual failure will be apparent, and will send the designer back to the drawing board. But sometimes the world does not clearly give the lie to the imagined success. The designer then persists in his illusion, and a full-fledged proper function results. The advantage of this intentionalist account over my non-intentionalist one is that by simply substituting selection based on imagined success rather than actual success, the phenomenological status of phantom functions as real functions is preserved.

But Griffiths's proposal will not work, either. The phantom function problem is not, as he suggests, the problem of seeing how a selection-based explanation could work without any successful performances to operate on, but, rather, the more general problem of how any account that involves *reproduction* could work without appeal to successful performance, because reproduction in the face of consistent failure would be arbitrary or irrational. This shows that the heart of Griffiths's proposal is not the imaginary selection process, or even the false beliefs about the world that are involved in it, but only the false perception of successful performance. It does not even really matter exactly how that perception of success is generated. In particular, it need not depend on the falsity of any beliefs about the world. A false perception of success could be generated by wishful thinking, for example. So extrapolating from the details of Griffiths's solution, an intentionalist solution to the phantom function problem simply says: If we substitute perceived success for actual success, we can account for phantom functions in exactly the same way we account for any other proper function. The fact that in some cases the perception is veridical and in other cases mistaken is an external consideration that need not concern us.

But this very elegant, general solution runs into difficulty, because it implicitly assumes that only a sincerely mistaken assessment of performance on the part of the designer could possibly account for the reproduction of an item of material culture that does not actually do what it is supposed to do. The intuition behind this assumption is that since material culture is produced to satisfy human needs, and since human beings are on the whole rational, only sincerely mistaken perceptions of success could account for the ubiquity in material culture of items that do not actually succeed in fulfilling the needs they are supposed to fulfill. But this intuition fails to take into account the actual complexities of human social relationships and interactions in the reproduction and circulation of material culture. Let us first consider the designer. As Marx pointed out in *Capital,* in any economic system of any sophistication, items of material culture not only have use values, they have exchange values—that is, they are commodities. And for a person with a commodity to sell, its use value is of little interest. Indeed, it need not have any use value for him, so long as it does have use value for the buyer. If a designer designs a coat and makes six of them, but only needs one for herself, the other five have no use value for her but do have exchange value insofar as they have use value for others. Similarly, if the coat is of a type used exclusively by women and the designer is a man, none of them have use value for him under ordinary circumstances, but they all have exchange value insofar as they have use value for female consumers. Because of this slippage between use value and exchange value, a designer of commodities may even be motivated to produce something he himself believes to have *no* real use value—that is, to have *no* capacity for success-ful performance with regard to its alleged function. The only thing that matters is whether he can persuade other people to buy it. And of course the designer may engage in deceptive or fraudulent marketing practices to induce them to do so. Examples are legion: From the snake oil salesmen of yesteryear, to the captains of the contemporary cosmetics industry, the ques-tion in the designer's mind often enough is not 'Does it work?' but 'Will it sell?' Thus, perception of success on the part of the designer is by no means a necessary accompaniment of the design process. Consequently, a solution to the phantom function problem that depends on designers' perceptions of success will have to treat differently a product sincerely believed by its designer to work as advertised and a product believed or known outright *not* to work. This solution will have to say that the product in the first case has a perfectly good (phantom) proper function, whereas the product in the second case has *no* function at all. But this is hardly satisfactory, especially since the two cases might be identical in all details except for the designer's personal assessment of performance. Thus, sincerely mistaken perceptions of successful performance on the part of the designer cannot be counted on to occur, and as a result many phantom functions will not be accounted for.

But perhaps the problem here is Griffiths's focus on the designer. Perhaps the more general solution is viable so long as the *users* of the commodity perceive it to perform successfully. This would accord better with our discus-sion of the novel prototype problem, which traced the failure of intentionalist solutions in that case to an overemphasis on the designer and a concomitant neglect of the user. A user-oriented solution to the phantom function prob-lem, then, would hold that the intentions and beliefs of the designer *qua* designer are not relevant to the establishment of a phantom function. Instead, what is relevant is a history of reproduction that, in turn, is dependent on user demand. And users will not continue to demand an item unless they believe it to perform its function successfully. In the case of normal proper functions, users are right about the success of this performance. But in some cases, users are systematically mistaken about the success of the performance, and then a phantom proper function results. As in the designer-oriented version of the solution, we may hold that whether the perception of success is veridical or mistaken is an external consideration that is not relevant to the establishment and maintenance of the proper function.

But there are difficulties here, too. We may begin with the simple observation that the requirement cannot be that *all* the users of a product perceive it to be successful. There are all sorts of motivations and reasons for the acquisition and use of products, and they are not necessarily contingent on a belief in the successful performance of the alleged proper function. Thus, the user demand that drives reproduction may not all spring from a perception of the successful performance of an item's proper function. For example:

- Users often acquire products in order to try them out. They may have no firm conviction one way or another whether they will work, or they may be outright skeptical about this. All they need is sufficient motivation to take a chance, or at least a lack of motivation to refrain. ('It's only $4.99. What the hell!')
- Users sometimes acquire items of material culture for purposes other than their proper function, that is, for system-functional purposes. Here again, they need have no conviction about whether an item is successful in performing its proper function, or they may be skeptical about this. ('I can't imagine this rabbit's foot will have any effect on my luck. But it will make a really interesting pull for my ceiling fan.') The only exception would be in cases where the success of the system-functional performance depends on the success of the proper-functional performance. ('Vitamin C prevents colds, so it should prevent flu—after all they are both caused by viruses.')
- Many items of material culture have more than one proper function. Users may acquire items for their successful performance of one of these functions, while having no conviction as to their successful performance of their other functions. ('I don't think this rabbit's foot will bring me luck, but it's a really cool souvenir of my trip to Las Vegas.')
- An important phenomenon that might constitute a subcategory of either the system-function or the multiple-function category is the acquisition of items of material culture for aesthetic purposes. ('I don't believe in demons or bad *qi*, but it's a really nice mirror and it will fit right in with the Chinese theme in the living room.')
- Users often acquire and use items of material culture as a matter of adhering to tradition. ('I don't believe in demons or bad *qi*, but I do want my house to be set up in accordance with the traditions of *fengshui*.')
- Users often acquire and use items of material culture in response to peer pressure of various sorts. ('I don't think rabbit's foot amulets really bring good luck, but everybody who is anybody has one.')

- Users often acquire and use items of material culture in deference to authority. ('I don't believe Vitamin C really prevents colds, but my doctor insists it does, so I take it.')
- Conversely, users may acquire and use items of material culture as a protest against authority. ('I don't believe this mirror will deflect bad *qi,* but putting it up in a conspicuous position over the front door shows I don't give a damn for the state orthodoxy.')[6]

What this list shows us is that just as there is slippage between perception of success and the designing of items of material culture, so there is slippage between perception of success and their use. And the slippage can be substantial. Items of material culture do serve human needs, right enough, but those needs are heterogeneous, multiple, and shifting. Thus, needs are connected to what we think of as the proper functions of items of material culture in very complex, and sometimes very tenuous, ways. Consequently, perception of success in the performance of those proper functions is not necessarily the predominant factor driving demand and reproduction.

But there is an obvious objection the intentionalist can make here that is not available in the case of the designer. If the whole weight of a proper function ultimately rests on a designer's perception of its successful performance, then the slippage only has to affect that one individual to derail the establishment of the proper function. But users are multiple, both in the horizontal plane of contemporary use and in the vertical plane of historical use. So it might be objected that in the case of the user-based solution, the slippage cannot derail the establishment of the proper function. So long as *some* users at *some* point in the history of reproduction perceive the item to perform successfully, that is all that is needed. And surely cases in which an item has been reproduced and has proliferated even though *no* users at all perceived it to perform successfully must be vanishingly rare. Pursuing this line would require some further work, of course. For instance, we would have to answer the Sodom-and-Gomorrah-like question of whether just *one* believing user would be enough, or if not one, then how many? We may agree that this number need not be very precise, but we would still need to say what sort of a pattern of perception of success among users would be required. In addition, we would need to say something about cases like rabbit's foot amulets, which may once have been widely believed to bring good luck, but which now are almost certainly being reproduced without any significant number of users really perceiving them to be successful in that respect. Perhaps we should say that attracting good luck used to be their proper function back in the day, but that now their only proper function is as tourist souvenirs, and it is their successful performance in this role, which is now accounting for their reproduction.

This user-oriented intentionalist option would require some complicated maneuvering with regard to the details. But this is no reason to rule it out, in principle. There are considerations weighing against it from another direction, though. We must remind ourselves that the *reason* for appealing to perceptions of success was to account for the reproduction of items of material culture through which proper functions are established. In particular, this appeal seemed to be required to account for reproduction establishing phantom functions, because reproduction in such cases cannot be explained by any real success. But as we have just seen, people have a variety of reasons and motivations for designing, making, acquiring, and using items of material culture—reasons and motivations that are often independent of assessments of success in performance of the erstwhile proper function. But this means that the perception of success in performing the function cannot by itself explain the reproduction of material culture, because it is only one factor among many that may be required for such an explanation. It is not necessarily even the predominant factor. And if it cannot explain reproduction, it cannot serve as the ultimate anchor for phantom proper function, as required by Griffiths's account.

The objector might reply that this picture is not as bleak as it looks. We already are aware that items of material culture often have more than one proper function. Perhaps each reason or motivation is really connected to a different proper function of the item. We tend to focus on the more narrowly utilitarian functions of items of material culture, but as we noted in Chapter 5, items of material culture also have sociofunctions and ideofunctions in addition to technofunctions (Schiffer 1992). A throne, for example, has the technofunction that all chairs have—supporting human beings in a seated position. But it also has the ideofunction of representing royal power and authority. A diamond engagement ring, on the other hand, does not have any obvious technofunction, but it does have the sociofunction of marking the person wearing it as engaged to be married. Similarly, a screwdriver has the technofunction of driving in screws, but no obvious sociofunction or ideofunction. Some items of material culture have all three types of functions. A white bridal gown has the technofunctions of any other dress, but it also has the sociofunction of marking the person wearing it as the bride, and its white color represents purity or virginity. This tripartite distinction is orthogonal to the proper function-system function distinction we have been operating with in the last two chapters (Preston 2000). A technofunction can be either a proper function or a system function, and similarly for sociofunctions and ideofunctions. For example, a perfectly ordinary chair with only its usual proper technofunction might be adopted by a person of power and authority as her regular seat, and might thus come to have the system ideofunction of representing her power and authority among her followers, whereas a seat that is made to be a throne has representing power and authority as a proper ideofunction.

In light of this, the intentionalist might argue that the reasons and motivations the users have for acquiring and using an item of material culture are typically connected not with its technofunction(s), but with sociofunctions or ideofunctions. Consider, for example, the *fengshui* practitioner who recommends a mirror over the front door to his clients only because he has a stockpile of mirrors to sell, and not because he believes that these mirrors really deflect bad *qi*. It might be argued that this practitioner does perceive the mirrors to be successful in the performance of a sociofunction—the function of being a commodity. Similarly, the client who buys and puts up a mirror may be interested only in an ideofunction—manifesting his resistance to the state orthodoxy—which he perceives the mirror to perform successfully. The intentionalist could then argue that the reproduction of items of material culture does ultimately depend on perception of success in performance of their proper functions, but since these functions are multiple, so are the reasons and motivations individuals have for acquiring and using these items. The reproduction of an item of material culture thus depends on contributions from a number of different directions reflecting its various proper functions. But the factor that accounts for the contribution to reproduction made by each of these proper functions is still perception of success in performing that function. So, the overall account for any particular item is more complicated only because there are more proper functions involved than we might have thought, and not because perception of success is swamped by other considerations.

But this move will at best buy the intentionalist some time. The problem is that most of the alleged proper functions involved are not what we usually think of as proper functions. Being a commodity, for instance, is certainly a role items of material culture play in certain kinds of economies. But in those economies pretty much *everything* is in principle a commodity, including raw materials and even, sometimes, people. So, it does not seem appropriate to say this is the specific proper function of any of them. The commodities that are items of material culture do have proper functions, but connected with their specific uses, not to their generic exchangeability. Similarly, while it is true that sometimes particular items of material culture acquire the proper ideofunction of signifying resistance to authority, in many cases it is not a particular type of thing but rather a set of practices involving whole suites of things that signifies resistance. This is the case with *fengshui,* for instance. It is the practice of *fengshui* in general that signifies a refusal to accept the centralized and rationalistic control of the government, not the use of *fengshui* mirrors in particular. In short, much of what people do successfully with material culture does not point directly at proper functions. Sometimes it points at system functions, and sometimes it points at more general kinds of projects people have that are not tied very closely to the specific proper functions or system functions of items of material culture.

Where does this leave intentionalist solutions to the phantom function problem? Rather than focusing only on perception of successful performance, it would have to encompass the panoply of motivations and reasons broached above. So, behind every case of reproduction, there would be some complicated, interacting set of motivations and reasons explaining it. The individuals involved would not necessarily entertain the whole set, and different individuals might entertain different subsets. For example, one person might participate in the traditional practices of *fengshui* out of a sincere belief in their efficacy and a desire to follow tradition, while her neighbor might be thoroughly skeptical about their efficacy, but intent on exhibiting resistance to authority by following tradition. Meanwhile, the practitioner they both hire to 'see' *fengshui* for their houses might be in it only for the money. Or partly for the money and partly out of a sincere belief in the efficacy of the practices. And so on. So not only does perception of success-ful performance turn out not to be the sole, or even the predominant inten-tional factor accounting for the reproduction of material culture; we are left instead with multiple and shifting intentional factors that are not very well suited to connect the reproduction of an item clearly with its antecedently identified proper function(s).

In our discussion of the novel prototype problem, we witnessed the break-down of the idea that the intentions of designers are sufficient for establishing proper functions. In consequence, we recommended looking to the subse-quent history of reproduction to establish the proper function. Here we are witnessing the breakdown of the correlative idea that the history of repro-duction is really the history of the intentional states of users—specifically, their intentions that a given item of material culture serve a given purpose, based on their perception that it has performed successfully in that role in the past. So now, we are faced anew with the question: How can we account for phantom functions as full-fledged proper functions if their bearers are never able to perform them?

In the case of novel prototypes, we gave up on the insistence that they have proper functions. But that does not seem like an option in this case, because there is a perfectly good history of reproduction, just as in the case of non-phantom proper functions. What we can give up on here is the idea that the history of reproduction is contingent on successful performance, real or imagined. Instead, we can simply look to the pattern of use to which the item is put, as judged by the actions of users in which it plays some part, including what they are disposed to say in response to the question 'What is that for?' This pattern of use is not going to be univocal, although it should be substantially more so than users' intentions to which it is relatively insen-sitive in somewhat the same way the outcome of a vote is relatively insensi-tive to the intentions of the voters. Out of 10 voters all voting the same way, you might have 10 different sets of reasons and motivations for doing so. But all of the voters are opting for *doing* the same thing, for example, hiring the same job candidate or spending money on the same program. Similarly, the users of rabbit's foot amulets typically do the same thing with them, namely, carry them about their person, as is commonly done with most good luck charms and amulets. People do this whether or not they believe in the effectiveness of these amulets. There will be some anomalies—the person who uses the amulet as a pull for his ceiling fan, for instance, or who buys two and makes them into earrings. But precisely because these are anomalous uses, they are easily categorized as system-functional rather than as proper-functional. On the other hand, in the rabbit's foot amulet case, we may also be witnessing a transition from one proper function to another, as the original use as an amulet gives way to use as a tourist souvenir. Or perhaps what we are witnessing is the addition of a second proper function (tourist souvenir), with the original use (amulet) remaining. And what we would need to do to settle this question is look at the specific patterns of use—where and under what conditions do people acquire these items, and most importantly, what do they do with them after acquiring them? Do they keep them in a drawer with the pictures from their Vegas vacation? Or do they carry them around on their person, and take special care to have them about their person when playing cards, taking exams, and so on?

This proposed solution to the phantom function problem follows up on our solution to the novel prototype problem by appealing to the history of reproduction rather than designers' intentions for the establishment of proper functions. But it specifies in more detail what is involved in a history of reproduction. It is not a matter of users' intentions, but rather of patterns of actual use that contribute significantly to demand for an item of material culture, and thereby drive its reproduction. These patterns of use are not contingent on real success in performance of the erstwhile function, or even upon perceived success, but rather emerge on the basis of a congeries of individual motivations, reasons, beliefs, and so on, that are not necessarily all consistent with each other either across individuals or with regard to particular individuals across time. Patterns of use may, of course, be quite complex in and of themselves. But they are much more clearly connected to the reproduction of items of material culture, on the one hand, and to their functions on the other. In particular, patterns of use point to proper function just as clearly in the case of phantom functions as in the case of non-phantom functions—the proper function is the effect the item of material culture would have to have to make sense of the pattern of use to which it is put. For example, in the case of *fengshui* mirrors, the practice is to put them up over the front door of your house. This is what the person who believes in their efficacy does, but also what the person who is merely following tradition does, and what the person whose interest is in resisting the central authority of the government does. And the best explanation of this practice, given everything we can find out about *fengshui* practices in general, what the users are disposed to say, and so on, is that the mirrors are acquired and placed there to deflect bad *qi*. Whether or not they really do that, and whether or not they are even believed to do that by the majority of their users, is not at issue. What is at issue is what explains the use, which in turn explains the continued reproduction of these items.

At the end of Chapter 5, we proposed a provisional definition of proper function. We must now revise that definition to reflect the conclusion of this chapter that, unlike in biology, successful performance does not account for reproduction in material culture. This requires reformulating the definition in terms of patterns of use rather than in terms of usefulness, because 'useful-ness' implies successful performance:

> A current token of an item of material culture has the proper function of producing an effect of a given type just in case producing this effect (whether it actually does so or not) contributes to the best explanation of the patterns of use to which past tokens of this type of item have been put, and which in turn have contributed to the reproduction of such items.

This new formulation reflects our conclusion that to account for proper function in material culture, we must look first to what people *do*—what uses they make of items of material culture, and how those uses contribute to the reproduction of those items—rather than to the intentions and other intentional states people may have. So just as in Part I our action-theoretic foundations for a philosophy of material culture de-emphasized intention and intentional action, so here in Part II the function-theoretic foundations de-emphasize the role of intention in the establishment of function in mate-rial culture. And in both cases, it is resistance to the centralized control model that ultimately accounts for this de-emphasis. Rather than under-standing action and function as fundamentally mental constructs and so fundamentally in the purview of individual human beings, we have come to understand them as constructed through the constant interaction of indi-viduals with their environment and with each other.

But, even if we now have a viable account of proper function in material culture, we have problematized the notion of reproduction in the process. In Chapter 5, the problem that surfaced was that in material culture reproduc-tion is apparently a matter of *being* reproduced by us. And here in Chapter 6 we have discovered that how we go about doing this is a complicated matter, depending on patterns of use that are very difficult to analyze and that have a fraught relationship with the intentions of individuals. So, in Chapter 7, we will focus on reproduction in material culture. This will bring us back to the theme of sociogenerism we broached in Part I, as we examine more closely the interaction of individual and society in the reproduction of mate-rial culture. The theme of creativity will re-emerge as well, as we consider what leeway the individual retains in light of the social structures embodied in the material culture into which she is born—structures that constrain her use and reproduction of it. Oddly enough, we will also find ourselves mov-ing back in the direction of biology as a model for reproduction in mate-rial culture, in spite of having jettisoned the biologically inspired notions of selection, fitness, and successful performance in the process of constructing an account of proper function in material culture.

7 Reproduction and Innovation

Materialism holds that it is likely that actions determine thoughts at least as often as thoughts determine action, that behavior is a guide for 'culture' at least as often as 'culture' is a guide for behavior.

—Marvin Harris, 'Why a Perfect Knowledge of All the Rules
One Must Know to Act Like a Native Cannot Lead to
the Knowledge of How Natives Act'

The main purpose of this chapter is to examine the crucial phenomenon of reproduction in greater depth. In the course of this examination, the themes of sociogenerism and creativity familiar from the discussion of action theory in Part I emerge as equally central to the discussion of function theory here in Part II. The first section begins with a question about making. This has traditionally been understood in accordance with the centralized control model, as a matter of individual human agents imposing structure and function on raw material, in accordance with their purposes. This sharply distinguishes it from growing, in which structure and function unfold from within rather than being imposed from without. But there is reason to doubt the integrity of this distinction, because the traditional understanding ignores the full extent of the reproduction that takes place in material culture. It is not merely the reproduction of material structures, but of functions, of the human purposes corresponding to those functions, and of particular types of human agents corresponding to the particular configuration of the material culture into which they are born and within which they develop into fully competent adults. Thus, it is just as correct to say that our purposes are imposed on us by the material culture we inhabit, as that we impose our purposes on it. And this means a sociogeneric approach to the reproduction of material culture is required.

The second section begins with a question raised by sociogenerism, which problematizes individual cultural creativity and innovation by emphasizing the extent to which agents are themselves products of their material culture. We can begin to account for innovation by understanding human interaction with material culture from the bottom up, starting with use rather than production. Specifically, while proper-functional use reflects the influence of a pre-existing material culture on the formation of human purposes and ultimately whole human agents, system-functional use reflects the ability of human agents—acting individually or collaboratively—to turn existing items of material culture to relatively novel purposes, and ultimately to change their material culture from the inside. This confirms our conclusion from Part I— social constraints and structures enable the activities of individuals while still leaving them considerable creative leeway to manage those constraints and to change those structures. And it does so by drawing on the account of function in material culture that we worked out in Chapters 5 and 6.

GROWING AND MAKING

In both biology and material culture, we encounter reproduced, functional structures. A time-honored account—traceable, ultimately, to Aristotle— holds that biological structures grow on their own, and that their form and their function are therefore natural to them, whereas cultural structures are made, and their form and function are therefore non-natural, imposed on them by their makers and/or users. Traditionally, then, there is an insistence on a stark difference between biological reproduction and cultural reproduction. Moreover, this difference is traditionally assimilated to the difference between non-intentionalist and intentionalist accounts of function. Biological functions are natural characteristics precisely because these functions do not depend on the intentions of an external, intelligent creator. In contrast, functions in material culture are non-natural characteristics, because they depend entirely on the intentions of intelligent human producers and/or users. The upshot is that making and growing, despite their superficially shared character as processes of reproduction, are understood as essentially different kinds of processes resulting in essentially different kinds of products.

This account is so entrenched as to have the appearance of common sense. But it has recently been challenged by Tim Ingold (2000a, 2000b), who refers to it as the 'standard view.' We will first lay out Aristotle's original version of this view. Ingold does not trace it to Aristotle, but doing so will shed more light on its fundamental structure and assumptions. Then we will examine Ingold's challenge to the most recent version of the standard view. His argument is specifically addressed to the reproduction of structure (morphogenesis) and does not address function. This leaves open the possibility that growing and making might yet be different with regard to the reproduction of function in material culture. But we can employ Ingold's approach to construct a parallel argument challenging the standard view with regard to these functional aspects, as well. Our ultimate conclusion will be that growing and making are more alike than the standard view allows. This opens up the possibility of a fresh approach to the study of reproduction in material culture. But Ingold's argument also has one important weakness that might allow a proponent of the standard view to keep his foot in the door. Specifically, Ingold does not handle the question of the role of mental representations in the activities involved in reproduction in an optimal way. Addressing this weakness will allow us not only to further strengthen Ingold's case against the standard view, but will strengthen our own case for a non-intentionalist account of function in material culture.

Aristotle

Aristotle's concern is to provide an account of nature (*physis*), and he does this in part by contrasting growing with making, that is, nature with culture. The first remark we will consider occurs at the end of an argument demonstrating that there is teleology in nature just as there is in art. Aristotle notes that since the *telos*, or end, determines the intermediate steps leading up to it, growing and making look exactly alike from the outside:

> Thus if a house, e.g., had been a thing made by nature, it would have been made in the same way as it is now by art; and if things made by nature were made not only by nature but also by art, they would come to be in the same way as by nature. (*Physics* 199a10–15)

So, as Tim Ingold (2000a) remarks, if you were an alien visitor from another planet, you would have no particular reason to distinguish a seed sprouting into a plant from a house under construction. But Aristotle thinks they are different, because the causes of the changes are different in the two cases:

> All the things mentioned [animals, plants, elements] plainly differ from things which are *not* constituted by nature. For each of them has within itself a principle of motion and of stationariness . . . On the other hand, a bed and a coat and anything else of that sort, *qua* receiving these designations—i.e. in so far as they are products of art—have no innate impulse to change. (*Physics* 192b10–20)

In the first instance, then, the difference is between internal and external causes of change.

This is linked to a second difference in the origin of the thing:

> Every craft is concerned with coming to be; and the exercise of the craft is the study of how something that admits of being and not being comes to be, something whose origin is in the producer and not in the product. For a craft is not concerned with things that are or come to be by necessity; or with things that are by nature, since these have their origin in themselves. (*Nicomachean Ethics* 1140a10–15)

Now this seems like an odd thing to say about natural things, since it is clear, for instance, that the origin of a seed is a mature plant. But Aristotle's point is that natural things have their origin in other things of the *same type,* whereas products of art do not. As he pointedly remarks, 'man is born from man but not bed from bed' (*Physics* 1935b–10). Thus, natural things share their form, or essence, with their parent(s), whereas products of art do not share their form with their makers. Products of art do *get* their forms from their makers, of course. The maker mentally entertains the formula of the essence of the product, and shapes the product in accordance with it (*Metaphysics* 1032a25–1033a5). Thus, the maker imposes an alien form, whereas a parent transmits a shared form.

There is a similar difference with regard to the matter that realizes the form:

> In the products of art, however, we make the material with a view to the function, whereas in the products of nature the matter is there all along. (*Physics* 194b5–10)

All the matter that makes up the full-grown plant is not in the seed, of course, but the growing plant has the capacity to gather to itself the matter it needs and shape itself into its adult form. The house, on the other hand, depends on the builder to supply the matter and shape it into the completed house.

Finally, there is a difference in the teleology of the two processes. As we noted above, Aristotle thinks the outward similarity of growing and making shows that both nature and art act for an end. But the similarity ends there. Natural teleology and artful teleology are so different that, as André Ariew (2002, 9) suggests, Aristotle really ought to have distinguished them terminologically, as well. Peter McLaughlin (2001, 143–45) supplies us with the requisite terminology—in material culture we have *external* teleology, whereas in biology we have *internal* teleology. The ends of items of material culture are not *their* ends, but rather *ours.* In contrast, the ends of natural things, and in particular the ends of biological organisms, are their own ends—ends they would have in any case, and regardless of any contact with outside intelligent agents.

On Aristotle's view, then, growing is a process engaged in by something that is self-sufficient with regard to its form, its matter, the series of changes required to realize the form in the matter, and the formal and functional ends at which the whole process aims. Making, in contrast, is a process undergone by something that is dependent in all these respects on an intelligent agent who supplies the matter, the form, the right series of changes, and the ends for which the product exists or is to be used. Moreover, all of the ultimate causes reside in the mind of the maker, who then gathers together all of the proximate causes, such as raw material, tools, and so on. Thus, this Aristotelian account of growing and making has two salient features: first, it depends on a strict distinction between internal and external causes; and, second, it characterizes the ultimate external causes involved in making as mental.

Ingold's Challenge

Although Tim Ingold does not credit Aristotle with originating the view he wishes to challenge, it is clearly a view that elaborates Aristotle's account in modern dress, with reference to design theory and genetics:

> Now it is very often assumed, in the study of both organisms and artefacts, that to ask about the form of things is, in itself, to pose a question about *design,* as though the design contained a complete specification that has only to be 'written out' in the material. This assumption is central to the standard view which . . . distinguishes between living and artificial things on the criterion of the interiority or exteriority of the design specification governing their production without questioning the premise that the resultant forms are indeed specified independently and in advance of the processes of growth or manufacture wherein they are realised. Thus it is supposed that the basic architecture of the organism is already established, as a genetic 'blueprint,' from the very moment of conception; likewise the artefact is supposed to pre-exist, fully represented as a 'virtual object' in the mind, even before a finger has been lifted in its construction. (Ingold 2000a, 58–59)[1]

This 'standard view' is clearly our old friend the centralized control model, extended to growing as well as making. And Ingold's criticism is, as we shall see, entirely in line with our criticism of the centralized control model in Part I.

Ingold's argument focuses specifically on morphogenesis. He notes that the idea that biological structure is completely due to a genetic 'blueprint' or 'program' has been undermined by recent evidence that genes do not fully specify form, but only set parameters for its development (Ingold 2000a, 59–60). These challenges to the Aristotelian idea that the causes of growth are internal to the organism can be characterized under two main heads— the abandonment, first, of the idea that all the causes of organic structure are internal to the organism; and, second, of the idea that genes are even the sole internal cause. Ultimately, some theorists prefer to abandon the very vocabulary of internal versus external causes, as well as associated distinctions, such as that between nature and nurture. This is also Ingold's preference. Instead, the organism should be understood as developing within a 'morphogenetic field' that operates across erstwhile boundaries between organism and environment (Ingold 2000a, 60).

The second step in Ingold's argument is to show that the genesis of structure in making can be understood in terms of this non-Aristotelian model currently emerging in biology. To illustrate the phenomena that ground this part of his argument, he describes the actions of a woman using the coiled basketry technique to construct a basket:

> Taking a bundle of fibres, placed lengthwise alongside one another to form a kind of rope of about one centimetre in diameter, she deftly

begins to turn it between her fingers to produce a flat coil, at the same time using somewhat broader fibres to wrap transversely around successive turns of the coil so as to keep it compact and prevent it from unravelling. After a while, the wrapped coil becomes recognisable as the base of the object. Then, as the work proceeds—evenly, rhythmically and repetitively—the turns of the coil are drawn tighter, so that each rises partly upon the base of its predecessor, thus forming the sides. (Ingold 2000a, 54)

Ingold's (2000a, 53–57) consideration of this simple and very ancient basket-making technique yields three points:

- The standard view suggests *transformation of a surface* as the paradigm of making, where the surface represents the boundary between internal and external, maker and product, etc. But the surface of the basket is *built up* rather than transformed from some pre-existing surface; and in the process there is no simple relationship between the surfaces of the fibers and the emerging surface of the basket.
- The standard view suggests that form is due to the *external application of force* to raw material. But the form of the basket depends largely on the tensile character of the plant fibers used to construct it, so there is a *play of internal and external forces* at work in its construction.
- The standard view suggests that the origin of form is the *idea in the mind* of the maker. But although the basket maker may well have some idea of what she wants the finished basket to look like, the actual form it takes has its proximate origin in the *skilled movements* involved in its construction. And lest anyone object that these skilled movements are themselves controlled by representations in the mind of the maker, Ingold asserts that skills are typically inculcated through practice and experience, and are 'fundamentally resistant to codification in the form of representations or programmes' (Ingold 2000a, 67).

The negative conclusions from Ingold's argument are, first, that neither growth nor making is the kind of transcription process envisioned by the standard view. Consequently, any distinction between these two processes grounded in the direction of the transcription evaporates. Second, the role of mental representations in making has been vastly overestimated and the role of skilled movement concomitantly underestimated. The corresponding positive conclusions are, first, that both growth and making take place in a field of forces that cannot readily be partitioned into internal and external causes. So, growth and making are fundamentally the same sort of process. Second, the role of skilled activity must be central to an adequate account of making as a reproductive process.

Ingold's argument concerns only the genesis of structure. But both biological and cultural structures are functional—indeed, that is the point of reproducing them. And the view Ingold rejects with regard to the generation of structure might still have some leverage with regard to the reproduction of function in material culture. For the functions of biological organs are natural to them, and thus come into existence along with the biological structures that subserve them. In contrast, the functions of items of material culture are thought to depend on the purposes of their producers, and thus are not natural. So a proponent of the standard view might argue that, even if Ingold is right about the genesis of structure, function might still be amenable to the standard, Aristotelian type of account, at least in the case of material culture.

We must now see if we can counter this move by constructing a parallel argument focusing on function. The ultimate aim is to show that the relationship between function and structure is no more or less natural in material culture than in biology—or better, that the standard vocabulary of external *versus* internal, of natural *versus* non-natural sources of function, is unable to capture the real character of the phenomena in either biology or material culture. An important clue is that knowledge of a structure is not, in general, sufficient for knowledge of its function. In the case of material culture, for instance, archaeologists frequently are in a quandary as to what functions to ascribe to the structures they unearth. At best, the structure constrains the function.[2] An interesting example is a pair of small, semi-tubular gold objects found in the grave of the Amesbury Archer.[3] One view is that they are ornaments that would have been braided into the hair. Another possibility is that they are ear cuffs that would have been wrapped around the edge of the ear. As far as their structure goes, they would be equally suited to either proper function. *A fortiori,* any system functions for which they might have been used on specific occasions are not determinable from their structure alone.

Biologists, like archaeologists, are often puzzled about the functions of biological structures. This is especially a problem in the case of extinct organisms and organisms that cannot be readily observed going about their daily business using the structures in question. For example, a large number of plants and animals have bioluminescent organs, but their functions (if any) are still not known in many cases. This difficulty is also manifest in the case of vestigial organs. The human appendix no longer does much of anything—other than become infected and rupture, of course—and not surprisingly, its function is a matter of dispute. What this suggests is that a thing, whether biological or cultural, does not have a function in virtue of its structure alone. If it did, you would be able to read its function right off its structure.

It might be objected that this is just a matter of the exercise of the function, and does not have any bearing on the having of the function in the first place. What we are looking for, after all, are the causes of the functionality of a structure; or more precisely, perhaps, the conditions (some of which might be causal only in an extended sense) that must obtain in order to reproduce a structure with a specific function, as opposed to a structure in abstraction from any function, as described by Ingold in the basket-making case. And it might be objected that this is a different matter from the conditions necessary for the exercise of a function. But in the case of system functions, this objection does not hold water. A system function is defined in terms of exercise—in terms of the role a thing plays, or at least has a current disposition to play, in an embedding system. This means that reproducing a system-functional structure requires not just the reproduction of the structure, but of its situation in an appropriate embedding system supplying appropriate inputs of energy and/or materials, appropriate interactions with other system components, and so on. For example, suppose a museum decides to make reproductions of the gold objects from the Amesbury Archer's grave, but their marketing manager, having observed few ear cuffs or braided-in hair ornaments on the museum's clientele, thinks they will sell better as pendants on a necklace. The museum might then reproduce the gold objects, but sell them strung on a silk cord or a gold chain, with a little information booklet explaining their hypothesized original proper functions and their recommended present system-functional use as pendants. Here what is reproduced is not just the structure of the gold objects, but their insertion into a different sector of the personal adornment arena than they are thought to have originally occupied. It would, of course, be open to a customer to buy two and use them as ear cuffs. But in the meantime, the system function (which is in the process of being standardized and might well in the long run become an additional proper function) is clearly indicated and its exercise reinforced by the packaging.

Ingold argued that morphogenesis takes place within a field of forces that cannot be easily partitioned into external and internal causes. It now seems that the same is true with regard to the reproduction of system-functional structures. The embedding system is not just an inert, external container, but is a source of energy and materials and the locus of other components that may have to interact with the component under consideration in order for it to have a specific system function. Thus, the embedding system is, in an etymological sense, a *context,* something 'woven together' with the component under consideration. Neither is it easy to partition the conditions generative of system functions into internal and external ones. In particular, inputs of energy and materials are difficult to classify in this way, because they are taken in and often changed in some way by their interaction with the functional structure during the exercise of the function (e.g., fuel in a combustion engine or leavening in a cake). Similarly, interactions with other components are difficult to categorize as either internal or external conditions of system functionality, because it is the engaged and active *relationship* between components that is essential. For example, it is not just the proximity of the tubular gold object to a string of some sort that makes it a (system-functional) pendant, but its being strung on a string of a particular sort and worn around a human neck. In short, because having a system function is defined in terms of the exercise of that function, because exercising a function requires factors over and above the sheer structure of the functional item, and because these other factors are difficult to partition into internal and external causes or conditions, the reproduction of system-functional structures fits Ingold's model better than it does the standard, Aristotelian one.

In the case of proper functions, the objection that we must be careful to distinguish having a function from exercising that function carries more weight, since having a proper function is not essentially bound up with exercising it, as in the case of system functions. As we noted in Chapter 5, a proper function is a performance a biological or cultural thing is *supposed* to engage in, regardless of whether it is actually able to do so. Thus, having a proper function is not contingent on exercising that function, or even on having the capacity to exercise it. But it is *supposed* to exercise that function under relevant conditions, because it belongs to a particular lineage defined in terms of historical patterns of fitness enhancing performance (biology) or of use (material culture), leading in both cases to reproduction. What our clue indicates in this case, then, is that you cannot read proper function off structure, because many of the essential conditions for reproducing proper-functional items are historical, not structural. If it often seems like you can tell what a thing's proper function is simply by observing its structure, this is very commonly due to your having been trained in the proper use of items of this type, where part of the training is learning to associate their observable structure with their (sometimes unobserved) proper function. Or you may have observed trained people using items of the type in question often enough that you tumbled to the association between structure and proper function. Someone who does not know how to cook, for instance, may have been in and around kitchens enough to recognize the proper functions of many of the items found there. Somewhat less commonly, you may have been trained to directly associate an observable structure with a proper function without ever interacting with the type of thing in question. Picture books for children are a very common way of doing this in our culture, for instance. In these examples, training provides access to the history of the item so that its observable structure is firmly linked to its proper function. It is important to note here that what an item of material culture *can* be used for is not a completely reliable guide to what it *is* (or was) properly used for—the distinction between proper functions and system functions rests on this divergence.

So here again, function is not contingent on structure alone. Reproducing a proper-functional structure—whether biological or cultural—is not just a matter of reproducing a structure, but of reproducing it under conditions that constitute its belongingness to a particular lineage. In biology, these conditions are basically a matter of genetics, and the relationships and processes involved in sexual or asexual reproduction. In material culture, these conditions involve factors such as how, where, or by whom items of a particular structural type are made; how, where, by, or to whom, and in conjunction with what other sorts of items they are distributed; and how, where, and by whom they are used. The most common way in which these conditions are realized is for there to be a continuous tradition of making, distributing, and using items of a given type. Consider the Amesbury Archer again. Fifteen flint arrowheads were among his grave goods. There is no real controversy about the proper function of these items, because there has been a continuous tradition of making and using archery equipment in Europe since well before the Amesbury Archer's time and extending through to our own. What is necessary for the reproduction of proper-functional items, though, is not that anyone actually *know* the history, but that there *be* such a history. In this respect, material culture is no different than biology, where what matters are the actual evolutionary and genetic relationships, not whether anybody knows about them.

To conclude, there are two important points here. First, lineage-constituting conditions are, if anything, even less amenable to the kind of division into internal and external factors required by the standard view. Belongingness to a lineage is a matter of having a complex network of historical relationships to other items of the same type, and, in material culture, to associated items of other types involved in the processes of production, distribution and use, and to agents of various types with various historically established roles and practices. So, the situation in the proper function case is the same as in the system function case—the lineage is a relational context that is woven together with the proper-functional items making up its most recent generation. It is precisely this interweaving that makes it the case that proper-functional items, and not bare structures, are reproduced. Second, the existence of historical, lineage-constituting conditions for the reproduction of proper-functional items in both material culture and biology prompts us to acknowledge that reproduced proper-functional items of material culture, like proper-functional biological traits, come into the world with their functions already attached, as it were. It is not up to me or any of my coworkers in the spoon factory—not even the managers or the owners—what proper functions the spooniform structures we are turning out have, for instance. This is a matter of their history, a history we do not even have to know much about in order to reproduce them in accordance with it. So, proper functions are as natural to items of material culture as they are to biological traits. In this regard, a material culture is literally a second nature to the human beings born into it. And the overall conclusion we can now draw is that the reproduction of proper-functional structures, like the reproduction of system-functional structures, fits Ingold's model better than it does the standard, Aristotelian model.

PROPER FUNCTIONS AND PURPOSES

Unfortunately, there is still a weak point in Ingold's argument that could be leveraged by proponents of the Aristotelian standard view. Ingold explicitly intends to divert theoretical attention away from the product and toward the process in order to correct what he sees as an entrenched overemphasis on mental design, and simultaneously to divert attention away from the role of mental representations in the activity of production and toward the situatedness of the activity itself:

> The notion of making, of course, defines an activity purely in terms of its capacity to yield a certain object, whereas weaving focuses on the character of the process by which that object comes into existence. To emphasize making is to regard the object as the expression of an idea; to emphasize weaving is to regard it as the embodiment of a rhythmic movement. Therefore to invert making and weaving is also to invert idea and movement, to see the movement as truly generative of the object rather than merely revelatory of an object that is already present in an ideal, conceptual or virtual form, in advance of the process that discloses it. (Ingold 2000b, 346)

This current of activity is a complex process of interaction between skilled human agents and the specific characteristics of various features of their environments, including raw materials, tools, work spaces, and so on. It does include mental representations the human agent has, but these are not the sole source of form, as the standard view holds, but only one of many contributing sources. In particular, Ingold thinks, the role of mental representations is primarily to set parameters that guide the process of construction, not to specify the characteristics of the final product:

> [T]he properties of materials are directly implicated in the form-generating process . . . Finally, the templates, measures and rules of thumb of the artisan or craftsman no more add up to a design for the artefacts he produces than do genes constitute a blueprint for the organism. Like genes, they set the parameters of the process but do not prefigure the form. (Ingold 2000a, 61)

As we noted above, the standard view of making is a special case of the centralized control model of action we criticized in Part I. And now we can see that Ingold's alternative to the standard view is consonant with our own improvisation-oriented alternative. Like Ingold's emphasis on skilled activity, our emphasis on improvisation directs attention to action as a process structured in an ongoing way, not a product prefigured in intention. Similarly, according to our alternative, the structure of action has its source not just in plans, goals, or other mental representations an agent may have, but also in features of the situation in which the action unfolds, including items of material culture, other agents, serendipitous events, and so on.[4] So far so good. But we have had to extend Ingold's argument to cover the functional aspects of items of material culture. This extension gives an opening to an objector wedded to the standard view.

It is relatively easy to concede that the physical structure of items of material culture owes a lot to characteristics of raw materials or of other features of the environment upon which human agents implicitly depend, but which they do not explicitly or fully represent. It is much harder to shake the idea that the functions of items of material culture depend on consciously represented human purposes. To take a literary example, in the Finnish national epic, the *Kalevala,* Kalevatar (daughter of the eponymous Kaleva) is depicted in Runo XX inventing beer (Lönnrot 1985). She makes a drink by boiling barley and hops in water, but is disappointed when it does not ferment. She tries a succession of additives—pine cones, fir shoots, foam from the mouth of a ravening bear, and finally honey. This last works, as well it might, since honey contains wild yeasts. But beer has been brewed for six or seven millennia, while the role of yeast in fermentation has only been understood since the work of Louis Pasteur less than two hundred years ago. So the fermented drink Kalevatar represents as her goal can be produced without the procurement of yeast or its operation being explicitly represented by her. Physical structure, in other words, does not depend on explicitly represented purposes and knowledge—representing some of the parameters necessary to the production process is sufficient. On the other hand, the *functions* of items of material culture do seem to depend on purposes human beings have and explicitly represent to themselves in some fashion. In the *Kalevala,* for instance, beer is represented as a beverage from the start. Indeed, as soon as Kalevatar finishes making the first batch, heroes come from all around to drink it. Indeed, the topic of beer comes up in the first place because Louhi, the mistress of Pohjola, is planning a wedding feast and needs great quantities of beer for her guests to drink. But she does not know how to make it and wonders, in any case, how it was invented. So, it seems that the function of beer as a beverage, and even more specifically as a beverage particularly appropriate for festive occasions, is dependent on the purposes its inventors and users have with regard to beer, and is intimately connected with other purposes and goals they have, such as putting on wedding feasts.

Marx, for one, is unequivocal about this dependence of function on consciously represented human purposes:

> Man not only effects a change of form in the materials of nature; he also realizes [*verwirklicht*] his own purpose in those materials. And this is a purpose he is conscious of, it determines the mode of his activity with the rigidity of a law, and he must subordinate his will to it. (1976, 284)

And Peter McLaughlin, who may serve here as representative of contemporary versions of this view, is equally unequivocal:

> The function of an artifact is derivative from the purpose of some agent in making or appropriating the object; it is conferred on the object by

the desires and beliefs of an agent. No agent, no purpose, no function. (2001, 60–61)

This view seems all the more plausible if the purposes are allowed to be socially distributed or collective, as both Marx and McLaughlin suggest. In the *Kalevala,* for instance, the function of beer as a beverage does not depend on Kalevatar's representation of it alone, but on its representation as a beverage by the heroes, who immediately show up to drink it, and by subsequent givers of feasts, such as Louhi.

We said above that reproducing system-functional items requires embedding them in a suitable system, and reproducing proper-functional items requires reproduction in accordance with a historical lineage. But the objector may now argue that with regard to function, the operative factor in the embedding in systems and the continuation of lineages is the conscious representation of the corresponding purposes by the human agents involved. In the case of beer, for instance, its proper function as a beverage especially suitable for festive occasions has been transmitted to batch after batch of beer down the ages by the human agents who brewed, distributed, and served it with that purpose in mind, and who transmitted that purpose to subsequent generations of human agents. Similarly, in the case of the many system functions of beer, it is the role of human agents and their purposes that is paramount. Consider the use of beer by organic gardeners to trap and kill slugs, for instance. This is a use that fits into the system of organic gardeners, their practices, and the items of material culture deployed in those practices. But, the objector may argue, beer originally acquires this system function because some enterprising organic gardener conceived the purpose of ridding her gardens of slugs by some means other than the ridiculously toxic commercial products available, and hit on beer as an environmentally safe alternative. And this system function is reproduced, because this gardener communicated the success of this method to other organic gardeners, who duly conceived the same purpose when bedeviled in their turn by slugs. The objection, in short, is that although lineages and systems are essential to the reproduction of items of material culture, it is the transmission and sharing of purposes among agents that really runs the show as far as the specifically functional aspects of these items are concerned. The only situation in which this account might seem to fail is latent function, such as the socioeconomic display functions of corsets in nineteenth-century Europe, or shoes for bound feet in China.[5] But even purposes such as these may be dimly represented by at least some people in the culture. Or they may be represented unconsciously, prevented from surfacing by conscious and more explicitly represented ideologies. In any case, the objector may insist, these are just minor complications, not problems in principle. The vast majority of functions are not latent, and it is the vast majority we are trying to account for here. So McLaughlin has it right, provided he is willing to accept a reformulation in the plural: *No agents, no purposes, no functions.*

Clearly, what we are dealing with here is an avatar of the intentionalist account of function. If the objector is right, the functions of items of material culture *are* prefigured in the mentally represented purposes of human agents, *contra* Ingold. These purposes do not merely set parameters for the process of producing functional items, but account completely for their functional aspects. In Chapter 6, we succeeded in showing that the intentions of designers, in particular, are not sufficient for the establishment of proper functions, and that instead we need to look at patterns of use leading to reproduction. But our present objector is arguing that the operative feature of these patterns of use is the transmission of consciously represented purposes among users. Thus, even if the intentions of individual designers are not sufficient for the establishment of functions, the patterns of use through which functions are not only established but continually reproduced down the generations *do* depend on the purposes of the human agents involved, considered collectively rather than individually. To deal with this objection, we will have to look more closely at the transmission of purposes from agent to agent.

As we saw in Chapter 6, Houkes and Vermaas have an intentionalist theory that grounds functions in use plans devised by human agents and communicated by them to other agents:

> The number of plans autonomously constructed by individual users is bound to be relatively small—we learn from others how to use toasters, pneumatic hammers, and bicycles. There seem to be three important sources of use plans for a user. First, innovative fellow users may invent clever use plans, such as removing candle wax by ironing with brown paper. Second, groups or traditions of users construct use plans gradually through processes of trial and error, e.g., the use of salt and sugar in preserving foodstuffs. And finally, designers produce use plans, which are likely to be grounded in scientific knowledge, e.g., in designing cellular phones. (2004, 60)

Although designers may have a role to play, it is a strictly subsidiary one. There are two main reasons for this. First and most importantly, the vast majority of things people acquire and use on a daily basis—things such as spoons, towels, shoes, wastepaper baskets, rakes, sofas, cheese, perfume, and so on—come with no instructive communication from their designers, or even from their manufacturers. You are expected to know what to do with most of the items making up your material culture, or failing that, to consult other competent users. Second, even complicated modern appliances, such as printers or automobiles, are not usually an exception. Here, the user acquires a user's manual or instruction sheet along with the appliance, and this may indeed be regarded as a communication from the designer to the user, if only indirectly through technical writers. But user's manuals and instruction sheets do not normally instruct the user about the overall proper function of the appliance—only about the functions of some of its

202 A Philosophy of Material Culture

component parts. The manual that came with my office printer, for instance, clearly assumes that I know what printers are for, and even what most of their components are for, and only need instruction about the newer details of this model. So, even in these cases, communication between designer and users is sketchy, and does not really amount to the communication of a complete use plan of the sort Houkes and Vermaas describe. Rather, the transmission of use plans—and, thus, of purposes from agent to agent—is overwhelmingly a matter of transmission from user to user. So, it is this transmission from competent to novice users we must examine in order to understand the relation between the reproduction of function and collective human purposes.

Use is in general more difficult to investigate than making, for several reasons. First, making is typically a temporally compact process occurring at the beginning of an item's existence, whereas use is typically sporadic and distributed over the whole course of its existence. Second, making is a relatively homogeneous cluster of operations, whereas use is heterogeneous, involving a number of different sorts of activities. For example, it may involve activities having to do with maintenance, repair, and recycling, and others having to do with ownership transfer (gift, sale, trade, or what have you). Third, items of material culture often have multiple proper functions. And finally, some uses are system-functional, not proper-functional. So with the understanding that what follows is nothing like an exhaustive phenomenology of use, let us look at some examples of typical activities involving the proper-functional use of a wastepaper basket.

- You are sitting at the desk in your office going through your snail mail. Periodically you deposit empty envelopes and sheets of paper in the wastepaper basket next to your desk. Sometimes you crumple them up or tear them in pieces before depositing them.
- By the time you have gotten through your mail, the basket is full. You pick it up, carry it out to the large trash receptacle in the hallway, empty it, and carry it back to your office.
- Before putting it back beside your desk, you dust it off with a feather duster.
- Then you write a note to yourself to stop at Walmart on your way home to get a new, larger wastepaper basket in a nicer color, since this one is both too small and rather dilapidated.

One important thing these examples show is that using a wastepaper basket involves skilled, repetitive actions, just as making a basket does. The repetition, in this case, is distributed sporadically over relatively long periods of time. Crumpling up a piece of paper and dropping it into the wastepaper basket is a simple action you may repeat many times a day, and hundreds or thousands of times over the course of weeks or years. Similarly, emptying and dusting the wastepaper basket are repeated tasks that you might do either on a sporadic basis as needed, or on a regular schedule of some sort. Finally, although buying a new wastepaper basket is something you may do only a few times in your life, it is a special case of the repetitive activity of buying household necessities—something you surely do every week, if not every day.

The skill involved in these activities is not as obvious as in the activity of making a basket described by Ingold, because it is a skill (or more precisely, a set of related skills) acquired by everyone in wastepaper basket cultures rather than by only a few specialists, as is more commonly the case with making. It is in the exercise of this skill that the proper function of wastepaper baskets is manifested; it is, therefore, in the passing on of this skill that the proper function is reproduced and perpetuated. So we need to look closely at how such common, everyday skills are acquired.

As is the case for everyday items in general, experience with wastepaper baskets begins in early childhood. You hand your toddler a crumpled piece of paper, for instance, and say 'Could you put this in the wastepaper basket for me?' Long before this, of course, the child has watched you putting crumpled pieces of paper in the wastepaper basket, and has also interacted with it in non-proper-functional ways—as something to peer into, pull over, and so on. Nevertheless, complying with your request takes some effort, since the child's 'naïve physics' is still in a nascent state, as is her command of hand-eye coordination. So, this is not likely to be one-trial learning—the child will have to practice putting things in the wastepaper basket for some time in order to become skilled at it. Furthermore, really good judgment about what goes in a wastepaper basket and what does not must also be acquired, on the basis of repeated admonishments against the child putting her toys in the wastepaper basket, for instance, or (worse yet) pouring her juice into it. When the child is older and has acquired more strength and dexterity, she can go on to wastepaper basket maintenance tasks. Indeed, collecting and taking out the trash is a job typically delegated to older children in a household. And in the end, the teenager or young adult will probably even be able to tell you explicitly what wastepaper baskets are for, where to buy them, how to maintain them, and so on. In other words, along with skill in using the wastepaper basket, the novice user eventually acquires an explicit representation of its function.

What we see here is an apprenticeship learning system, with children performing component activities under the tutelage of already competent adults, and working up through mastery of these subtasks to their own full-fledged competence. According to cognitive anthropologists, apprenticeship learning of this sort is also typical of adults, even for complex or highly technical tasks (Wynn 1993; Marchand 2010). Kim Sterelny (2012) has recently argued that this kind of transmission of information across generations through apprenticeship learning is a crucial factor in explaining our rapid evolutionary divergence from our nearest relatives. But the important point for us is that it bears little resemblance to the explanation-based communication of fully formed use plans from designer to user that Houkes and Vermaas take as their paradigm.

Ingold points out that the application of skilled, repetitive actions in making a basket is not the application of external force to an inert and infinitely malleable raw material, but rather an interactive engagement. The material exerts its own forces that interact with the forces exerted by the basket maker, and it is this field of forces operating across the erstwhile thing-environment boundary that results in the reproduction of the basket structure. Moreover, the forces specific to the basket material continue to operate in the fully formed basket, thus allowing it to retain its structure. We can now see that something similar is true of the reproduction of proper function through use. In our wastepaper basket example, the skill involved in use is acquired through active engagement with the structural and physical properties of the basket and the things deposited in it; and the fully skilled practitioner continues to engage these properties when exercising their skill. So, just as structure is, on Ingold's view, not merely the result of the maker imposing a preconceived form on inert material, so we may say that proper function is not merely the result of the user imposing a preconceived purpose on an inert object. This is a crucial point and requires further elucidation.

As we pointed out previously, one of the typical *results* of the process of acquiring skill in using everyday items of material culture is explicit representation of their proper functions. A child starts out with no idea what the proper functions of the items making up his environing material culture are, and gradually acquires more or less refined ideas about this in a piecemeal and indirect fashion, largely through apprenticeship learning. This is not to deny that adults, in particular, sometimes acquire knowledge about the proper functions of items of material culture in other ways—by regular observation of use, for instance, or by explanation. It is only to claim that apprenticeship learning is the fundamental process through which proper functions come to be explicitly represented, and that learning by observation or explanation are secondary processes parasitic on it. More importantly, though, the representations of proper function acquired in this fundamental way are representations of items that already exist in the surrounding culture. And the point of insisting on the ubiquity of apprenticeship learning of everyday skills is to emphasize that such representations of proper function are acquired as much through direct interaction with material culture itself as through interaction with other human agents. Competent adults do play an important role, but it is more one of facilitating interactions with material culture than of explaining it in the abstract. Thus we encounter wastepaper baskets as always already proper-functional. And as individuals we then *acquire* ideas about the proper functions of such things through facilitated interaction with them.

But representations of proper functions are not all we acquire. This is the surface manifestation of a deeper acquisition—that of the relevant *purposes* themselves. Infants initially have no purposes corresponding to the proper function of wastepaper baskets. They acquire these purposes; and they acquire them in wastepaper basket cultures through facilitated, skill-generating interactions with wastepaper baskets. This is not to deny that human agents, particularly as adults, sometimes acquire knowledge of the proper functions of items of material culture without acquiring the relevant purposes. For example, an inveterate urbanite might read a book about the history of farming and learn about the proper functions of farm equipment, without either learning how to use it or forming any of the relevant purposes. Nor is it to deny that sometimes, particularly as adults, we form a purpose and then go looking for some item of material culture with a corresponding proper function, or even contrive to make such an item from scratch. Rather it is to claim that these are secondary processes parasitic on the basic process of acquiring the standard sets of purposes adults are expected to have with regard to a given material culture by apprenticing with already competent users of that culture. Even when we form a purpose and then look for something with which to carry it out, this purpose is almost never radically novel, but is rather itself a standard, culture-relative purpose we have acquired in this way. Thus, it is as correct to say that the purposes we have depend on the functions of items of our material culture, and are externally imposed on us, as to say that the functions of items of material culture depend on our purposes, and are externally imposed on them.

Furthermore, the purposes an individual is expected to have vary. Some purposes are expected of every competent adult—those relevant to common items used by everyone, such as wastepaper baskets and spoons in contemporary Western culture. After that, there is variation depending on such factors as gender, age, ethnicity, socio-economic status, occupation, hobbies, and so on. So women in Western cultures are expected to have purposes corresponding to the proper functions of dresses but not neckties, whereas the reverse expectation obtains for men; and farmers are expected to have purposes corresponding to pitchforks, whereas inveterate urbanites are not. It is these sets of expected purposes that to a large extent define culturally relative types of agents, or more generally (to use a locution of Michel Foucault), types of subjects. So, the reproduction of purposes through facilitated interaction with material culture is part and parcel of the sociogeneric formation of the individual we discussed in Part I.

Marx elaborates this view in his later work, detailing how the economic conditions prevailing in a given society result in the reproduction of individuals equipped with the requisite beliefs and purposes to operate under those conditions, and by so doing, to perpetuate them. So capitalist economic conditions reproduce capitalists on the one hand and wage laborers on the other; and capitalists and wage laborers then interact to reproduce capitalist economic conditions.[6] This theme is even more pervasive in the work of Foucault, who specifically analyzes the role of material culture in the social reproduction of types of individuals. The notorious Panopticon of *Discipline and Punish,* for instance, is introduced precisely to show how features of the built environment, just in virtue of their physical form and the uses to which they are put, inculcate beliefs and purposes that define types of individual agents suited to live, work, and play in precisely these built environments. In short, then, it is as correct to say that material culture reproduces individual human agents as that material culture is reproduced by them.

Putting these points together, we now find we must reverse McLaughlin's slogan. Rather than: *No agents, no purposes, no functions,* we now must say: *No functions, no purposes, no agents.* But it would be wrong to simply rest content with the reversal, for what we have in fact discovered is that, properly understood, *both* formulations are correct. We may grant that if there were no human agents, there would be no material culture. But we must insist, on the other hand, that if there were no material culture, human beings would not have the purposes they have or be the individuals they are. Arguably, without material culture, biologically human individuals would not even *be* human in the sense they now are. Culture in general, and material culture in particular, are essential to being human, not incidental. Thus, the reproduction of material culture is at the very same time, and indissolubly, the reproduction of human purposes and of types of human individuals.

To frame this important point another way, in Chapter 6 we argued for the claim that proper functions are not established by the authority of designers, but rather through processes of use, and reproduction contingent on that use. Thus, the establishment of proper functions is not a short-term individual accomplishment; it is a long-term social one. But this means there is no longer any real possibility of understanding the relationship between agents' purposes and proper functions in a unidirectional way. In other words, the common view expressed so clearly by McLaughlin, that proper functions depend on the prior purposes of human agents but not *vice versa,* evaporates with the authority of the designer—but so does its opposite. The only viable view is one that sees human purposes and the proper functions of items of material culture indissolubly linked in patterns of use and reproduction. Thus, it no longer seems reasonable to ask which came first, the purpose or the proper function. Both are produced and reproduced through the self-same social process. This point is analogous to Ingold's insistence that the only viable view of morphogenesis is one in which structure is seen as arising out of a field of forces that cannot be readily partitioned into internal and external causes. Here, we have discovered that the only viable view of the reproduction of the proper-functional aspects of material culture is one in which they are seen as arising out of a field of social forces that cannot easily be partitioned into agents and patients.

Finally, we can now see that we have arrived by a different route at the sociogeneric view of the individual we broached in Chapter 3. As we said there, individuals do not create the social, as on the suigeneric view, but rather are themselves created by the social environment into which they are born, and in which they develop and acquire their competences. In turn, because they are the individuals they are, and are enculturated in the way they are, they transmit this social environment to the next generation of individuals.

We have just verified this view specifically with regard to the relationship between the proper functions of items of material culture, on the one hand, and the purposes of individual human agents, on the other hand. Thus, the objector's argument does not support an intentionalist conclusion. The fact that the lineage-constituting conditions required for the reproduction of proper functions are social conditions created and maintained purposively by human agents does not succeed in establishing the priority of purposes with regard to proper functions, because it ignores the equally important fact that those very purposes are created and maintained by the proper-functional material culture into which human beings are born and in interaction with which they acquire the purposes they have and become the kinds of individuals they are.

SYSTEM FUNCTIONS AND INNOVATION

We can give system function an analysis along the same lines as the one we have just given proper function. System functions occur where an item of material culture is used for a purpose other than the one corresponding to its proper function; or less commonly, where a naturally occurring object is used for some purpose. The important point for our analysis is that the purposes involved are overwhelmingly standard purposes acquired in the way described in the previous section, not radically novel purposes. For example, I used my safe deposit box key to tighten the screws fastening the lock to my garage door (Preston 1998b). The purpose I had was an entirely standard one, acquired as a result of growing up in a culture with screws and screwdrivers. I do have screwdrivers, but using the safe deposit box key on the key ring in my hand saved me the time and trouble of going inside and retrieving a screwdriver. Later on, this same lock developed an internal problem requiring the services of a locksmith. When I mentioned to him that I was also having a problem with the screws working loose, he fixed that, too—by picking up some pine twigs lying on the driveway, inserting them into the holes for the screws and then putting the screws in through the twigs. The screws have not worked loose since. So, the locksmith, too, accomplished an entirely standard purpose, this time by means of a system-functional use of a naturally occurring object with no human-related proper function.

The picture emerging here is one in which system functions are dependent on standard purposes, and thus ultimately on agents defined in part by configurations of such purposes. Similarly, system functions depend on existing items of material culture that can be turned to account for purposes other than the ones corresponding to their proper functions. What is novel, then, is just the non-standard pairing of purpose with item of material culture (or with naturally occurring object). This is not to deny that on rare occasions an entirely novel purpose may be conceived by an otherwise well-acculturated agent or group of agents. Nor is it to deny that on rare occasions, a purpose may be accomplished by the construction of some entirely novel item of material culture. But such radical novelties are the exception, not the rule. What we need to account for here is the rule—the non-standard pairing of a purpose with an item of material culture.

This phenomenon is important not only in its own right, but because it has a bearing on an issue raised by the sociogeneric view that re-emerged in the last section. This view problematizes individual innovation and autonomy by emphasizing the extent to which individual agents are products of their culture rather than suigeneric producers of it. In particular, if even our most intimate and commonplace purposes are inculcated rather than *sui generis,* then our understanding of the individual as autonomous, self-determining, or culturally innovative is compromised. Indeed, the idea of the autonomous, creative, self-determining individual begins to look like a fantasy of the Enlightenment cult of individual rationality and self-sufficiency, just as the privileged designer we discussed in Chapter 6 ultimately turned out to be a fantasy of the nineteenth century's cult of individual genius and heroic invention. There is, of course, a substantive as well as a historical connection between these fantasies, both of which revolve around the idea of the individual as, in principle, free in both thought and deed from cultural constraints. But if this is a fantasy, it is clearly a very persistent and culturally important one that may yet be shown to contain a kernel of truth. A more detailed consideration of system functions will help us confirm that.

The relationship between the individual and society has come to seem deeply problematic over the last century or so. In archaeology and anthropology, for instance, functionalism has problematized it, as Ian Hodder explains:

> Another limitation of the functionalist perspective of the New Archaeology is the relationship between the individual and society. The functional view gives little emphasis to individual creativity and intentionality. Individual human beings become little more than the means to achieve the needs of society. The social system is organized into subsystems and roles which people fill. The roles and social categories function in relation to each other to allow the efficient equilibrium of the whole system. In fact, however, individuals are not simply instruments in some orchestrated game and it is difficult to see how subsystems and roles can have 'goals' of their own. Adequate explanations of social systems and social change must involve the individual's assessments and aims. This is not a question of identifying individuals . . . but of introducing the individual into social theory. (1992, 98–99)

In philosophy, postmodernism and affiliated lines of thought are the primary locus of this problematization. One of the sharpest critics of postmodernism is Jürgen Habermas, who echoes Hodder's concern. Habermas locates the beginning of the problem in Nietzsche's philosophy of will to power, which in its starkest form construes the ordinary individual—the 'herd animal'—as merely a shifting confluence of various exercises of power, and not in any sense *causa sui*. Habermas traces the lasting influence of this view in the work of Michel Foucault and Arnold Gehlen:

> In place of socialization as individuating (which remains unconceptualized) . . . [Foucault] puts the concept of a fragmenting empowerment, a concept that is not up to the ambiguous phenomena of modernity. From his perspective, socialized individuals can only be perceived as exemplars, as standardized products of some discourse formation—as individual copies that are mechanically punched out. Gehlen, who thought from opposite political motives, but also from a similar theoretical perspective, made no secret of this: 'A personality: that is an institution in a *single* instance.' (Habermas 1987, 293)[7]

The worry, then, is that this is where we, too, have ended up. We have said that the interaction of the individual with her material culture—an interaction that pervades action in general—is constitutive of the individual's purposes and overall character as an individual. So what prospects are there for showing that the lives and activities of individuals are not simply orchestrated by impersonal, social forces outside of their control, and, in most cases, outside of their understanding?

This question has been hotly debated in social and political theory, where its implications are very pressing, since what is at stake are notions of social progress, justice, emancipation, and the like. But it does not seem that an acceptable solution is in sight. Habermas, for example, has attempted to salvage what is left of the Enlightenment through a theory of communicative rationality. His theory acknowledges the force of the postmodernist critique of a purely individualistic and subjective origin for political freedom and creative expression, but tries to preserve the emancipatory force of Enlightenment notions of social progress by understanding communicative rationality in terms of an 'ideal speech situation,' which provides complete freedom of expression to individuals, and through this provides for the critique and revision of existing institutions (Habermas 1984). Although Habermas acknowledges that this is an ideal not achieved in practice for the most part—and perhaps not even achievable for the most part—this alternative has seemed unconvincing to many of his critics. Even as an ideal, they think, it underestimates the pervasiveness and robustness of tradition on the one hand, and of the exercises of power elucidated by Nietzsche and his postmodern followers on the other (Dews 1999; Warnke 2002).

On the other side, many theorists in the postmodernist camp have tried to build the possibility of social critique and emancipation right into their understanding of power. Foucault, for instance, theorizes freedom and resistance as inherent to power:

> When one defines the exercise of power as a mode of action upon the actions of others, when one characterizes these actions by the government

of men by other men—in the broadest sense of the term—one includes an important element: freedom. Power is exercised only over free subjects, and only insofar as they are free. By this we mean individual or collective subjects who are faced with a field of possibilities in which several ways of behaving, several reactions and diverse comportments may be realized . . .

The relationship between power and freedom's refusal to submit cannot therefore be separated . . . At the very heart of the power relationship, and constantly provoking it, are the recalcitrance of the will and the intransigence of freedom. Rather than speaking of an essential freedom, it would be better to speak of an 'agonism'—of a relationship which is at the same time reciprocal incitation and struggle; less of a face-to-face confrontation which paralyzes both sides than a permanent provocation. (1982, 221–22)

But this move has not met with any better success than attempts such as Habermas's to rescue the Enlightenment from the Nietzschean onslaught. As Nancy Fraser (1981) points out, Foucault leaves political and ethical action without any normative foundation. Resistance is a permanent possibility, but which exercises of power should be resisted and which left alone? Which modes of resistance are legitimate and which should be prohibited? Questions such as these do not seem to have an answer within the localist and relativist framework of postmodernism and the philosophies of power stemming from Nietzsche. In yet another twist, as Fraser (1985) emphasizes in a subsequent article, feminist theory has problematized the idea of autonomy from a different direction, debating whether it is something women should demand, or something they should reject as a masculinist ideal of self-sufficiency that ignores values of caring and relatedness to others (Cooke 1999). In short, as a political and ethical issue, the relationship between individual and society is at present an arena of deeply divided camps and increasingly complex debates, with no resolution in sight.

But the relationship between individual and society is not articulated only in personal interactions at the level of ethics and politics. It is articulated equally, and often less tendentiously, at the level of everyday activities involving material culture. This provides another arena in which to examine the relationship between individual and society and, more particularly, in which to assess the leeway individuals have with regard to social constraints. At this level, the leeway is typically a matter of simple deviation from social norms rather than outright, politically charged resistance to them. On the other hand, ordinary items of material culture sometimes mediate exercises of political and ethical power. For example, the clothes women are encouraged or discouraged, required or forbidden to wear (corsets, veils, trousers, and so on) are arguably instrumental in their political and social positioning. Moreover, these same items of material culture can also mediate resistance—burning your corset, for instance, or using it as a system-functional element in an (metaphorically, this time) incendiary work of conceptual art. This suggests that we may ultimately be able to get some purchase on the debate at the political and ethical level through a better understanding of how individuals interact with their societies through their material cultures in general.

Our conclusion from the previous section was that learning proper-functional uses results in individuals acquiring culturally standard purposes relevant to their material culture; and that configurations of such purposes in part define culturally standard types of individuals. Thus, proper function in material culture—as might be expected from its Normative nature—operates on the side of social constraint. On the other hand, system function in material culture is mostly a matter of non-standard use of proper-functional items. So it operates on the side of individual autonomy with regard to social constraints. This autonomy is clearly limited in a number of ways. We have already noted that the typical system-function scenario involves the use of a familiar item of material culture to carry out a perfectly standard purpose. Thus, system functions usually operate within the ambit of already available cultural options, not from some standpoint outside it. And system-functional uses often become relatively standardized and lose any hint of novelty, while yet stopping short of becoming proper functions. Standing on a chair to change a light bulb or opening a can of paint with a screwdriver is not likely to strike anyone as an exercise of individual freedom, for instance. Nevertheless, to the extent that we as individuals have readily available and significant leeway with regard to the proper-functional constraints of material culture, system functions provide it. So what makes this leeway possible?

On the side of material culture itself, what makes system-functional use possible is, in the first instance, the multiple realizability of function and the multiple utilizability of structure—the twin features we noted at the beginning of Chapter 5. Function and structure are mutually constraining, but also mutually underdetermining. So any function can in principle be accomplished using a number of alternative structures; and any existing structure can, in principle, be used to carry out a number of alternative functions. Thus, in principle, function and structure can be separated and recombined in different pairings. But we can be more precise about the underpinnings of this phenomenon. Things have a multitude of physical properties and dispositions. First of all, unless they are malfunctioning, proper-functional items of material culture have whatever properties are needed to subserve their function. A flat head screwdriver, for instance, must be rigid but not brittle, long enough to provide leverage, and with a thin, flat tip. In addition, there has to be some source of torque, which may be partly incorporated into the screwdriver in the form of an electric motor rather than being supplied by the user. But these properties, singly or in combination, can be coopted for other purposes:

> [The flat head screwdriver is] the most common tool on the planet. The flat head is also one of the most abused tools, often substituted for any

number of other tools that might not be available. The fact is the flat head screwdriver is quite useful for more than tightening screws. Used for light prying, scraping, nudging or holding it can be pretty versatile. Treat it too badly, though, and it'll snap, leaving you with a fishing weight in your toolbox.[8]

In addition, the screwdriver has other properties not directly required for the exercise of its proper function, such as being heavy. These, too, can be co-opted for other purposes.

This disquisition on screwdrivers has still more to tell us in the context of what makes system functions possible from the side of the user. In the previous section, we explored the genesis of the patterns of activity corresponding to the proper functions of items of material culture. These are culturally standard patterns of activity into which we are trained early on, and which are continually reinforced by social expectations and/or sanctions thereafter. So, these patterns of activity manifest the social nature of individuals—the kinds of social constraints that are built right into their everyday behavior through acculturation. Like most constraints, these patterns of activity are on the whole *enabling* for the individual (Giddens 1984). Training children in the proper use of wastepaper baskets, for instance, enables them to coordinate their activities with the activities of other people and with the rest of the complex material culture in which they find themselves. This represents a huge gain in practical and cognitive efficiency for the individual, who is not burdened with the impossible task of reinventing his material culture and its associated practices from the ground up. It also represents a huge gain in technical and social efficiency, since both individuals and groups can count on an accumulated foundation of material culture and practices on which they can build. Given the enabling character of proper-functional use, it is no surprise that the vast majority of uses of material culture by individuals on a day-to-day basis are proper-functional—a fact you can easily verify by keeping track of your own interactions with items of material culture for a day or two.

But the positive and socially necessary nature of the constraints embodied in proper function has built into it various kinds of restrictions on the actions—and, ultimately, sometimes even the prospects—of individuals. First, in order for enabling to occur and for social order at the level of material culture to be maintained, individuals must in general be encouraged to adhere to the proper uses of items of material culture and sanctioned for departing from them. Screwdrivers are for putting in screws, not for opening paint cans; teaspoons are for stirring your tea, not for eating soup; corsets are female attire, not male attire; communion chalices are for the administration of the sacrament, not for drinking beer at football games; Oxy-Contin is for relieving pain, not for recreation; and so on. Second, because proper-functional use is socially enforced, it can be used as the basis for further restrictions of a political or legal sort, as in the case of OxyContin.

Nevertheless, individuals do regularly violate these constraints and use items of material culture in non-proper ways. The violation is often referred to as abuse, but this is a surprisingly complex phenomenon. The simplest case is the purely instrumental one illustrated in the disquisition on flat head screwdrivers. Here, 'abuse' refers primarily to non-proper uses that may damage the screwdriver, and the sanction is a natural one—the damage may render the screwdriver unusable for its proper function.[9] When the proper function is mediating other social restrictions, though, the issue is not usually damage to the item, and the sanctions do not follow naturally, but are socially constituted and enforced. Corsets are, in general, an item of female attire, the acknowledged proper function of which is to give a certain shape and support to the upper bodies of women.[10] So, even though the wearing of a woman's corset by a man does it no damage, this non-proper use may incur sanctions, in the form of ostracism, ridicule, or even punishment under the law. The picture so far, then, is one in which the individual's interactions with material culture are carefully policed for adherence to proper-functional use.

But the alert reader probably detected a certain amount of ambivalence about this in the disquisition on flat head screwdrivers. Although it foregrounds a complaint about how often screwdrivers are 'abused' through non-proper use, it also acknowledges not only that people often use flat head screwdrivers for such non-proper purposes, but that screwdrivers are useful and versatile in this respect. Moreover, it supplies one of the most common motives for non-proper use—unavailability of a tool with the appropriate proper function—and lists some apparently acceptable non-proper uses of a screwdriver, such as light prying and scraping. The overall message is: 'Go right ahead and use your flat head screwdriver for non-proper purposes; just be careful not to damage it in the process, on pain of no longer being able to use it for its proper function.' Similarly, off-label uses of drugs such as OxyContin are tolerated, both legally and socially, provided they are medical uses advised by properly licensed medical professionals. Here again, the message is that non-proper use is fine provided abuse—which in this case is any use that is recreational rather than medical—is avoided. Nor are you likely to be criticized for using your teaspoon as a measuring spoon. Etiquette is just not an issue when cooking, as it is when eating in company. Indeed, in the days before special-purpose measuring spoons were introduced, everybody used ordinary teaspoons and tablespoons for measuring. It was a second proper function, now perhaps vestigial.

For items that are common, cheap, and/or disposable, there usually *is* no issue of abuse. Paper napkins are properly for keeping yourself clean and tidy while eating; but no one is likely to upbraid you for writing a note or blowing your nose on one. Similarly, items that have served their proper function and are worn out or disposable can be used for alternative uses without fear of criticism. No one is likely to upbraid you for keeping nuts and bolts in an empty peanut butter jar or for cutting up worn out clothes to make a quilt. Indeed, such reuses are often encouraged. Not surprisingly, it is precisely cheap, common items or items that have already served their proper function that most frequently turn up in non-proper use situations, from hobby or craft uses to idiosyncratic or standardized system-functional uses around the house and yard. For example, craft stores sell things such as popsicle sticks, clothespins (both the old-fashioned peg type and the newer clip type), and pipe cleaners (nowadays sometimes larger, longer, brightly colored, and going under the appellation of 'chenille stems') for various uses not corresponding to their proper functions. Similarly, gardeners often use popsicle sticks for plant labels or clothespins to fasten crop row covers (which may themselves be secondhand sheer curtains from a thrift store) to wire hoops (which may themselves be short lengths of leftover fencing wire) over the row. Neither criticism nor sanctions are likely to ensue from non-proper uses of such items, unless they are locally in short supply, or unless there is a further, social restriction piggy-backing on the instrumental restriction to proper function. Communion wafers are cheaply and easily produced, for example, but furnishing your backyard birdfeeder with them might nevertheless be frowned upon in some circles.

These observations change the picture somewhat. Clearly, non-proper use is not only acceptable in many circumstances, but is even encouraged where abuse is not an issue or where it can be avoided with a little forethought and care. Indeed, we can go further. Non-proper use is learned by children simultaneously with the learning of proper-functional use. First, many of the hobby and craft uses of things such as popsicle sticks and clothespins originate in creative projects for children. The old-fashioned peg clothes-pins are often used as the basis for homemade angel and toy soldier figures to hang on a Christmas tree, for instance. In this kind of creative produc-tion, children can experiment with non-proper uses of some things, while at the same time learning the proper-functional uses of other things—scissors, glue, paint, and so on. A second area in which such non-proper uses of things are encouraged is in pretend play. For example, the mother of a four-year-old once told me how her son used laundry baskets as pretend trans-portation devices. Sometimes, he would get in a basket and pretend it was a car; with the addition of a baseball bat as a paddle, the basket became a canoe; placing the bat transversely across the basket to serve as wings made it an airplane; and several laundry baskets end to end made a train. Since this inventive child clearly had a whole transportation theme going, he may well have been consolidating his learning about the proper functions of devices such as airplanes, trains, and their component parts through pretend play involving non-proper use of the laundry baskets and the bat.

Psychologists recognize this connection between non-proper use and creativity.[11] Tests for creativity and for certain cognitive styles associated particularly with the arts traditionally include questions asking the test sub-jects to think up as many different uses as they can for some familiar items of material culture, such as paper clips or blankets. Of necessity, most of the responses reflect non-proper uses. Liam Hudson reports the following response for the blanket from a young, male student, for example:

> (Blanket) To use on a bed. As a cover for illicit sex in the woods. As a tent. To make smoke signals with. As a sail for a boat, cart or sled. As a substitute for a towel. As a target for shooting practice for short-sighted people. As a thing to catch people jumping out of burning skyscrapers. (1966, 46)

Here, the first response reports the proper use, whereas the others are all non-proper. Of these, some appear to be intended humorously (cover for illicit sex); others are standardized system functions for blankets the student may have heard or read about (making smoke signals, catching jumpers); but some seem idiosyncratic and imaginative (substitute for towel, target for short-sighted people). This tradition in psychological creativity testing is significant for our analysis, because it confirms that people are used to thinking of items of material culture in non-proper-functional ways; are familiar not only with the proper functions of common items of material culture, but with their common system functions as well; and—if reporting the proper function first is significant—are sensitive to which is which. Non-proper, system-functional uses of proper-functional items of material culture are, thus, not only common, they are perfectly well understood by users of material culture, and are indeed encouraged especially in contexts where creativity is fostered.

At the level of interaction with items of material culture, then, the restrictions embodied in the more culturally salient proper functions do not straightjacket individual action. Rather, individuals have—and understand that they have—quite a bit of leeway to use items of material culture in alternative ways without criticism or sanction. And, of course, they sometimes do so even when they are criticized or sanctioned. This is where relatively harmless deviations from proper-functional use shade into genuine social or political resistance (Certeau 1984). Foucault spent a lot of time investigating the proper functions of modern prisons and their component devices. But, to my knowledge, he says nothing at all about the well-known and famously creative use by prison inmates of proper-functional items for non-proper purposes. One motivation for this is the provision of forbidden creature comforts or tools for forbidden activities in a spirit of what John Irwin calls 'making do':

> Another part of making do is a spirit of improvisation. Besides appropriating things, prisoners replace or manufacture useful articles from any available material. An ex-prisoner at Santa Rita, the Alameda County jail, told me:
>
>> They take two [metal] spoons and put a piece of plastic they get from cheese packages between them and wrap the ends of electrical cord around the ends of the spoons. This is a pretty good stinger [device for

heating water], but it blows the fuses pretty often. You should see the tattoo needles they make. They take a little electrical motor from some toy or something, attach it to a couple of needles, and they have a motorized tattoo needle. They make ink from soot. They burn checkers for the soot. Or they grind up colored pencil leads. (1985, 89)

An even more subversive motivation is the provision of weapons and tools for engineering escapes. Chris Ryder, in his book on the infamous Maze prison in Northern Ireland, reports that:

Several prison officers said that there was hardly a single item of material or equipment within the prison that had not been adapted or misused for some unintended purpose. Some of the most ingenious invention took place in support of the almost constant tunnelling operations . . . Food scoops and other kitchen utensils were flattened or reshaped to become digging implements. A trolley to convey spoil along the tunnel was made from a food tray with wheels fashioned from wood, and a chain was made to pull it in and out . . . Ventilation came by way of an electric motor removed from a heater and a propeller shaped from the metal lid of a Fray Bentos steak and kidney pie tin. (2000, 130)

You can find reports like these in practically any book on prison life, academic or popular, which makes it all the more significant that Foucault neglected to mention this phenomenon. He really should have, given his (admittedly somewhat later) insistence on resistance as inherent to exercises of power. On the other hand, so far as I have been able to determine, no other writers about prisons have made a study of this phenomenon, either—it is just mentioned in passing.

It might be doubted, though, that even cases of system-functional use in the service of political or social resistance have any significant effect on material culture or society at large. The shivs (knives) improvised by prison inmates from spoon handles, razor blades, and the like have, to my knowledge, had no effect on proper-functional weaponry, for instance. Indeed, it is likely that the vast majority of system-functional uses are not by themselves productive of significant cultural change or innovation. But system-functional uses are sometimes fundamental to broader processes of significant cultural innovation. In Chapter 6, for instance, we noted that the invention of the electric guitar, a diffuse, long-term process involving many individuals, depended heavily on system-functional uses of existing devices, such as microphones. And the electric guitar changed the character of Western popular music dramatically, along both aesthetic and technical dimensions (Preston 2000, 44–46). Similarly, organic gardening furnishes many examples of practices that depend on system-functional uses of readily available items—beer as slug bait, lengths of foundation drain to aerate the compost pile, rain barrels made from trash cans, and so on. And organic gardening is now spreading rapidly and changing food-growing practices from backyard gardens to large-scale farming. So, even if most system-functional uses are quite mundane deviations from proper-functional use, and even if most of these mundane deviations remain quite isolated and have in and of themselves little noticeable effect on the culture at large, there is a non-negligible fund of system-functional uses that contribute to pervasive and fundamental cultural changes.

Arguably, then, it is at this ground-floor level of interaction with material culture that the basic activity patterns necessary for acts of political or social resistance on the one hand, or for participation in significant cultural innovation on the other hand, are established. If you acquire the ability as a child to interact with items of material culture in the system-functional mode of alternative use as well as in the proper-functional mode of standard use, you end up as an adult with the ability to deal with items of material culture not just in terms of their established, socially approved proper functions, but in terms of other possible uses that may contribute to innovative or even revolutionary social processes. Like the skills involved in the proper-functional use of common items of material culture, the skills requisite to the non-proper use of these same items are acquired by everybody (*modulo* divisions of labor and leisure along lines of gender, class, age, and so on).

We can further characterize these skills by drawing on the results of our discussion of action in Part I. At the very end of that discussion, we briefly considered the role of practices and habits in implementing actions structured by the improvisatory strategies of appropriate-and-extend, proliferate-and-select, and turn-taking. Everyday activity involving the use of material culture—making breakfast, cleaning up the yard, working in the office, doing the shopping, and so on—is largely improvisatory in this sense. And proper-functional uses of items of material culture are stellar examples of the practices involved in implementing these activities, since they are culturally constituted, pre-existing action structures that individuals can deploy. A musician in the improvisatory process of writing a song, for example, relies on practices such as keys and modes, standard tunings for instruments, common song structures, and the like. But among these practices are also many proper-functional uses of items of material culture, such as the use of a capo to change the key, of pegs to tune strings, of tuners to tell you when you have tuned the strings correctly, of tape recorders to save the music you compose, of paper and pencil to write down the lyrics, and so on. Similarly, when making breakfast you rely on culturally specific practices concerning which foods are appropriate for the first meal of the day, but equally on proper-functional use practices, such as the use of frying pans for cooking eggs, of small glasses for juice and cups with handles for hot drinks like coffee, of knobs for turning the stove on and off, and so on.

We noted two things about such practices. First, they are still rather too general to be applied directly, and so must be implemented in their turn by personal habits. So, for example, you might have several frying pans, and which one you ordinarily use to fry your eggs is a matter of habit, as is the length of time you fry them. Similarly, you may well develop some fairly fixed habits over time with regard to the sequence in which you perform necessary sub-actions, such as getting out the juice, putting on the water for coffee, starting the eggs, and so on. Second, and much more importantly for our purposes at this point, we noted that practices are not infrequently honored in the breach rather than the performance. Some examples from songwriting were writing songs that deviate from the traditional verse-chorus structure, making up chords or tunings, and surreptitiously writing down lyrics in a notebook instead of taking notes at a business meeting. And, of course, this also pertains to the proper-use practices we have been looking at here. You might smash a guitar or set it on fire to create a spectacle during a performance rather than use it for its proper function, for example. Or you might use something that has a non-musical proper function for musical purposes. Guitar slides are a good example. Nowadays, you can buy specially made slides in metal, glass, or ceramic. But fundamentally, a slide is anything you can use to play a guitar string without fretting it. The most common item used was a glass bottleneck, but many other options are recorded, including a table knife (Cedell Davis), a lipstick tube (Bob Dylan, on his first album), and the T-bone from a steak (Fred McDowell—although this one may be apocryphal, it is a nice reminder of the fact that naturally occurring objects with biological proper functions may be pressed into service as easily as items of material culture). The non-proper, system-functional uses of items of material culture we have been discussing in this chapter thus turn out to be a special case of a general phenomenon remarked earlier. There is more than one way of deploying practices as a resource for structuring actions. Just as a practice such as taking notes at a business meeting can be subverted for other purposes, such as writing down song lyrics or composing love letters, so the material culture involved, which embodies the practices associated with proper-functional use, can be subverted for system-functional uses.

There is also more we can say about how this subversion proceeds. Although some system-functional uses become standardized and, thus, operate more like accepted practices, many are invented (or reinvented) on the fly by people intent on accomplishing their ordinary purposes. And these inventions typically are themselves improvisatory; that is, they proceed by application of the strategies we examined in Chapter 4. Let us start with appropriate-and-extend. First and most generally, a system-functional use of a proper-functional item of material culture can be seen as the appropriation of the item and the extension of its usefulness to new purposes. Thus, just as a songwriter may appropriate a traditional tune and write new lyrics for it, so anyone may appropriate a screwdriver and use it for a new purpose. Second, we emphasized in Chapter 4 that appropriation often alters what is appropriated rather than leaving it as is. Many system functions do not alter the item used. Indeed, the burden of complaints about abuse is precisely that they *should* not alter it; that the item should be left in its original state and with its original capacity to perform its proper function intact. But many system-functional uses do require modifications. You have to fold a sheet of writing paper in order to make a paper airplane, and chew it to a pulp to make a spitball. Its capacity to perform its proper function is compromised by the first operation, and destroyed by the second, although given the cheapness and disposability of writing paper, this might not qualify as abuse. Finally, we noted in Chapter 4 that the appropriation is often itself implemented by an application of proliferate-and-select—the generation and sorting through of a number of candidates for appropriation. This, too, is common in the invention of system functions, because an agent typically starts with a purpose she wants to accomplish and casts about for something that will do the trick. Thus, if you need to tighten a screw, you might try out a key (too thick), a nail file (too pointy), and finally a table knife (perfect!).

The collaborative nature of improvisatory action is also evident in system-functional uses. Collaborative applications of both proliferate-and-select and appropriate-and-extend often occur when people are already working or playing together. Thus, just as bandmates may appropriate and extend bits of music generated by others, so housemates may appropriate and extend candidate items generated for accomplishing some common purpose. ('Find me something to tighten this screw with, will you?' 'How about this key?' 'Nope, too thick. Can you find me something thinner?' 'Here's a table knife.' 'Great, thanks!') Turn-taking, which is necessarily collaborative, is also in evidence. Many proper-functional uses of items of material culture require turn-taking. Simple examples involve things that must be used by two people alternating their actions, like seesaws. More complex examples involve things that are used simultaneously by many people, like city buses. Here, negotiating turns may be a dicey business. In any case, because turn-taking is a familiar strategy in proper-functional use contexts, it is easily transferable to system-functional contexts. Thus, two prison inmates might take turns with the tedious task of sharpening a spoon handle on the cement floor of their cell to make a shiv—one sharpening while the other keeps an eye out for the guard, for instance, and switching roles whenever the sharpener becomes tired.

To sum up, then, the picture we have here is one in which proper-functional uses are central to the structuring of individual and collaborative action. They provide a supportive scaffolding and productive base for activity. At the same time, they represent constraints imposed by society on its members—constraints that are enforced in a variety of ways and with a variety of sanctions. But in cases where damage to the item can be avoided or where replacing it is easy, these constraints are not likely to be enforced with any great rigor, if at all. Moreover, while children are held to these constraints quite strictly in many contexts, in others they are encouraged to subvert or ignore them. The result of this ambivalent training regimen is ambivalently skilled adults, who are equally able to use material culture in proper-functional ways and in system-functional ways, and who are sensitive to the differences between these use patterns.

The purposes of individuals with regard to their material culture are formed by interaction with that material culture itself. So, subverting or ignoring a proper-functional use is not a way of stepping outside your culture, but rather a way of operating creatively or even subversively within it, and possibly of contributing to the process of changing it piecemeal from the inside. At the end of a supplement to the English edition of *Truth and Method*, Hans-Georg Gadamer characterizes the relationship between language and thought this way:

> To sum up, I would say that the basic misunderstanding concerning the linguistic character of our understanding is one of language, as if language were an existing whole composed of words and phrases, concepts, points of view and opinions. In reality, language is the single word whose virtuality opens up the infinity of discourse, of discourse with others, and of the freedom of 'speaking oneself' and of 'allowing oneself to be spoken'. Language is not its elaborate conventionalism, nor the burden of pre-schematism with which it loads us, but the generative and creative power unceasingly to make this whole fluid. (1975, 498)

What we have discovered about the relationship between material culture and individual purposes yields an analogous point. Material culture is misunderstood if it is viewed only in terms of proper-functional constraints on action and on the purposes people acquire. These constraints are real, and they do 'pre-schematize' actions and purposes. But the phenomena of system-functional use show that material culture is even more fundamentally an opening up of possibilities for creative action. Thus, material culture, like language, is at every point potentially fluid.

Gadamer also points us in the direction of an answer to the more general question about the relationship between the individual and society. Early in Habermas's career, he defended a revamped version of the Enlightenment view of this relationship, not against Foucault and the postmodern juggernaut, but against Gadamer's tradition-oriented philosophical hermeneutics. There are major differences between the philosophies of Gadamer and Foucault, and more generally, between hermeneutics and postmodernism. But they share a distrust of Enlightenment thinking, especially insofar as it revolves around the idea of individual autonomy and rational self-reflection *vis-à-vis* the social order. They share a fundamental belief that autonomy and self-reflection are subject to important limitations, especially given the developmental requirements of human individuals. And they share a suspicion that the kind of autonomy and rational self-transparency envisioned by the Enlightenment may not even be desirable as an ideal, since it compromises full-blooded notions of community, rootedness, tradition, emotional and social connection to others, and so on. Habermas has done his level best to address these issues, and to produce a version of the Enlightenment ideal that will stand up to the critiques of thinkers such as Gadamer and Foucault.

But, doubts remain and the criticisms resurface in new forms rather than being quelled once and for all.

Our account of action and material culture will be of little comfort to Habermas and the other devotees of the Enlightenment ideal, who are in essence committed to what we have been calling here the suigeneric view. The opposing sociogeneric view we have argued for is much more in consonance with the anti-Enlightenment tendencies of hermeneutics and postmodernism. In particular, it depicts the relationship between individual and society as ambivalent. On the one hand, the individual is formed in and through her interaction with material culture, such that her goals, purposes, motivational structure, and so on, are constituted in part by this interaction. In this sense the individual is not autonomous, but rather heteronomous—regulated to her core by the goals, purposes and motives of others, especially as they are embodied in the proper functions of the material culture she inherits. On the other hand, this same material culture is the springboard for individual and group departures from proper-functional usage in the pursuit of local purposes and goals. But, these departures are more in the nature of spin-offs than of unique inventions from scratch. So, we can grant Ian Hodder what he claims—as far as material culture goes, individuals are definitely not just instruments in a fully orchestrated game. They have a say in the orchestration, and sometimes that say eventuates in significant cultural innovation. But any notion of the individual abstracting herself completely from her material culture, even temporarily, as the Enlightenment ideal seems to require, must be abandoned.

Conclusion

So, where are we with regard to a philosophy of material culture? Our project was to lay some foundations, and to do so from within the discipline of philosophy. We did this, first, by looking at material culture from the side of the producer and user, and then by shifting our perspective and looking at it from the side of the things produced and used. As a result, we now have action-theoretic and function-theoretic foundations on which to build. But most importantly, we found that these two kinds of foundation share some unifying characteristics.

First, the centralized control model had to be dismantled before our foundation could be laid down. The centralized control model manifests itself in action theory as an entrenched view that understands intentions as plans, and actions as the execution of these plans. It manifests itself in function theory as the view that functions in material culture are established by the intentions of the designer. We countered the individualistic centralization aspect of this model with an emphasis on collaboration as the typical mode of human action, and also by de-emphasizing the role of intention in both action and the establishment of function in material culture. We countered the control aspect of the model with an account of improvisation as the predominant structure of human action.

Second, our discussion led us to a view we have called sociogenerism—a well-known view existing in many variations, the burden of which is that the individual is formed by her society, and would not be the individual she is without this. On the contrary, the centralized control model implies that fully fledged individuals exist prior to any social relationships into which they enter. We called this contrasting view suigenerism. It manifests itself in action theory as the view that individuals create social relationships by committing themselves to joint action. It manifests itself in function theory as the view that material culture, including its functional aspects, is reproduced by us, whereas organisms, including human beings, reproduce themselves. We countered suigenerism in action theory by showing that individuals are always already social, and that the social character of joint actions is determined by this pre-existing sociality, not created out of whole cloth by the individuals involved. We countered suigenerism in function theory by showing that the reproduction relationship between human beings and material culture is not a one-way street. Types of human purposes and individuals specific to a given society are reproduced through the interactions of human beings with the material culture of that society. Thus, we are reproduced by our material culture just as surely as we reproduce it.

Finally—and fortunately, since it supplies an antidote to sociogenerism's problematization of individual autonomy and innovation—our discussion led in both cases to a consideration of the creativity of human action. In the planning-oriented view of traditional action theory, the creativity of action is individual mental creativity, bound up with the devising of plans. Our account of improvisation gave us a different perspective. Creativity is distributed throughout the course of the action itself, as people take advantage of opportunities and resolve difficulties on the fly, often in concert with others and always in ongoing interaction with their material culture. Our account of function enhanced our understanding of this interaction with material culture by emphasizing the distinction between proper function and system function. In turn, this provided a reading of the creativity of action specific to the functional aspects of material culture. Learning to use items of material culture in accordance with their proper functions is central to the sociogeneric process of reproducing types of purposes and individuals. But at the same time, the permanent possibility of using proper-functional items in system-functional ways manifests the permanent possibility of individual inventiveness and creative intervention in material culture. In turn, this underwrites large-scale processes of cultural change and innovation.

So, that is where we are. How can we build on these foundations? We have touched on a number of topics that are essential for a philosophy of material culture, but that we have not been at leisure to address—the role of material culture in cognition, in social life, and in the good life as an aspect of human flourishing. Pursuing these topics would require building connections between the action-theoretic and function-theoretic foundations we now have, and work in other areas of philosophy, as well as in a number of other disciplines. We can briefly sketch some directions for future work along these lines.

Although we did not investigate the role of material culture in cognitive processes involving knowledge, belief, and the like, some of our conclusions do have a bearing on this topic. For example, the distinction between proper function and system function suggests a possible difference in the cognitive processes with which we engage our material culture, perhaps along the lines of the distinction between logical thought and *bricolage* drawn by Claude Lévi-Strauss (1968). But more importantly, the centralized control model of action implies that cognition is in the first instance an individual, mental process. Our collaborative improvisation model, on the other hand, implies that cognition is in the first instance a social process carried out in constant commerce with material culture and with others. This links our conclusions closely to the recent philosophical literature on the extended mind hypothesis, which holds that cognitive processes extend outside the skull and skin of the individual organism (Clark and Chalmers 1998; Clark 2008; Menary 2010). The predominant line of inquiry concerns individual cognition extended by items of material culture such as notebooks or astrolabes, but there has been some discussion of socially extended cognition as well (Tollefsen 2006). This philosophical literature connects with work in cognitive anthropology and archaeology which focuses not only on the role of material culture in cognitive processes, but also on how cognition may have changed over the course of human history as a result of the evolving involvement of human beings with material cultures (Knappett 2005; Boivin 2008; Renfrew, Frith, and Malafouris 2009; Malafouris and Renfrew 2010). In these disciplines, the collaborative use of material culture and the social nature of cognition are emphasized much more strongly than in the philosophical literature. So, there is considerable potential for using the accounts of action and function developed here to contribute to this new interdisciplinary approach to cognition.

Both parts of our investigation here called for a sociogeneric approach to the relationship between individual and society. In particular, we found that function in material culture is an essential factor in explaining how the individual is formed by her society, as well as how and to what extent the individual nevertheless has the capacity for creativity and self-determination. So, we did touch on the social aspects of material culture to some extent. But there is a lot more to be said on this topic. Especially important here is the role of material culture in the circulation of power in society, which we addressed only in passing. Our sociogeneric approach suggests that material culture is not just a passive tool used by human beings to exercise power, but rather has a kind of agency of its own (DeMarrais, Gosden, and Renfrew 2004; Latour 2005; Knappett and Malafouris 2010). Thus, just as the extended mind hypothesis takes aspects of material culture as actual components of cognitive processes, so a philosophy of power may take aspects of material culture as actual agents in exercises of power. This view is implicit in Foucault's later work, especially *Discipline and Punish* (1977), and explicit in actor-network theory (Latour 2005). The account of function in material culture we have developed here, thus, has potential to contribute to an understanding of how this material agency operates and what effects it has for ordinary people going about their everyday lives.

Finally, a topic we have not really touched on at all here is the evaluation of material culture as an element of human flourishing—or lack of flourishing, as the case may be. This topic is perhaps most obviously the province of philosophy of technology, which began with wide-ranging critiques of modern technology and its allegedly dire effects on human existence by Martin Heidegger, Jacques Ellul, and others. But it is also related to more descriptive attempts by archaeologists and anthropologists to understand how the evolving involvement with material culture might have changed the social (in addition to the cognitive) possibilities for human beings over the course of our history as a species (Ingold 2000b; Hodder 2006). In short, the topic here is the role of material culture in explaining what it is to be human, and change in what it is to be human. Both parts of our discussion have a bearing on these issues. If we are primarily improvisers, we are quite a different kind of animal, with quite a different kind of trajectory through the world, than if we are primarily planners. We are more the inventive animal than the rational animal. And the distinction between proper function and system function, as we deployed it in Chapter 7, helps to explain how individuals can be free and self-determining within the ineluctable, shaping forces of their culture (Ingold 2011). Indeed, function theory has become a standard component of work in recent philosophy of technology, especially in the Netherlands (Houkes and Vermaas 2010; Vermaas et al. 2011). So, last, but not least, the accounts of action and function we have developed here also have much to contribute to the evaluation of material culture and its role in human flourishing.

Appendix

THE SONGWRITING STUDY

The account of improvisation in Chapter 4 rests largely on an interview-based study of songwriting I conducted myself. The reasons for choosing songwriting as the domain for this study are given in detail there, so I will just review them briefly here. As published interviews with songwriters attest, songwriting is an improvisatory activity and frequently collaborative, as well. In addition, songwriting is one component in the larger complex of music-making activities, which has some very attractive features from the point of view of the study of action and material culture. First, there appear to be no human cultures devoid of music making, so cross-cultural studies are possible. Second, the domain of music making exhibits a rich and diverse material culture, ranging from musical instruments, to various kinds of texts, to musical works themselves. Finally, music making often involves improvisation in performance, a special kind of improvisatory activity that should be studied in addition to, and in comparison with, the more common, non-performance kinds of improvisation we are concerned with here.

The idea for the study began with the realization that existing, publically available interviews with songwriters contained a wealth of interesting and suggestive material from the point of view of an investigation of improvisation and collaboration. But there were a number of problems with using this material. First, there was a lack of consistency between interviews in terms of what questions were asked. Moreover, it was impossible to know how the interviews had been transcribed, and to what extent they had been edited. These problems led to the idea of doing a set of interviews with songwriters myself, to supply the missing consistency and a foundational set of data. The publically available interviews could then be used as supplementary data.

The plan for the study was to record interviews with 10 songwriters. The only official criterion for choosing the participants was songwriting experience. It was also required that roughly half of them be songwriters who typically write collaboratively, and the other half songwriters who typically write on their own. This could be judged ahead of time by looking at the songwriting credits on releases, and through information in published interviews and articles in the popular press. Potential participants were contacted directly by email or letter, or through their manager if they had one. They were told that the interview would concern their songwriting practices, and that the purpose of the research was to find out more about how people make cultural artifacts, especially the improvisatory and collaborative aspects of the creative process. They were also told that participants would be identified by name in resulting publications. In return, participants were promised an opportunity to review pre-publication drafts in case they wished to withdraw their participation at that point.

Two aspects of this study depended on the agreement of the participants to have their participation be public rather than anonymous or confidential. First, and most importantly, much of the interest of this material resides in the discussion of particular songs and how they came to be written. It would have been impossible to disguise the identities of the songwriters without disguising the identities of the songs. That would have been difficult to do in many cases without losing significant details, as well as some quotable quotes. And it would have prevented interested readers from listening to the songs to hear for themselves the end results of the improvisatory activity described. Second, publically available material could be used in a supplementary role.

Of the 10 people who agreed to an interview, five were women and five were men. With one exception (Miria), all were songwriters working in Athens, Georgia, where the University of Georgia is located. This made it possible to do the interviews in person. (Miria was interviewed in person as well, but in Milford, New Hampshire.) Some of the participants were in bands at the time of the interview, and typically wrote in collaboration with one or more of their bandmates. So, where possible, more than one person from the band was interviewed (Russ Hallauer and Jason Slatton from The Lures; Mamie Fike Simonds, Kathy Kirbo, and Kelly Noonan from Jackpot City). Some of the participants make their living in the music business; others have day jobs. Some have considerable formal training in music; others have little or none. Most are performers as well as songwriters.

The interviews were conducted in person, usually in my office, and lasted about an hour. They were semi-structured. I had a list of basic questions about songwriting I asked every participant, but I asked some additional, individually tailored questions as well. The individually tailored questions were based on what I had been able to glean from publically available sources about the songwriting practices and history of the participant. In addition, whenever an interesting direction was opened up by an answer, I followed up in a flexible manner. I also prepared for the interviews by listening to the live and/or recorded music of the participants, which made it possible to ask about particular songs and to follow up in an informed way on remarks made about the experience of writing particular songs.

The interviews were recorded on audiotape. I transcribed the tapes myself. Initially, this decision was due to a lack of funding to hire a professional transcriber, but it turned out to be an invaluable first pass in the interpretation process. By the time all the tapes had been transcribed, some basic patterns had already become apparent. I then went back over the transcripts, coding passages for the occurrence of these patterns and their variations, as well as for some additional patterns that emerged on this second pass through the data. The end result of this process was the conceptual framework for the account of improvisation in Chapter 4. The examples and quotations from songwriters used in Chapter 4 are drawn from this set of interview transcripts, supplemented occasionally with examples and quotations from publically available interviews with the participants, and/or their bandmates and other collaborators.

Finally, it is important to say something about the relationship between this kind of work and the recent movement called 'experimental philosophy' (Alexander 2012; Knobe and Nichols 2008). Experimental philosophy is methodologically just that—experimental. Subjects are normally brought into a laboratory setting and asked specific questions, their answers are recorded, and the results are analyzed. The idea is to get at the intuitions of ordinary folk about some important philosophical issues, such as free will, or when an action is judged intentional and when not. Often an attempt is also made to get at the cognitive processes underpinning the intuitions. This is valuable work, in my view, and a valuable empirical adjunct to more traditional philosophical methodology. But the methodology of experimental philosophy would not have been appropriate for my project. Because it is aimed at eliciting intuitions, understandings, and the like, it is focused on what people think. My interest, in contrast, is in what people do. So, bringing them into a laboratory setting to answer questions with one word or a short phrase would not help at all. There were two other options— interviews in which my subjects could tell me what they did, or participant observation. Ideally, of course, one should do both. But since I did not have the wherewithal to do participant observation, I settled for interviews.

This is usually termed qualitative research, as opposed to the quantitative paradigm favored by experimental philosophy. (For example, an experimental philosopher might ask what proportion of subjects, when presented with a given scenario, judged it to be an example of an intentional action.) These two methodological paradigms have different strengths and weaknesses, and are consequently good for generating different kinds of data. So, in adopting a qualitative methodology, I do not intend to challenge the methodology of experimental philosophy in any way, but only to complement it by showcasing another methodological option that may be more useful for some philosophical purposes.

STUDY PARTICIPANTS

Mamie Fike Simonds was keyboard player and vocalist for Jackpot City at the time of the interview. Jackpot City changed its name to Heavy Feather in 2009 and has now, for the most part, disbanded. Fike Simonds also plays violin with the Athens Symphony Orchestra.
   www.myspace.com/heavyfeatherband

Russ Hallauer was the guitarist for The Lures at the time of the interview. The Lures have disbanded, but Hallauer continues to record on his own and with a bluegrass band, The Welfare Liners, for whom he plays mandolin. He is also the proprietor of Ghostmeat Records.
   www.ghostmeat.com/home.html
   www.thewelfareliners.com/index.html

Kevn Kinney was a singer/songwriter based in Athens, Georgia, at the time of the interview. In addition, he is a founding member of Drivin' N' Cryin', which continues to perform and record. Kinney also records and performs both on his own and with various other collaborators.
   www.kevnkinney.com
   www.drivinncryin.com

Kathy Kirbo played bass and guitar and sang with Jackpot City at the time of the interview. Jackpot City changed its name to Heavy Feather in 2009 and has now, for the most part, disbanded. Kirbo has a new band, The Spinoffs. She is also the executive director of the Reef Ball Foundation.
   www.facebook.com/spinoffs
   www.myspace.com/heavyfeatherband
   www.reefball.org/

Mike Mills was the bass player and multi-instrumentalist for R.E.M. at the time of the interview. R.E.M. disbanded in 2011, but Mills continues to pursue musical projects on his own and with various collaborators.
   www.remhq.com/index.php

Miria is a songwriter who was based in Milford, New Hampshire, at the time of the interview. After moving to Los Angeles to pursue her musical career, she co-produced the first Los Angeles Women's Music Festival in 2007 and released an album, *Under the Surface,* with producer Amir Efrat. Her single, 'Lullabye of Mars,' won second place at the 2004 Mars Society Roget de Lisle song contest, and her song, 'Break Your Heart,' from the album, won second place in the DBSA 'Facing Us' Song Contest in 2008.
   www.miriamusic.com
   www.lawmf.com

Kelly Noonan was the guitarist and vocalist with Jackpot City at the time of the interview. Jackpot City changed its name to Heavy Feather in 2009 and has now, for the most part, disbanded. Noonan is also the proprietor of Doggie Styles, a dog-grooming establishment in Athens, Georgia.

www.myspace.com/heavyfeatherband

Debbie Norton was the main songwriter, singer, and guitarist for the band Where's Anita? at the time of the interview. Although Where's Anita? has disbanded, Norton still occasionally performs her music in local venues in the Athens, Georgia, area.

Nathan Sheppard is a singer/songwriter based in North Georgia. Although he had worked with bands at an earlier point in his career, at the time of the interview he was pursuing a solo path. He continues to perform and record, both on his own and with others.

www.nathansheppard.net/?section=home

Jason Slatton was the lead vocalist and guitarist for The Lures at the time of the interview. He has also co-written and/or collaborated on five albums with songwriter Randall Bramblett. He has since obtained a degree in creative writing and literature; he currently teaches a course in American modernism at the Alabama School of Fine Arts in Birmingham, Alabama.

www.ghostmeat.com/lures.html

Notes

NOTES TO THE INTRODUCTION

1. Besides Brooks himself, whose early papers on subsumption architecture were influential for my dissertation and subsequently for my "Heidegger and Artificial Intelligence" (1993), this group included John Batali, Peter Cudhea, Gary Drescher, Anita Flynn, Marty Hiller, Ian Horswill, David Kirsh, and Maja Mataric.
2. For a description of these robots and their capabilities, see Brooks (1990), also reprinted as chapter 7 of Brooks (1999).
3. This point is also made by Randall Dipert, whose own *Artifacts, Art Works, and Agency* (1993) is an important exception.
4. See Baker (2007), Elder (2004), Thomasson (2007), and the essays in Part I of Margolis and Laurence (2007). An exception is Hilpinen (1992, 2011), who focuses more squarely on artifacts and not only on metaphysics.
5. See Heidegger (1993a), Dusek (2006), and Pitt (2000). An exception is Mitcham (1994), who suggests that technology should be broadly characterized to include everything from toys, to art works, to objects of religious veneration.
6. See Pitt (2000), Kroes and Meijers (2002), or Ihde (1991). Recent English language anthologies of philosophy of technology often manifest this narrowing of focus as well. See Scharff and Dusek (2003) or Kaplan (2004). An exception is Dusek (2006).
7. See Myers (2001) for a valuable and sophisticated discussion of this issue. In Myers's view, the general issue is really the multiple sources of value that things have, and the ways they circulate—or fail to circulate—through various cultural contexts.
8. Dipert (1998) acknowledges that outside philosophy the term 'artifact' is often used in ways that do not assume intentional, individual authorship.
9. See Dipert (1993) for the argument that performances are indeed artifacts. The very fact that an argument was called for is evidence of the strength of the implicit bias toward durable, tangible things.

NOTES TO CHAPTER 1

1. 'Centralized control' is terminology commonly used in military and business contexts to refer to hierarchical organizations in which decisions are made at the top and transmitted to the rank and file. Mitchell Resnick (1994) generalized this terminology to everything from national political organization, to ant colonies, to minds. On Resnick's view, the assumption of centralized

control reflects a misunderstanding of how all these things are typically organized. Instead, he claims, they are typically self-organizing systems in which order and complexity are created solely from the interaction of multitudes of simple and initially disorderly elements. Although I am in sympathy with his complaint—hence my adoption of the same terminology—I am not in sympathy with the self-organizing system alternative, because I think it badly underestimates the role of the environment, including the social environment, in structuring activity.

2. Some exceptions are Brett (1981), Pollard (2006a, 2006b), and Sutton (2007).
3. An exception is Clarke (2010).
4. On Aristotle's view there really is only one activity that is perfectly energic—always chosen for itself and never for some further end—and that is theoretical activity or contemplation (*Nicomachean Ethics* 1177a10–1178b35).
5. See *Capital* (Marx 1976), Volume I, chapters 13 and 14, *et passim.*
6. Marx articulates this vision in several versions, particularly in the chapter entitled 'Private Property and Communism' in *Economic and Philosophic Manuscripts* (Marx 1997, 301 ff.). The issue of ownership and its disappearance under full-fledged communism is also most clearly discussed in this chapter.
7. Chuck Berry's 'Sweet Little Sixteen' originally appeared on *One Dozen Berries* (Chess 1958). The Beach Boys' retitled version is on the eponymous *Surfin' USA* (Capitol Records 1963). Memphis Minnie's original version of 'When the Levee Breaks' can be found on *Kansas Joe and Memphis Minnie, 1929–1934* (Document 1991). Led Zeppelin's version is on their untitled fourth album (Atlantic 1971). Both the Beach Boys and Led Zeppelin credited the originators of the appropriated songs.
8. Big Joe Williams recorded 'Baby, Please Don't Go' several times. One of these versions is on his *Complete Works, Volume I, 1935–1941* (Document 1991).
9. This is clear from the discussion of Dipert's work, but see also Houkes, Vermaas, Dorst, and Vries (2002) for an explicit application of planning theory to design of artifacts.
10. This is often explicit in the artificial intelligence planning literature. See Pollack (1992, 44 ff.) for an example.
11. My thinking on this issue owes a lot to Suchman (2007), Agre and Chapman (1990), Chapman (1991), and Agre (1997). I should also stress that I am talking about relatively experienced cooks. Novice cooks do tend to follow recipes rather more slavishly. But novice cooks by definition do not yet know how to cook—in particular, they do not yet have the fund of habits and background knowledge the experienced cook has accumulated. Consequently, there is no reason to think that experienced cooks are merely doing *better* what novice cooks do, and some good reasons to think they are doing something *different* (Dreyfus and Dreyfus 1988).
12. Large organizations are too unwieldy to turn on a dinner plate, let alone a dime. Nor do they seem to be particularly well equipped for efficient planning. There is a question about scaling up here that needs attention, but I will not be able to devote any to it here.

NOTES TO CHAPTER 2

1. As action theorists routinely point out, you can have a plan without ever being committed to executing it. For example, a homeland security expert might ask herself: 'If I were a terrorist, what targets would I select, and how would I go about attacking them?' The resulting plans are not ones the expert herself has any intention of ever carrying out. Thus planning theories of intention

appeal to *executing a plan* as the relevant notion, not just to *having a plan* in the abstract.
2. As Bratman (1999b, 88–89) himself notes, personal policies are by nature defeasible.
3. 'Control' is Bratman's term here, and thus should not be construed in the technical sense given it in the first chapter for the purposes of explicating the centralized control model of production. 'Guidance' or 'governance' might better express Bratman's point, which is that the agent has some say in how things go, as opposed to being in the grip of a compulsion or a reflex and having no say at all.

NOTES TO CHAPTER 3

1. These articles are reprinted together as Part Two of Bratman (1999a).
2. The idea that nonhuman entities are actors of a sort, and thus capable of responding, has been explored in actor-network theory (Law and Hassard 1999; Latour 2005).
3. This actually makes perfect sense in terms of the game theoretic definition of cooperation as strategic interaction in which enforceable agreements are possible. Enforcing an agreement is a competitive action, not a cooperative one.
4. An exception is Miller (2001).
5. Some notable examples include Tuomela and Miller (1988), Gilbert (1989, 2008), Searle (1990), Velleman (1997), Bratman (1999a), Kutz (2000), Tollefsen (2002), and Roth (2004).
6. Plural subjecthood is explicated at length in Gilbert (1989, 1996, 2000). The best single exposition of this idea is probably the essay "Walking Together: A Paradigmatic Social Phenomenon" (1996, 177–94).
7. This argument takes up the whole of Chapter III of *On Social Facts* (Gilbert 1989, 58–145).
8. The content certainty and privacy theses also rule out content externalism, the view that the content of our mental states is in part social, not individual (Putnam 1975; Burge 1979).
9. Seumas Miller (1997) also makes this point. It resonates as well with Kenneth Shockley's (2004) worry that there is no reasonable sense in which the individual obligations flow from the joint commitment; and with Deborah Tollefsen's (2002) criticism that Gilbert's theory involves a circular analysis in which social concepts are presupposed in the formation of the plural subject rather than created by it.
10. Gilbert (2008, 489) does issue this disclaimer, for instance.

NOTES TO CHAPTER 4

1. A list of the songwriters interviewed and information about their past and current musical activities may be found in the Appendix.
2. That this is sometimes possible with actions as well as with freestanding products may not be obvious. But consider, for example, restating in a quite different way something you just said; or having failed to find something you have lost, starting over and conducting the search in a different way. On the other hand, a product is not always revisable in every respect. Once the casserole is cooked, you may *wish* you had put in less salt than the recipe called for, but it is too late to do anything about it.

3. This crucial point is missed in R. Keith Sawyer's (2001) otherwise interesting attempt to understand group improvisation in conversation using improv theater as a model (see also Crease [1994]). Sawyer proposes a 'Yes, and' rule, in accordance with which an improvising agent accepts at face value a contribution from another agent and then tacks on a contribution of her own. Improvisation on stage necessarily proceeds in this beads-on-a-string fashion, because of the restrictions imposed by performance. You do have to interpret the contributions of the other actors in some way in order to formulate your own. But you can't revise or reject their contributions without ruining the performance for the audience. Sawyer also misses the importance of unintentional contributions, for similar reasons—in performance you have to focus on what your fellow performers intend as their contributions, and indeed on what they intend *by* them.

4. Sawyer (2001) also misses this crucial point as a result of using improv theater as his model for improvisation in general. On stage, you can't try out a number of options before selecting one. Instead, you must generate one option and stick with it, no matter what. So Sawyer's model effectively restricts his analysis to this limiting case of proliferate-and-select.

5. A good and very readable introduction to conversation analysis, which also details its historical relationship to ethnomethodology, is Hutchby and Wooffitt (1998). See also Psathas (1995) and Have (1999). The classic introduction to ethnomethodology is Heritage (1984); see also Coulon (1995).

6. This is pointed out by Paul ten Have (1999, 8–9).

7. The official rules for professional baseball can be found on the Major League Baseball website at http://mlb.mlb.com/NASApp/mlb/mlb/official_info/index.jsp (accessed June 7, 2012). Many thanks to Randolph Clarke for helping me with this example.

NOTES TO CHAPTER 5

1. 'System function' is my term.

2. Michael Schiffer (1992) distinguishes between technofunctions, sociofunctions and ideofunctions. Technofunctions subserve practical purposes—for example, the technofunction of a carving knife is to cut meat. Sociofunctions subserve social purposes—for example, the sociofunction of a wedding ring is to display marital status. And ideofunctions subserve communicative or symbolic purposes—for example, the Christian cross has the ideofunction of communicating the connection between Christ's suffering and the salvation of the believer. This taxonomy of function is descended from Lewis Binford's (1962) distinction between technomic, socio-technic and ideo-technic categories of artifacts. It is understood by both Schiffer and Binford that an item of material culture may belong to more than one of these categories at the same time. For example, a white wedding dress does keep you warm, while at the same time displaying your social status as a bride.

3. See http://www.ipm.iastate.edu/ipm/hortnews/1996/6–14–1996/bugzapper.html (accessed June 12, 2012), for instance.

4. I owe this example to Amie Thomasson.

5. Karen Neander (1991a, 1991b) calls Cummins's functions 'causal role' functions, and this terminology has taken hold in the literature. I prefer 'system' function because not all such functions correspond straightforwardly to an identifiable causal role. For example, one of the functions of the queen in the chess system is to capture pawns. But her capacity to do this does not cause pawns to be captured in the straightforward way that the capacity

of the heart to pump blood causes blood to be circulated through the body. Moreover, Cummins (1983) himself explicitly contrasts functional analysis (or interpretive explanation, as he also calls it) with analysis in terms of causal laws. So the term 'causal role' is misleading in general, and is especially so in the case of function in material culture.

6. This is disputed by Davies (2001) and Hardcastle (2002). But there is wide agreement that theories of proper function lend themselves naturally to accounts of malfunction, whereas theories of system function do not.

7. I have argued that in spite of her overt support for a pluralist theory, Millikan, in fact, subsumes system function under proper function as an unwanted side effect of her account of derived proper function (Preston 1998b).

8. You can find this history on the 3M website at http://www.3m.com/us/office/postit/pastpresent/history.jhtml (accessed June 13, 2012).

9. Walsh and Ariew canvas them very thoroughly, for instance (1996, 505 ff.).

10. This label refers to the phenomenon noted by Heidegger (1962) that items of material culture typically make sense only in relation to other types of items with related functions. Writing paper makes sense only in conjunction with writing instruments, erasers, wastepaper baskets, paper clips, and so on. These suites or toolkits have rather fluid boundaries, but then so do the correlative conspecific groups or populations on the biology side of the chart.

11. As Peter Godfrey-Smith (2009, 88–91) points out, this divide is not so sharp if we take into account the many different modes of reproduction in biology. Among them is what he calls 'scaffolded reproduction,' where biological entities are reproduced by some other entity or as part of some larger entity. Examples are viruses and chromosomes, which are reproduced by the cells they inhabit, and so might as well be termed reproducees as reproducers. Godfrey-Smith (2009, 153) says that although scaffolded reproduction is rare in biology, it is common in the case of cultural entities. This might provide an alternate route for bridging the divide between natural reproduction and cultural reproduction—and thus ultimately between nature and culture—although it is not the route we will take in Chapter 7.

NOTES TO CHAPTER 6

1. The following discussion is based on Millard (2004) and Bacon and Day (1993).

2. Bacon and Day (1993) quote Ted McCarty, the president of Gibson at the time, who says those involved included himself, John Huis, Julius Bellson, Wilbur Marker, sales manager Clarence Havenga, and 'one of the fellows in charge of the wood department, and one of the guitar players in the final assembly' (13).

3. Thanks to Sarah Wright for this suggestion.

4. Thanks to David Chapman for suggesting this analogy.

5. Thanks to Amie Thomasson for pointing out some of these problems to me.

6. Ole Bruun (2003, 6 ff.) gives this as a major reason for the resurgence of *fengshui* practices in rural China. The state orthodoxy has been rationalistic and secular, and has attempted to impose corresponding practices on local populations from a position of central authority. This has been resisted in many cases by simply resurrecting or continuing local practices and traditions, particularly *fengshui*. Bruun also looked into the question of whether people in his study area believe in the efficacy of *fengshui* practices. Some clearly did and some clearly did not; but overall what Bruun concluded was that this is usually not even the right question to ask if you are trying to understand the practices and their persistence.

NOTES TO CHAPTER 7

1. A revised, shorter form of this essay appeared as chapter 18 of Ingold (2000b). The basic argument is the same.
2. How much structure constrains function and what methods we can reliably use to infer function on the basis of structure are matters of debate (Kirsh 2010). What is not controversial is that structure and function underdetermine each other—the point we captured in Chapter 5 under the headings of multiple realizability of function and multiple utilizability of structure. And that is all we need in order to proceed here.
3. This astonishing early Bronze Age burial is described in detail on the website of Wessex Archaeology, the commercial firm responsible for the excavation and analysis of the finds, at http://www.wessexarch.co.uk/projects/amesbury/archer.html (accessed June 19, 2012). Thanks to Ervan Garrison for drawing my attention to this example.
4. This consonance is further borne out by Ingold's own more recent work on improvisation (Hallam and Ingold 2007), discussed in Chapter 2.
5. Marianne Thesander (1997) argues that tightly laced corsets make it impossible for women to do strenuous work. So, if the women of a household wore corsets this showed they did not have to work, and thus displayed the socioeconomic status of the family. Similar arguments apply to the practice of foot binding in China at the same period.
6. See Marx (1976), especially Part Eight (chapters 26–33) and the Appendix (III and IV). The sociality of the individual does not sort particularly well with the view that material culture is the expression of human purposes. Marx was convinced of the fundamental sociality of individual agents, and, on the other hand, was committed to individual self-determination as an ethical and political ideal. I do not think he ever really explains how these views can be reconciled.
7. The Arnold Gehlen quote is the last line of *Man in the Age of Technology* (Gehlen 1980, 166).
8. See Wright (2012).
9. Damage and loss of proper-functional capacity may also result from overly rough proper use or from lack of maintenance, such as leaving your screwdriver out in the rain to get rusty. These cases, too, may be categorized as abuse, and are an aspect of the complexity of this phenomenon. But for present purposes, we will limit our consideration to cases of abuse involving alternative, non-proper uses. Another complication is that what counts or does not count as abuse is relative to the particulars of the situation. If you broke your screwdriver using it to help pry a heavily bleeding accident victim out of a wrecked car when no better implement was to hand, you would not be criticized as you would if you broke it prying up floor tiles when you had plenty of time to find or purchase a more suitable tool. We will ignore this complication, as well.
10. Both historically and currently, there are corsets designed for and used by men. But for the most part, corsets have been, and continue to be, designed for and used by women; and even men wearing corsets designed as male attire are often criticized as effeminate (Steele 2001, 36–39). The unacknowledged, latent proper function of socioeconomic display connected with the wearing of corsets in the nineteenth century depends on this gender specificity.
11. Thanks to Bonnie Cramond for alerting me to this tradition in creativity testing.

References

Agre, Philip E. 1997. *Computation and Human Experience*. Cambridge, UK: Cambridge University Press.

———, and David Chapman. 1990. "What Are Plans For?" *Robotics and Autonomous Systems* 6:17–34.

Alexander, Joshua. 2012. *Experimental Philosophy: An Introduction*. Cambridge, UK: Polity Press.

Allen, Colin, and Marc Bekoff. 1995. "Biological Function, Adaptation, and Natural Design." *Philosophy of Science* 62: 609–22.

Appadurai, Arjun, ed. 1986. *The Social Life of Things: Commodities in Cultural Perspective*. Cambridge, UK: Cambridge University Press.

Arendt, Hannah. 1958. *The Human Condition*. 2nd ed. Chicago: University of Chicago Press.

Ariew, André. 2002. "Platonic and Aristotelian Roots of Teleological Arguments." In *Functions: New Essays in the Philosophy of Psychology and Biology*, edited by André Ariew, Robert Cummins, and Mark Perlman, 7–32. Oxford, UK: Oxford University Press.

———, and Mark Perlman. 2002. "Introduction." In *Functions: New Essays in the Philosophy of Psychology and Biology*, edited by André Ariew, Robert Cummins, and Mark Perlman, 1–4. Oxford, UK: Oxford University Press.

Aristotle. 1984a. *Physics*. In *The Complete Works of Aristotle: The Revised Oxford Translation, Volume One*, edited by Jonathan Barnes, 315–446. Princeton, NJ: Princeton University Press.

———. 1984b. *Metaphysics*. In *The Complete Works of Aristotle: The Revised Oxford Translation, Volume Two*, edited by Jonathan Barnes, 1552–1728. Princeton, NJ: Princeton University Press.

———. 1985. *Nicomachean Ethics*, translated by Terence Irwin. Indianapolis: Hackett Publishing Company.

Audi, Robert. 1973. "Intending." *The Journal of Philosophy* 70(13): 387–403.

Bacon, Tony, and Paul Day. 1993. *The Gibson Les Paul Book*. San Francisco: GPI Books.

Baier, Annette C. 1997. "Doing Things With Others: The Mental Commons." In *Commonality and Particularity in Ethics*, edited by Lilli Alanen, Sara Heinämaa, and Thomas Wallgren, 15–44. New York: St. Martin's Press.

Baker, Lynne Rudder. 2007. *The Metaphysics of Everyday Life: An Essay in Practical Realism*. Cambridge, UK: Cambridge University Press.

Binford, Lewis R. 1962. "Archaeology as Anthropology." *American Antiquity* 28(2): 217–25.

Boivin, Nicole. 2008. *Material Cultures, Material Minds: The Impact of Things on Human Thought, Society, and Evolution*. Cambridge, UK: Cambridge University Press.

Bourdieu, Pierre. 1977. *Outline of a Theory of Practice*, translated by Richard Nice. Cambridge, UK: Cambridge University Press.

Brand, Myles. 1970. "Action and Behavior." In *The Nature of Human Action*, edited by Myles Brand, 3–21. Glenview, IL: Scott, Foresman and Company.

———. 1986. "Intentional Actions and Plans." In *Midwest Studies in Philosophy, Volume 10*, edited by Peter A. French, Theodore E. Uehling, Jr., and Howard K. Wettstein, 213–30. Minneapolis: University of Minnesota Press.

Bratman, Michael E. 1983. "Taking Plans Seriously." *Social Theory and Practice* 9(2–3): 271–87.

———. 1999a. *Faces of Intention: Selected Essays on Intention and Agency*. Cambridge, UK: Cambridge University Press.

———. 1999b. *Intention, Plans, and Practical Reason*. Reprinted in *The David Hume Series of Philosophy and Cognitive Science Reissues*. Stanford, CA: CSLI Publications. Originally published by Cambridge, MA: Harvard University Press, 1987.

Brett, Nathan. 1981. "Human Habits." *Canadian Journal of Philosophy* 11: 357–76.

Brooks, Rodney A. 1990. "Elephants Don't Play Chess." *Robotics and Autonomous Systems* 6: 3–15.

———. 1999. *Cambrian Intelligence: The Early History of the New AI*. Cambridge, MA: MIT Press.

Bruun, Ole. 2003. *Fengshui in China: Geomantic Divination Between State Orthodoxy and Popular Religion*. Honolulu: University of Hawai'i Press.

Buchli, Victor. 2002. "Introduction." In *The Material Culture Reader*, edited by Victor Buchli, 1–22. Oxford, UK: Berg.

Buller, David J. 1998. "Etiological Theories of Function: A Geographical Survey." *Biology and Philosophy* 13: 505–27.

Burge, Tyler. 1979. "Individualism and the Mental." *Midwest Studies in Philosophy* 4(1): 73–121.

Certeau, Michel de. 1984. *The Practice of Everyday Life*, translated by Steven Rendall. Berkeley: University of California Press.

Chapman, David. 1991. *Vision, Instruction, and Action*. Cambridge, MA: MIT Press.

Charmaz, Kathy. 1995. "Grounded Theory." In *Rethinking Methods in Psychology*, edited by Jonathan A. Smith, Rom Harré, and Luk Van Langenhove, 27–49. London, UK: Sage Publications.

Churchland, Paul M. 1970. "The Logical Character of Action Explanations." *The Philosophical Review* 79: 214–36.

Clark, Andy. 1997. *Being There: Putting Brain, Body, and World Together Again*. Cambridge, MA: MIT Press (Bradford).

———. 2008. *Supersizing the Mind: Embodiment, Action, and Cognitive Extension*. Oxford, UK: Oxford University Press.

———, and David Chalmers. 1998. "The Extended Mind." *Analysis* 58: 10–23.

Clarke, Randolph. 2010. "Skilled Activity and the Causal Theory of Action." *Philosophy and Phenomenological Research* 80(3): 523–50.

Collier, Graham. 1995. *Interaction: Opening Up the Jazz Ensemble*. Stuttgart: Advance Music.

Conkey, Margaret W. 2006. "Style, Design, and Function." In *Handbook of Material Culture*, edited by Christopher Tilley, Webb Keane, Susanne Küchler, Michael Rowlands, and Patricia Spyer, 355–72. Los Angeles: Sage Publications.

Cooke, Maeve. 1999. "Habermas, Feminism and the Question of Autonomy." In *Habermas: A Critical Reader*, edited by Peter Dews, 178–210. Oxford, UK: Blackwell.

Coulon, Alain. 1995. *Ethnomethodology*, translated by Jacqueline Coulon and Jack Katz. *Qualitative Research Methods Series, Volume 36*. Thousand Oaks, CA: Sage Publications.

Crease, Robert P. 1994. "The Improvisational Problem." *Man and World* (now *Continental Philosophy Review*) 27: 181–93.

Crilly, Nathan. 2010. "The Roles That Artefacts Play: Technical, Social and Aesthetic Functions." *Design Studies* 31(4): 311–44.

Cummins, Robert. 1975. "Functional Analysis." *The Journal of Philosophy* 72: 741–64.

———. 1983. *The Nature of Psychological Explanation.* Cambridge, MA: MIT Press.

———. 2002. "Neo-Teleology." In *Functions: New Essays in the Philosophy of Psychology and Biology,* edited by André Ariew, Robert Cummins, and Mark Perlman, 157–72. Oxford, UK: Oxford University Press.

Davies, Paul Sheldon. 2001. *Norms of Nature: Naturalism and the Nature of Functions.* Cambridge, MA: MIT Press.

Davis, Wayne A. 1984. "A Causal Theory of Intending." *American Philosophical Quarterly* 21 (1): 43–54.

DeMarrais, Elizabeth, Chris Gosden, and Colin Renfrew, eds. 2004. *Rethinking Materiality: The Engagement of Mind with the Material World.* Cambridge, UK: McDonald Institute for Archaeological Research.

Dews, Peter, ed. 1999. *Habermas: A Critical Reader.* Oxford, UK: Blackwell.

Dipert, Randall R. 1986. "Art, Artifacts, and Regarded Intentions." *American Philosophical Quarterly* 23(4): 401–8.

———. 1993. *Artifacts, Art Works, and Agency.* Philadelphia: Temple University Press.

———. 1998. "Artifact." In *The Encyclopedia of Aesthetics,* edited by Michael Kelly, 121–23. Oxford, UK: Oxford University Press.

Dreyfus, Hubert L. 2007. "The Return of the Myth of the Mental." *Inquiry* 50(4): 352–65.

———, and Stuart E. Dreyfus (with Tom Athanasiou). 1988. *Mind Over Machine: The Power of Human Intuition and Expertise in the Era of the Computer.* New York: Free Press.

Dusek, Val. 2006. *Philosophy of Technology: An Introduction.* Malden, MA: Blackwell.

Elder, Crawford. 2004. *Real Natures and Familiar Objects.* Cambridge, MA: MIT Press (Bradford).

Elster, Jon. 1985. *Making Sense of Marx.* Cambridge, UK and Paris, France: Cambridge University Press and Maison des Sciences de l'Homme.

Endler, John A. 1986. *Natural Selection in the Wild.* Princeton, NJ: Princeton University Press.

Ennen, Elizabeth. 2003. "Phenomenological Coping Skills and the Striatal Memory System." *Phenomenology and the Cognitive Sciences* 2(4): 299–325.

Ferré, Frederick. 1988. *Philosophy of Technology.* Englewood Cliffs, NJ: Prentice Hall.

Foucault, Michel. 1977. *Discipline and Punish: The Birth of the Prison,* translated by Alan Sheridan. New York: Vintage Books.

———. 1982. "The Subject and Power." In *Michel Foucault: Beyond Structuralism and Hermeneutics,* edited by Hubert L. Dreyfus and Paul Rabinow, 208–26. Chicago: University of Chicago Press.

———. 1990. *The History of Sexuality, Volume I: An Introduction,* translated by Robert Hurley. New York: Vintage Books.

Fraser, Nancy. 1981. "Foucault on Modern Power: Empirical Insights and Normative Confusions." *Praxis International* 1: 272–87.

———. 1985. "Michel Foucault: A 'Young Conservative'?" *Ethics* 96: 165–84.

Furo, Hiroko. 2001. *Turn-Taking in English and Japanese: Projectability in Grammar, Intonation, and Semantics.* New York: Routledge.

Gadamer, Hans-Georg. 1975. *Truth and Method,* translated by Garrett Barden and John Cumming. New York: Seabury Press (Continuum).

Gehlen, Arnold. 1980. *Man in the Age of Technology,* translated by Patricia Lipscomb. New York: Columbia University Press.

Giddens, Anthony. 1984. *The Constitution of Society: Outline of the Theory of Structuration.* Berkeley: University of California Press.

Gilbert, Margaret. 1989. *On Social Facts.* London, UK: Routledge.

———. 1996. *Living Together: Rationality, Sociality, and Obligation.* Lanham, MD: Rowman and Littlefield Publishers.

———. 1997. "Concerning Sociality: The Plural Subject as Paradigm." In *The Mark of the Social: Discovery or Invention?* edited by John D. Greenwood, 17–35. Lanham, MD: Rowman and Littlefield Publishers.

———. 2000. *Sociality and Responsibility: New Essays in Plural Subject Theory.* Lanham, MD: Rowman and Littlefield Publishers.

———. 2008. "Two Approaches to Shared Intention: An Essay in the Philosophy of Social Phenomena." *Analyse & Kritik* 30: 483–514.

Godfrey-Smith, Peter. 1993. "Functions: Consensus Without Unity." *Pacific Philosophical Quarterly* 74: 196–208.

———. 2009. *Darwinian Populations and Natural Selection.* Oxford, UK: Oxford University Press.

Goldman, Alvin I. 1970. *A Theory of Human Action.* Englewood Cliffs, NJ: Prentice-Hall.

Griffiths, Paul E. 1993. "Functional Analysis and Proper Functions." *The British Journal for the Philosophy of Science* 44: 409–22.

Grumley, John Edward. 1992. "Two Views of the Paradigm of Production." *Praxis International* 12: 181–204.

Habermas, Jürgen. 1984. *The Theory of Communicative Action,* translated by Thomas McCarthy. Boston: Beacon Press.

———. 1987. *The Philosophical Discourse of Modernity: Twelve Lectures,* translated by Frederick Lawrence. Cambridge, MA: MIT Press.

Hallam, Elizabeth, and Tim Ingold, eds. 2007. *Creativity and Cultural Improvisation.* Oxford, UK: Berg.

Hardcastle, Valerie Gray. 2002. "On the Normativity of Functions." In *Functions: New Essays in the Philosophy of Psychology and Biology,* edited by André Ariew, Robert Cummins, and Mark Perlman, 144–56. Oxford, UK: Oxford University Press.

Harris, Marvin. 1974. "Why a Perfect Knowledge of All the Rules One Must Know to Act Like a Native Cannot Lead to the Knowledge of How Natives Act." *Journal of Anthropological Research* 30(4): 242–51.

Harrison, Andrew. 1978. *Making and Thinking: A Study of Intelligent Activities.* Hassocks, UK: The Harvester Press.

Have, Paul ten. 1999. *Doing Conversation Analysis: A Practical Guide.* Los Angeles: Sage Publications.

Heidegger, Martin. 1962. *Being and Time,* translated by John Macquarrie and Edward Robinson. New York: Harper and Row.

———. 1993a. "The Origin of the Work of Art." In *Martin Heidegger: Basic Writings,* 2nd ed., edited by David Farrell Krell, 143–212. New York: HarperCollins.

———. 1993b. "The Question Concerning Technology." In *Martin Heidegger: Basic Writings,* 2nd ed., edited by David Farrell Krell, 311–41. New York: HarperCollins.

Heritage, John. 1984. *Garfinkel and Ethnomethodology.* Cambridge, UK: Polity Press.

Hicks, Dan, and Mary C. Beaudry, eds. 2010. *The Oxford Handbook of Material Culture Studies.* Oxford, UK: Oxford University Press.

Hilpinen, Risto. 1992. "On Artifacts and Works of Art." *Theoria (A Swedish Journal of Philosophy)* 58: 58–82.

———. 2011. "Artifact." *The Stanford Encyclopedia of Philosophy (Winter 2011 Edition),* edited by Edward N. Zalta. http://plato.stanford.edu/archives/win2011/entries/artifact/ (Accessed June 30, 2012)

Hodder, Ian. 1992. *Theory and Practice in Archaeology*. London, UK: Routledge.
———. 2006. *The Leopard's Tale: Revealing the Mysteries of Çatalhöyük*. London, UK: Thames and Hudson.
———, and Scott Hutson. 2003. *Reading the Past: Current Approaches to Interpretation in Archaeology*, 3rd ed. Cambridge, UK: Cambridge University Press.
Houkes, Wybo, and Pieter E. Vermaas. 2004. "Actions versus Functions: A Plea for an Alternative Metaphysics of Artefacts." *Monist* 87: 52–71.
———. 2010. *Technical Functions: On the Use and Design of Artefacts*. Dordrecht: Springer.
———, Kees Dorst, and Marc de Vries. 2002. "Design and Use as Plans: An Action-theoretical Account." *Design Studies* 23: 303–20.
Hudson, Liam. 1966. *Contrary Imaginations: A Psychological Study of the Young Student*. New York: Schocken Books.
Huebner, Bryce. 2008. "Do You See What We See? An Investigation of an Argument Against Collective Representation." *Philosophical Psychology* 21(1): 91–112.
Hutchby, Ian, and Robin Wooffitt. 1998. *Conversation Analysis: Principles, Practices and Applications*. Cambridge, UK: Polity Press.
Hutchins, Edwin. 1995. *Cognition in the Wild*. Cambridge, MA: MIT Press.
Ihde, Don. 1991. *Instrumental Realism: The Interface between Philosophy of Science and Philosophy of Technology*. Bloomington: Indiana University Press.
———. 1993. *Postphenomenology: Essays in the Postmodern Context*. Evanston, IL: Northwestern University Press.
Ingold, Tim. 2000a. "Making Culture and Weaving the World." In *Matter, Materiality and Modern Culture*, edited by Paul Graves-Brown, 50–71. London, UK: Routledge.
———. 2000b. *The Perception of the Environment: Essays on Livelihood, Dwelling and Skill*. London, UK: Routledge.
———. 2011. *Being Alive: Essays on Movement, Knowledge and Description*. London, UK: Routledge.
Irwin, John. 1985. *The Jail: Managing the Underclass in American Society*. Berkeley: University of California Press.
Joas, Hans. 1996. *The Creativity of Action*, translated by Jeremy Gaines and Paul Keast. Chicago: University of Chicago Press.
Jonas, Hans. 1984. *The Imperative of Responsibility: In Search of an Ethics for the Technological Age*, translated by Hans Jonas with David Herr. Chicago: University of Chicago Press.
Kander, Mrs. Simon, ed. 1947. *The Settlement Cookbook*, 28th ed. Milwaukee: The Settlement Cookbook Company.
Kaplan, David M., ed. 2004. *Readings in the Philosophy of Technology*. Lanham, MD: Rowman and Littlefield Publishers.
Kincaid, Harold. 1986. "Reduction, Explanation, and Individualism." *Philosophy of Science* 53: 492–513.
Kirsh, David. 2010. "Explaining Artefact Evolution." In *The Cognitive Life of Things: Recasting the Boundaries of the Mind*, edited by Lambros Malafouris and Colin Renfrew, 121–44. Cambridge, UK: McDonald Institute for Archaeological Research.
Kitcher, Philip. 1993. "Function and Design." In *Midwest Studies in Philosophy, Volume 18*, edited by Peter A. French, Theodore E. Uehling, Jr., and Howard K. Wettstein, 379–97. Notre Dame, IN: University of Notre Dame Press.
Knappett, Carl. 2005. *Thinking Through Material Culture: An Interdisciplinary Perspective*. Philadelphia: University of Pennsylvania Press.
———, and Lambros Malafouris, eds. 2010. *Material Agency: Towards a Non-Anthropocentric Approach*. New York: Springer.
Knobe, Joshua, and Shaun Nichols, eds. 2008. *Experimental Philosophy*. Oxford, UK: Oxford University Press.

Kroes, Peter A., and Anthonie W. M. Meijers. 2002. "The Dual Nature of Technical Artifacts: Presentation of a New Research Program." *Techné* 6(2): 4–8.

Kutz, Christopher. 2000. "Acting Together." *Philosophy and Phenomenological Research* 51(1): 1–31.

Latour, Bruno. 1992. "Where Are the Missing Masses? A Sociology of a Few Mundane Artifacts." In *Shaping Technology/Building Society: Studies in Sociotechnical Change,* edited by Wiebe E. Bijker and John Law, 225–58. Cambridge, MA: MIT Press.

———. 2005. *Reassembling the Social: An Introduction to Actor-Network-Theory.* Oxford, UK: Oxford University Press.

Law, John, and John Hassard, eds. 1999. *Actor Network Theory and After.* Oxford, UK: Blackwell Publishers/The Sociological Review.

LeCompte, Margaret D., and Judith Preissle, with Renata Tesch. 1993. *Ethnography and Qualitative Design in Educational Research,* 2nd ed. San Diego: Academic Press.

Lévi-Strauss, Claude. 1968. *The Savage Mind,* translated by John Weightman and Doreen Weightman. Chicago: University of Chicago Press.

Lewens, Tim. 2004. *Organisms and Artifacts: Design in Nature and Elsewhere.* Cambridge, MA: MIT Press.

Lönnrot, Elias. 1985. *Kalevala: The Land of the Heroes,* translated by W.F. Kirby. London, UK: The Athlone Press.

Malafouris, Lambros, and Colin Renfrew, eds. 2010. *The Cognitive Life of Things: Recasting the Boundaries of the Mind.* Cambridge, UK: McDonald Institute for Archaeological Research.

Marchand, Trevor H.J., ed. 2010. *Making Knowledge: Explorations of the Indissoluble Relation between Mind, Body and Environment (Journal of the Royal Anthropological Institute Special Issue Book Series).* Chichester, UK: Wiley-Blackwell.

Margolis, Eric, and Stephen Laurence, eds. 2007. *Creations of the Mind: Theories of Artifacts and Their Representation.* Oxford, UK: Oxford University Press.

Marx, Karl. 1976. *Capital: A Critique of Political Economy, Volume I,* translated by Ben Fowkes. London, UK: Penguin Books in association with New Left Review.

———. 1997. *Writings of the Young Marx on Philosophy and Society,* translated and edited by Lloyd Easton and Kurt Guddat. Reprinted, with corrections. Indianapolis: Hackett Publishing Company. Originally published by Garden City, NY: Doubleday and Company, 1967.

———, and Friedrich Engels. 1994. *The German Ideology.* In *Karl Marx: Selected Writings,* edited by Lawrence H. Simon, 102–56. Indianapolis: Hackett Publishing Company.

———, and Frederick [sic] Engels. 1999. *The Communist Manifesto,* translated by Samuel Moore, edited by John E. Toews. Boston: Bedford/St. Martin's.

McDowell, John. 2007. "What Myth?" *Inquiry* 50(4): 338–51.

McLaughlin, Peter. 2001. *What Functions Explain: Functional Explanation and Self-Reproducing Systems.* Cambridge, UK: Cambridge University Press.

Mele, Alfred R. 1992. *Springs of Action: Understanding Intentional Behavior.* Oxford, UK: Oxford University Press.

———, and Paul K. Moser. 1997. "Intentional Action." In *The Philosophy of Action,* edited by Alfred R. Mele, 223–55. Oxford, UK: Oxford University Press.

Menary, Richard, ed. 2010. *The Extended Mind.* Cambridge, MA: MIT Press.

Millard, André. 2004. "Inventing the Electric Guitar." In *The Electric Guitar: A History of an American Icon,* edited by André Millard, 41–62. Baltimore: Johns Hopkins University Press.

Miller, Daniel. 1985. *Artefacts as Categories: A Study of Ceramic Variability in Central India.* Cambridge, UK: Cambridge University Press.

———. 2010. *Stuff.* Cambridge, UK: Polity Press.

Miller, Seumas. 1997. "Social Norms." In *Contemporary Action Theory: Volume 2: Social Action,* edited by Ghita Holmström-Hintikka and Raimo Tuomela, 211–27. Dordrecht: Kluwer Academic Publishers.

———. 2001. *Social Action: A Teleological Account.* Cambridge, UK: Cambridge University Press.

Millikan, Ruth Garrett. 1984. *Language, Thought, and Other Biological Categories: New Foundations for Realism.* Cambridge, MA: MIT Press (Bradford).

———. 1989. "An Ambiguity in the Notion 'Function.'" *Biology and Philosophy* 4: 176–81.

———. 1993. *White Queen Psychology and Other Essays for Alice.* Cambridge, MA: MIT Press (Bradford).

———. 1999. "Wings, Spoons, Pills and Quills: A Pluralist Theory of Function." *The Journal of Philosophy* 96(4): 191–206.

———. 2002. "Biofunctions: Two Paradigms." In *Functions: New Essays in the Philosophy of Psychology and Biology,* edited by André Ariew, Robert Cummins, and Mark Perlman, 113–43. Oxford, UK: Oxford University Press.

Mitcham, Carl. 1994. *Thinking Through Technology: The Path between Engineering and Philosophy.* Chicago: University of Chicago Press.

Moerman, Michael. 1988. *Talking Culture: Ethnography and Conversation Analysis.* Philadelphia: University of Pennsylvania Press.

Montero, Barbara. 2010. "Does Bodily Awareness Interfere with Highly Skilled Movement?" *Inquiry* 53(2): 105–22.

Myers, Fred R. 2001. "Introduction: The Empire of Things." In *The Empire of Things,* edited by Fred R. Myers, 3–61. Santa Fe, NM: School of American Research Press.

Neander, Karen. 1991a. "Functions as Selected Effects: The Conceptual Analyst's Defense." *Philosophy of Science* 58: 168–84.

———. 1991b. "The Teleological Notion of 'Function.'" *The Australasian Journal of Philosophy* 69: 454–68.

Nietzsche, Friedrich. 1974. *The Gay Science,* translated by Walter Kaufmann. New York: Vintage Books.

———. 1998. *On the Genealogy of Morality: A Polemic,* translated by Maudemarie Clark and Alan J. Swensen. Indianapolis: Hackett Publishing Company.

Perlman, Mark. 2004. "The Modern Philosophical Resurrection of Teleology." *The Monist* 87(1): 3–51.

Petroski, Henry. 1992. *The Evolution of Useful Things.* New York: Vintage Books.

Pettit, Philip. 1996. *The Common Mind: An Essay On Psychology, Society, And Politics.* Expanded edition. Oxford, UK: Oxford University Press.

———. 1998. "Defining and Defending Social Holism." *Philosophical Explorations* 1(3): 169–84.

———. 2003. "Groups with Minds of Their Own." In *Socializing Metaphysics: The Nature of Social Reality,* edited by Frederick F. Schmitt, 167–93. Oxford, UK: Rowman and Littlefield Publishers.

Pitt, Joseph C. 2000. *Thinking About Technology: Foundations of the iPhilosophy of Technology.* New York: Seven Bridges Press.

Plato. 1992. *Plato: Republic,* translated by G.M.A. Grube, revised by C.D.C. Reeve. Indianapolis: Hackett Publishing Company.

Pollack, Martha E. 1992. "The Uses of Plans." *Artificial Intelligence* 57: 43–68.

Pollard, Bill. 2006a. "Actions, Habits and Constitution." *Ratio* 19(2): 229–48.

———. 2006b. "Explaining Actions with Habits." *American Philosophical Quarterly* 43(1): 57–69.

Preston, Beth. 1993. "Heidegger and Artificial Intelligence." *Philosophy and Phenomenological Research* 53(1): 43–69.

———. 1998a. "Cognition and Tool Use." *Mind & Language* 13(4): 513–47.

————. 1998b. "Why Is a Wing Like a Spoon? A Pluralist Theory of Function." *The Journal of Philosophy* 95(5): 215–54.

————. 2000. "The Functions of Things: A Philosophical Perspective on Material Culture." In *Matter, Materiality and Modern Culture,* edited by Paul Graves-Brown, 22–49. London, UK: Routledge.

————. 2003. "Of Marigold Beer—A Reply to Vermaas and Houkes." *The British Journal for the Philosophy of Science* 54: 601–12.

————. 2009a. "Philosophical Theories of Artifact Function." In *Philosophy of Technology and Engineering Sciences (Handbook of the Philosophy of Science. Volume 9),* volume editor Anthonie Meijers, general editors Dov M. Gabbay, Paul Thagard, and John Woods, 213–33. Amsterdam: Elsevier.

————. 2009b. "Biological and Cultural Proper Functions in Comparative Perspective." In *Functions in Biological and Artificial Worlds: Comparative Philosophical Perspectives (Vienna Series in Theoretical Biology, Volume 9),* edited by Ulrich Krohs and Peter Kroes, 37–50. Cambridge, MA: MIT Press.

Psathas, George. 1995. *Conversation Analysis: The Study of Talk-in-Interaction. Qualitative Research Methods Series, Volume 35.* Thousand Oaks, CA: Sage Publications.

Putnam, Hilary. 1975. "The Meaning of 'Meaning.'" In *Language, Mind and Knowledge. Minnesota Studies in the Philosophy of Science, Volume 7,* edited by Keith Gunderson, 131–93. Minneapolis: University of Minnesota Press.

Renfrew, Colin, Chris Frith, and Lambros Malafouris, eds. 2009. *The Sapient Mind: Archaeology Meets Neuroscience.* Oxford, UK: Oxford University Press.

Resnick, Mitchell. 1994. *Turtles, Termites, and Traffic Jams.* Cambridge, MA: MIT Press (Bradford).

Reynolds, Peter C. 1993. "The Complementation Theory of Language and Tool Use." In *Tools, Language, and Cognition in Human Evolution,* edited by Kathleen R. Gibson and Tim Ingold, 407–28. Cambridge, UK: Cambridge University Press.

Robbins, Philip, and Murat Aydede, eds. 2008. *The Cambridge Handbook of Situated Cognition.* Cambridge, UK: Cambridge University Press.

Roth, Abraham Sesshu. 2004. "Shared Agency and Contralateral Commitments." *Philosophical Review* 113(3): 359–410.

Ryder, Chris. 2000. *Inside the Maze: The Untold Story of the Northern Ireland Prison Service.* London, UK: Methuen.

Sawyer, R. Keith. 2001. *Creating Conversations: Improvisation in Everyday Discourse.* Cresskill, NJ: Hampton Press.

————. 1997b. *Pretend Play as Improvisation: Conversation in the Preschool Classroom.* Mahwah, NJ: Lawrence Erlbaum.

————, ed. 1997a. *Creativity in Performance.* Greenwich, CT: Ablex Publishing.

Scharff, Robert C., and Val Dusek, eds. 2003. *Philosophy of Technology: The Technological Condition—An Anthology.* Malden, MA: Blackwell.

Schiffer, Michael B. 1992. *Technological Perspectives on Behavioral Change.* Tucson: University of Arizona Press.

————, with Andrea R. Miller. 1999. *The Material Life of Human Beings: Artifacts, Behavior, and Communication.* London, UK: Routledge.

Schwartz, Peter H. 1999. "Proper Function and Recent Selection." *Philosophy of Science* 66 (Proceedings): S210–22.

————. 2002. "The Continuing Usefulness Account of Proper Functions." In *Functions: New Essays in the Philosophy of Psychology and Biology,* edited by André Ariew, Robert Cummins, and Mark Perlman, 244–60. Oxford, UK: Oxford University Press.

Searle, John R. 1990. "Collective Intentions and Actions." In *Intentions in Communication,* edited by Philip R. Cohen, Jerry Morgan, and Martha E. Pollack, 401–15. Cambridge, MA: MIT Press.

————. 1995. *The Construction of Social Reality.* New York: Free Press.

Shockley, Kenneth E. 2004. "The Conundrum of Collective Commitment." *Social Theory and Practice* 30(4): 535–57.

Shumaker, Robert W., Kristina Walkup, and Benjamin B. Beck. 2011. *Animal Tool Behavior: The Use and Manufacture of Tools by Animals.* Baltimore, MD: Johns Hopkins University Press. Originally published as Benjamin B. Beck, *Animal Tool Behavior* (New York: Garland STPM Press, 1980).

Smith, Jonathan A. 1995. "Semi-Structured Interviewing and Qualitative Analysis." In *Rethinking Methods in Psychology,* edited by Jonathan A. Smith, Rom Harré, and Luk Van Langenhove, 9–26. London, UK: Sage Publications.

Sober, Elliott. 1984. *The Nature of Selection: Evolutionary Theory in Philosophical Focus.* Cambridge, MA: MIT Press.

Steele, Valerie. 2001. *The Corset: A Cultural History.* New Haven, CT: Yale University Press.

Sterelny, Kim. 2010. "Minds: Extended or Scaffolded?" *Phenomenology and Cognitive Science* 9: 465–81.

———. 2012. *The Evolved Apprentice: How Evolution Made Humans Unique.* Cambridge, MA: MIT Press.

Suchman, Lucy. 2007. *Human-Machine Reconfigurations: Plans and Situated Actions,* 2nd ed. Cambridge, UK: Cambridge University Press.

Sudnow, David. 2001. *Ways of the Hand: A Rewritten Account.* Cambridge, MA: MIT Press.

Sutton, John. 2007. "Batting, Habit and Memory: The Embodied Mind and the Nature of Skill." *Sport in Society* 10(5): 763–86.

———, Doris McIlwain, Wayne Christensen, and Andrew Geeves. 2011. "Applying Intelligence to the Reflexes: Embodied Skills and Habits Between Dreyfus and Descartes." *Journal of the British Society for Phenomenology* 42(1): 78–103.

Thesander, Marianne. 1997. *The Feminine Ideal,* translated by Nicholas Hills. London, UK: Reaktion Books.

Thomasson, Amie L. 2007. *Ordinary Objects.* Oxford, UK: Oxford University Press.

Tilley, Christopher, Webb Keane, Susanne Küchler, Michael Rowlands, and Patricia Spyer, eds. 2006. *Handbook of Material Culture.* Thousand Oaks, CA: Sage Publications.

Tollefsen, Deborah Perron. 2002. "Collective Intentionality and the Social Sciences." *Philosophy of the Social Sciences* 32(1): 25–50.

———. 2006. "From Extended Mind to Collective Mind." *Cognitive Systems Research* 7(2–3): 140–50.

Tuomela, Raimo. 1995. *The Importance of Us: A Philosophical Study of Basic Social Notions.* Stanford, CA: Stanford University Press.

———. 2000. *Cooperation: A Philosophical Study.* Dordrecht: Kluwer Academic Publishers.

———, and Kaarlo Miller. 1988. "We-Intentions." *Philosophical Studies* 53: 115–37.

Velleman, J. David. 1997. "How to Share an Intention." *Philosophy and Phenomenological Research* 48(1): 29–50.

Vermaas, Pieter E., and Wybo Houkes. 2003. "Ascribing Functions to Technical Artefacts: A Challenge to Etiological Accounts of Functions." *British Journal for the Philosophy of Science* 54: 261–89.

Vermaas, Pieter E., Peter Kroes, Ibo van de Poel, Maarten Franssen, and Wybo Houkes. 2011. *A Philosophy of Technology: From Technical Artefacts to Sociotechnical Systems.* San Rafael, CA: Morgan and Claypool.

Walsh, Denis M., and André Ariew. 1996. "A Taxonomy of Functions." *Canadian Journal of Philosophy* 26(4): 493–513.

Warnke, Georgia. 2002. "Hermeneutics, Ethics, and Politics." In *The Cambridge Companion to Gadamer,* edited by Robert J. Dostal, 79–101. Cambridge, UK: Cambridge University Press.

Wheeler, Michael. 2005. *Reconstructing the Cognitive World: The Next Step*. Cambridge, MA: MIT Press (Bradford).

Winch, Peter. 1958. *The Idea of a Social Science and Its Relation to Philosophy*. London, UK: Routledge and Kegan Paul.

Wittgenstein, Ludwig. 1973. *Philosophical Investigations*, 3rd ed., translated by G.E.M. Anscombe. New York: Macmillan.

Wright, Larry. 1973. "Functions." *The Philosophical Review* 82: 139–68.

Wright, Matthew. 2012. "Know Your Tools: Flat Head Screwdriver." About.com http://autorepair.about.com/od/tools/a/tools_flathed.htm. Accessed June 29, 2012.

Wynn, Thomas. 1993. "Layers of Thinking in Tool Behavior." In *Tools, Language and Cognition in Human Evolution*, edited by Kathleen R. Gibson and Tim Ingold, 389–406. Cambridge, UK: Cambridge University Press.

Zollo, Paul. 1997. *Songwriters on Songwriting*. New York: Da Capo Press.

Index